ARTIFICIAL INTELLIGENCE

Methodology, Systems, Applications

ARTIFICIAL INTELLIGENCE

Methodology, Systems, Applications

Proceedings of the International Conference on
Artificial Intelligence: Methodology, Systems, Applications (AIMSA '84)
Varna, Bulgaria, 17-20 September, 1984

edited by

W. BIBEL
TU- München
München
Federal Republic of Germany

and

B. PETKOFF
Bulgarian Academy of Sciences
Sofia
Bulgaria

1985

NORTH-HOLLAND
AMSTERDAM • NEW YORK • OXFORD

for the European Coordinating Committee for Artificial Intelligence

ISBN: 0 444 87743 6

Published by:
ELSEVIER SCIENCE PUBLISHERS B.V.
P.O. Box 1991
1000 BZ Amsterdam
The Netherlands

Sole distributors for the U.S.A. and Canada:
ELSEVIER SCIENCE PUBLISHING COMPANY, INC.
52 Vanderbilt Avenue
New York, N.Y. 10017
U.S.A.

Library of Congress Cataloging in Publication Data

International Conference on Artificial Intelligence:
Methodology, Systems, Applications (1984 : Varna, Bulgaria)
Artificial intelligence.

1. Artificial intelligence--Congresses.
2. Artificial intelligence--Data processing--Congresses.
I. Bibel, W., 1938- . II. Petkoff, B.
III. European Coordinating Committee for Artificial Intelligence. IV. Title.
Q334.I554 1984 001.53'5 85-4467
ISBN 0-444-87743-6

PRINTED IN THE NETHERLANDS

FOREWORD

AIMSA '84 was held at Golden Sands, Bulgaria, at the Black Sea, September 17–20, 1984. It was organized by the Bulgarian Academy of Sciences and the Bulgarian Industrial Association, and sponsored by ECCAI and IIASA. About 100 papers were selected by the international program committee for presentation from about 200 submitted extended abstracts.

This volume contains less than a third of the presented papers selected by the program committee after the conference for their high quality and their harmony with the topics of the conference. They address important actual issues in the field of Artificial Intelligence, describe running AI-systems and point out applications of AI technologies to various areas.

In comparison with other AI-conferences, AIMSA has laid a special emphasis on methodological issues in the field of Artificial Intelligence. As a relatively young subject, AI lacks a clearly defined way of carrying out research. This deficiency explains the recent interest in discussions of a methodological nature. Hopefully, these discussions will eventually result in a clearer identification of the basic principles underlying AI-research.

Another feature of this conference was its truly international character with a participation mainly from Europe, that is from all of Europe. In this sense both the conference and the activities connected with it took place in an atmosphere of cooperation and friendship which will be remembered with pleasure.

W. Bibel and B. Petkoff

CONFERENCE CHAIRMAN

Blagovest Sendov – Vice-President of the Bulgarian Academy of Sciences

INTERNATIONAL PROGRAM COMMITTEE

W. Bibel (FRG) – Chairman

L. Bolc (Poland)
B. Buchberger (Austria)
L. Carlucci (Italy)
I. Guevski (Bulgaria)
Ph. Jorrand (France)
D. Ochotsimsky (USSR)
T. O'Shea (UK)
O. Panov (Bulgaria)
L. Pereira (Portugal)
I. Plander (CSSR)

B. Petkoff (Bulgaria) – Secretary

A. Polikarov (Bulgaria)
D. Pospelov (USSR)
G. Pospelov (USSR)
E. Sandewall (Sweden)
V. Sgurev (Bulgaria)
G. Stanke (GDR)
V. Tomov (Bulgaria)
R. Trappl (Austria)
T. Vamos (Hungary)
W. Wahlster (FRG)

BULGARIAN ORGANIZING COMMITTEE

V. Sgurev – Chairman

V. Belenski
D. Bogdanov
D. Dochev
O. Katov
D. Kostadinova

Ch. Ditchev – Secretary

E. Michailova
B. Petkoff
Ch. Serbezov
N. Zlatareva

CONTENTS

METHODOLOGY

ARTIFICIAL INTELLIGENCE: Methodology, Systems, Applications
W. Bibel and B. Petkoff (Editors)
Elsevier Science Publishers B.V. (North-Holland)

ARTIFICIAL INTELLIGENCE IN EUROPE

Wolfgang Bibel

Technische Universität München
West Germany

In this article we give a brief account of the field of Artificial Intelligence from several points of view (historical, actual, methodological, taxonomic, etc.). In particular, the European scene in AI is discussed, pointing out weaknesses, strengths, and perspectives.

INTRODUCTION

Artificial Intelligence (AI) is in the headlines these days. Industry seems now determined to exploit AI-techniques for a broad range of applications. Scientists from nearly all disciplines are attracted by the idea of approaching their own specific problems by AI-methodologies. Ordinary people are stunned by the inconceivable capabilities of AI-systems and feel uneasy about the prospects of this technology.

The actuality of this extraordinary interest has three main sources: man's scientific curiosity, advances in computer technology, and the increasing complexity of our world. Let us briefly consider each of them.

By nature, man is curious to understand the phenomena in his world. His own intellectual capabilities are of course one of these phenomena, perhaps the most exciting one indeed. Consequently, science has attempted to clarify the nature of these capabilities from the very beginning in its long history.

With the methodologies available until recently progress in this endeavor was frustratingly slow. In particular, these methodologies did not make use of experimentation, a feature which since Galileo turned out to be crucial for the success of the natural sciences. The great pioneers like G. W. Leibniz and C. Babbage were clearly aware of this deficiency. Any means for experimenting in the area of processes realizing intelligent behavior, however, were not available until modern computers were developed.

Once general purpose computers became feasible,their use for such experiments was taken into consideration immediately (by J. v. Neumann, A. Turing, K. Zuse, and others). Today this potential of the new species of machines is becoming more or less common place. In particular, the advances in computer technology are reaching a level of performance where the machines might even become capable of competing with humans in restricted areas of cognitive behavior.

It is perhaps not by chance that this technological evolution takes place in a time when mankind faces problems of existential dimensions. The continuing explosion in the world population, the decrease of basic resources, the global environmental crisis, the rising demands and expectations of people, the critical status of the military balance are some of these problems for which human intelligence seems incapable of providing a solution. Could artificial intelligence give us advice in this critical situation?

A number of AI-systems have already demonstrated that AI-methodologies provide us with more flexible tools than traditional technologies do. Taking into account that AI is such a young enterprise, one may infer from these initial successes a tremendous influence on the technological evolution in general. Since man has no other choice for coping with his problems than by some kind of technology - including the prudent use of the technical machinery - we see that AI might indeed play a crucial role in the near future.

CHARACTERISTIC FEATURES OF AI

As we have seen, one of the aims of AI is the modeling of human intelligence in computers. That this might be feasible, at least in principle and to a large extent also in practice, is sometimes referred to as the **strong AI thesis.** On the more application-oriented side AI-systems are expected to technically realize functions for performing specific tasks that would otherwise require human intelligence if done by man. The feasibility of such limited systems is then referred to as the **weak AI thesis.**

The field of Artificial Intelligence extends between these two extremes. Apparently, it goes far beyond the paradigms of traditional computer science. Thus, despite the strong ties between the two, AI is a field in its own right, and in this capacity it would deserve a proper name such as **intellectics** (suggested by the author several years ago [2]). We will use both names synonymously.

The difference between the methodologies of intellectics and of computer science is also reflected in the architecture of the implemented systems. While computer science centers around the notions of **data, algorithms** and/or **functions,** AI-systems focus the attention on knowledge in various representations which is activated in a heuristically controlled way, whereby the conceptual separation of these three fundamental notions - **knowledge, control, heuristic search** - lies at the heart of any AI-methodology.

This distinction between intellectics and computer science is emphasized for no other purpose than that of clarification. As we already pointed out, both fields heavily rely on each other and in fact share a large common intersection. Nevertheless, their differences have important consequences in questions of enormous practical importance.

For instance, take the notion of a **knowledge base management system** (KBMS). A traditional computer scientist today tends to view such a KBMS as an upgraded version of a data base management system (DBMS) [5]. There is nothing wrong with such a view except for the confusion arising from the fact that in intellectics this notion has been used from the very beginning with quite a different interpretation in mind [4]. Hence to be clear we would actually have to make the distinction between a CS-KBMS and an AI-KBMS.

As we see, intellectics is characterized not only by its aims and paradigms but also by its methodology which in turn influences the notions and techniques realized in AI-systems. We already mentioned the three most fundamental notions. Others are **inference** (classical, non-monotonic, fuzzy, etc.), the distinction between **reasoning** and **meta-reasoning, representing** and **structuring** knowledge (by semantic nets, frames, on the object- and meta-level, etc.), **learning, judgmental** use of knowledge (beliefs, planning, etc.), and **cognitive modeling** (simulation, task analysis, user model, etc.), by far not an exhaustive list, of course.

Apart from this **methodological** characterization of intellectics, AI may also be seen simply as a field consisting of a taxonomic hierarchy of subfields like those distinguished in the various AI-conferences around the world (notably IJCAI, AAAI, ECAI, etc.) in the form of subsections. Among these the subfield of **expert systems** has currently attracted most of the attention. Many AI-scientists are not really

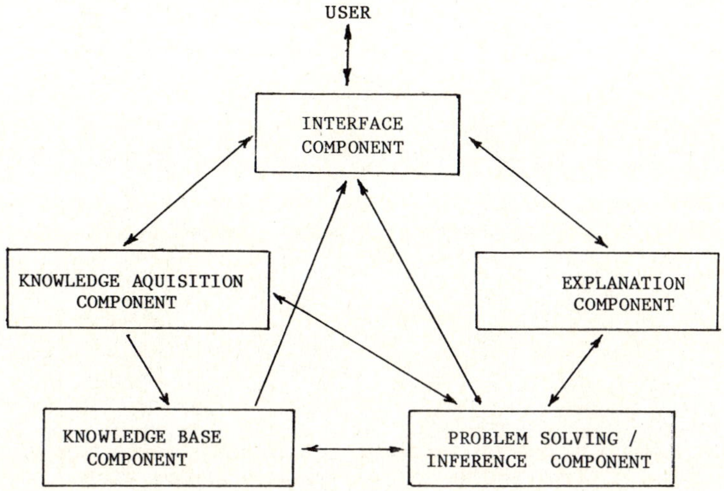

Figure 1
The basic structure of a KBS

happy with this term and rather prefer to speak more generally of **knowledge-based systems** (KBS).

Such systems heavily rely on a base of knowledge in some limited field of expertise (such as programming, subareas of mathematics, infectious blood deseases in medicine, domains of mineral exploration, computer configuration, aircraft design, contract configuration, and many more). This knowledge is often represented in the form of rules (eg. "if the spill is sulfuric acid, then use an anion-exchanger") although more general forms are also taken into consideration (or even required). For solving a given task these rules are matched against the actual situation which eventually results in a sequence of actions that will cary out the task. From a formal point of view the rule activation may be regarded as a deductive process controlled in various ways. As a general principle one may say that the deductive capabilities have to be the more powerful, the more general the form of represented knowledge actually is.

Further important components in such a system are, first of all, one for a comfortable user interface that provides the communication of the user with the system. Further there is usually a knowledge acquisition component that automatically integrates additional knowledge into the existing knowledge base. Last but not least, we mention the explanation component, which provides the user on request with a detailed analysis of the reasoning process. These components of a KBS are depicted in Figure 1.

Although any AI-system may be regarded as some sort of a KBS, the nature of the tasks to be tackled by them is so different that other subfields are naturally distinguished from the one of KBS (or expert systems). A particularly important one is that of **natural communications** which aims at an exchange of information between the user and the system in a natural human-oriented way. Natural language understanding, generation and translation, more demandingly speech understanding and

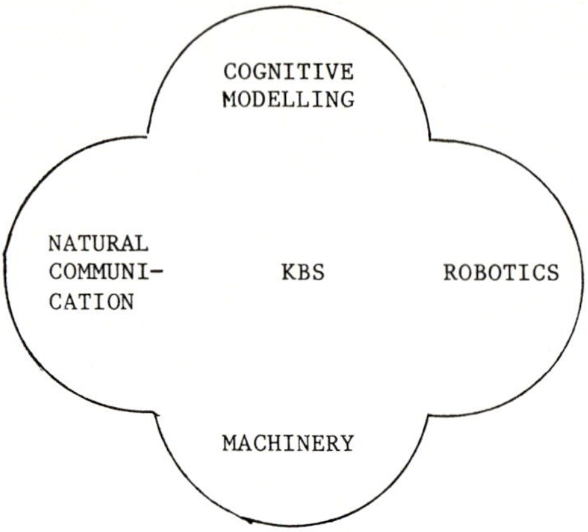

Figure 2
The five major subfields of intellectics

generation, graphical means of communication, and finally vision are the subfields which share this common goal. Clearly, an extra quality is required in order to achieve a system performance that copes with the enormous problems faced in natural communication.

The realization of the solution of a given task by a sequence of physical actions carried out by a machine within a realistic environment is again of a different nature in comparison with the tasks mentioned so far. Therefore **robotics** and **computer integrated manufacturing** (CIM) is another one of the subfields of intellectics. As before with KBMS we should perhaps talk more clearly about AI-robotics or AI-CIM since what we address here are **not** the devices that are able to no more than repeating a series of motions possibly reacting to an elementary perception. Rather it has been the goal of AI-research in robotics from the very beginning to develop devices that are able to perform a variety of tasks even under unexpected conditions. That sort of species is today sometimes called third-generation robots.

Clearly, an intelligent robot of that kind must have a basic knowledge about its environment. It must be able to plan its actions in accordance to what it "sees", "touches" and "hears". Perhaps most important of all, it must have the capability to learn from its experiences.

The last among these subfields is **cognitive modeling.** It is concerned with the AI thesis in its strong form mentioned further above and aims at a simulation of cognitive processes for the purpose of their exploration. This in turn has important applications, e.g. in education and psychology.

The work in these subfields relies on special hardware, systems, languages that are to an ever greater extent specialized for the use in intellectics. Therefore we may even add a subfield especially concerned with the machinery used for AI experiments.

Thus we have distinguished altogether five major subfields in this **taxonomic** characterization of intellectics shown in figure 2 : KBS, natural communication, robotics, cognitive modeling and AI machinery. They in turn consist of various subfields, some of which we have mentioned more or less explicitly.

THE EUROPEAN AI SCENE

In order to analyze the European situation in intellectics it is necessary to have a glance at the situation in general. While Europe clearly carried the role of leadership until the first and partially also the second world war politically, economically and technologically, the state of affairs at present is by far less satisfactory. "The decline of Europe" was the headline on the front cover of Newsweek's issue of April 9, 1984. The question is whether this is a temporary decline only or a definite decadence, as was pointed out by Oliver Wormser, the former president of the Bank of France.

The lack of leadership is naturally felt most in pioneering areas of any kind. In the present context we are more interested in that of information technology (IT). Thanks to the Japanese fifth generation computer systems (FGCS) initiative there are now numerous reports from individuals, national or supranational committees which emphasize the importance of IT in general and of AI technology in particular and warn of the tremendous gap between Europe and the technology leaders U.S. and Japan.

First of all the IT industry is a healthy employer. Worldwide it shares a market of up to $50 billion with a growth rate of more than 20% per annum. In Western Europe over half of all employed people is at present affected by IT to a high or medium degree. The sad side of the coin is that Western Europe in its overall demand in IT at a rate of 20% heavily relies on imports (compared with a low 4,6% for Japan). The rate is even much higher if we restrict the attention to advanced technology like supercomputers, VLSI, LISP machines, expert systems, etc.

The message should be clear, then. It has in fact been understood by government and industry at various levels. The ESPRIT program, launched by the EEC, the Alvey project in Britain, and similar programs in Germany, France, Sweden, the Netherlands, the third five-year plan for computing of the USSR in collaboration with Eastern European partners, the basis laboratory at Bratislava, supported by Eastern European countries, these and others are enough evidence for the intention to catch up in this area as soon as possible. This fact alone is of high significance. However, I am afraid that money and such limited intentions alone will not be enough to overcome the malaise which probably has much deeper reasons.

Obviously, Europe still suffers from the consequences of the two world wars. Its current division into an eastern and a western part, with an embarrassing barrier in between, is not an encouraging fact indeed. This status clearly contradicts the historical realities that continue to be alive in our minds. The variety of nations and languages adds to the confusion. So above all there is a crisis of identity which might be the deeper reason for many problems of detail (like the frictions in a family or any other community occupy and set a burden on its members, thus hindering their development).

It should be clear that Europe has a chance within the international competition only if it acts as a whole. If such an identification could be achieved, Europe's variety would even turn out to be a virtue, while in the present situation it tends to cause many frictions. The possibility of such a goal could be sensed in the encouraging cooperation of those involved in ESPRIT. If this spirit would spread out over all of Europe we might be very optimistic.

All this, unfortunately, also has an important effect on such limited endeavors like AI. Intellectics has a pioneering role for IT (and for science in general) which in turn plays a similar role for many other technologies. Most of Europe has ignored this potential for nearly 3 decades. Although its importance is finally recognized, the support is still half-measured. For instance, it is a fact that leading European AI scientists have to spend most of their time with activities **other** than research. They lack the infrastructure, struggle with a dominant bureaucracy, and are requested to explain the role, nature and needs of AI to numerous committees, magazines, individuals, etc. A community assured of its identity would not continue indefinitely to burden its pioneers with such a heavy load. As an aside we mention that other pioneering groups experience similar problems (eg. biotechnology, ecology, etc.).

Despite these apparent problems there are very promising trends. The recent European Conference on Artificial Intelligence, ECAI-84 in Pisa, has demonstrated that the level of quality of AI-research may well compete with that in any other area of the world. The best AI researchers from Europe are highly respected in the U.S. and in Japan (and therefore receive attractive offers from there). Many important ideas originally come from Europe. AI-research at an international level of quality is now being carried out at more than 40 universities in Europe and in a number of companies.

Particular strength can be observed in the use of logic as a formalism for programming (Prolog, program synthesis, etc.) and for the representation of knowledge, a crucial issue for expert systems. In close relation with this, the inference methods and systems developed in Europe rank among the best in the world. Here a rich tradition has found is continuation. Another area is natural language understanding where systems with an internationally respected performance have been produced. The influence of traditional fields (linguistics, logic) can be seen here also. In general one can say that AI in Europe has considerable strength in theory but not so much in practice, which is a good basis for catching up rather quickly, once the infrastructure has been prepared for such a purpose.

Naturally, European AI research is weak in areas which require big and continuous support by large groups and expensive equipment. For this reason there are no spectacular systems in robotics, vision, speech understanding, and industrial applications. This is not at all to say that we lack excellent work in these areas. For instance, work on understanding moving scenes was first carried out in Europe. But more concentrated efforts are required for building , say, an intelligent robot.

Typically, AI research at universities in Europe is carried out by relatively small groups, perhaps five people around a more prominent figure. This way the efforts are scattered in small pieces over many places. Moreover, communication over a computer net does not yet exist here in practice. Some groups have recently considerably grown, but there are doubts whether this rapid growth has been accompanied by an increase in quality. Hence Europe still lacks any centers of excellence which would attract more than just one or two prominent figures from the AI scene, in particular those who departed to the U.S. for obvious reasons. More seriously, the number of chairs (full professorships) in the field of AI at European universities can probably be counted with one hand. In connection with this fact, most universities still do not offer a coherent curriculum for intellectics. Also a coherent postgraduate education by advanced schools in AI does not exist so far.

EUROPE'S PROSPECTS

Europe's current weakness might at the same time be a great chance. The danger of decadence might be the driving force that eventually creates the strong feeling of identity which is lacking now. One might even hope that with the help of AI-systems we are able to rationalize the difference in the various political, economic and cultural communities in such a way that these could integrate themselves without sacrificing their individual identity.

Since in principle we do not lack the capabilities for a potential lead in any area of IT or AI, as I said before, we are still free to select and focus upon the most promising ones. In any case we have to start with a considerable improvement of the infrastructural support of scientists.

In the first place this means a drastic improvement of communication facilities among the many scattered groups. In a study for the OECD [1] it is stated that "the lack of communication facilities is a major obstacle to the development of a strong Artificial Intelligence community in Europe. Probably no one thing would help more than establishing network communications between research centers".

Of equal importance is the computational equipment. In the race for supercomputers I see the most promising perspectives for Europe in a focus on multiprocessor architectures rather than in the hardware technology where the U.S. and Japan enjoy a clear advantage. Anyway, AI is not so much interested in the big number-crunchers. It is not too late, however, for a substantial investment in the fifth-generation machines on a European level (done within ESPRIT). In any case, the existence of competitive European machines would not only help to balance the trade deficit in IT but also encourage the development of smart systems on top of them. The company ACT in Britain has demonstrated with its "Apricot" that this way is in fact viable - to mention just one example.

A further large area with excellent prospectives is that of advanced software systems. In particular, one should push forward the development of constructive software development tools towards automatic programming, as well as that of expert systems, bridging the compatibility gap between existing systems and new ones [3]. Clearly, logic programming will play a crucial role in a business of that sort. One should note that such systems would alleviate the dependency on imported machines and systems since imported systems could much more easily be made to run on home-made machines and vice versa.

The multilingual situation in Europe makes us strive for systems that support the communication between different languages. Natural language understanding lies at the heart of such an endeavor.

We notice that all these top priority suggestions take advantage of the strength of the European AI know-how mentioned in the previous section. One might therefore expect an early success in these areas. I am less sure in this respect in so far as the following other areas are concerned.

Obviously, robotics and CIM (computer integrated manufacturing) will become more and more essential for the survival of any kind of industry. The robots of the third generation, however, will not be developed unless engineers closely cooperate with AI experts. The capability for reasoning, planning, learning, required in such devices will hardly be developed by traditional engineers alone. Unfortunately, the barriers between disciplies are sometimes as high as those between nations in Europe (an analogy which is not accidental, as I tried to indicate in the previous section). I am optimistic that the market will eventually push us towards cooperation, as I pointed out at the beginning of this section.

Office automation might face us with even harder problems. The world of an office is ill-structured and will hardly be modeled by a neat uniform theory. This poses a problem to the Europeans' preferences for theory and their long tradition in the human sciences and arts. We have to learn from the American pragmatism in this respect (with some help from the British). I am afraid it will take quite a while until the resistance gives in to some degree.

To some extent this conservatism may even be an advantage. The speed with which the information technology is changing our lives, poses tremendous problems of adaptation, namely the technological adaptation of the systems to the humans and the human societies, but, even more problematic, the adaptation of the people and society to the new technology. Let us spend a lot of time to make sure that the new technology enhances the unique and rich life-style and culture of Europeans rather than endangers this precious treasure.

REFERENCES

[1] Barber, G. R., Trends in Artificial Intelligence, OECD, ICCP (84) 2 (1984).

[2] Bibel, W., "Intellektik" statt "KI" - Ein ernstgemeinter Vorschlag, Rundbrief FG KI der GI, Nr. 22, 15-16 (1980).

[3] Bibel, W., Software - Eine Studie aus der Sicht der Künstlichen Intelligenz, Report ATP-27-IV-84, Forschungsgruppe KI, Institut für Informatik, TUM (1984).

[4] Reimer, U., Knowledge Base Management System, Informatik-Spektrum, Bd. 7, Nr. 3, S. 173 (1984).

[5] Reuter, A., Knowledge Base Management Systems, Informatik-Spektrum, Bd. 7, Nr. 1, S. 44-45 (1984).

TYPESCRIPT: L. Zalevski

ARTIFICIAL INTELLIGENCE: Methodology, Systems, Applications
W. Bibel and B. Petkoff (Editors)
Elsevier Science Publishers B.V. (North-Holland)

METHODOLOGICAL PROBLEMS AND APPROACHES IN ARTIFICIAL INTELLIGENCE

A. Polikarov

Scientific Information Center
Bulgarian Academy of Sciences
Sofia, Bulgaria

From the viewpoint of the content of methodology (philosophy) of science a survey is made of methodological problems arising in the domain of AI (subject-matter, demarkation from related branches, critical considerations). On the other hand the impact of AI on methodology is outlined. It comprises growth and use of heuristics (heuretics), the problems of thinking, of mind-body, the relevance of functionalism, reductionism, analogy, etc.

I

1. To a more or less comprehensive examination of a special problem I have prefered a brief survey of an ample range of problems concerning the interrelation of methodology of science (M) and artificial intelligence (AI).

In this paper I aim to outline, on the one hand, the role of methodological posing of the problems and methodological statements in the development of the new branch (which may be interesting for the representatives of the latter), and on the other - the impact of scientific and methodological problems arising for M itself (which is closer to the interests of the philosophers of science).

2. I shall note the set of problems which M involves, namely:

a. Subject-matter and general principles.
b. Problems of the system: language (concepts), substantiation, interpretation.
c. Problems of dynamics of knowledge: methods and heuristics, historical development.
d. Explanation (understanding).
e. Criticism (validity, evaluation).
f. Interrelation with other sciences and activities.
g. Ontic (ontological) picture.
h. Goals and applications, as well as problems of M itself (metamethodological ones).

3. It is to the point to note especially the open nature of M, in the sense that methodological role may have different philosophical and scientific statements (to which, besides methods, also hypotheses, principles, theories etc. have to be referred) within the framework of a discipline or outside it. Every time when the posing of a problem and its solution is based on some more general (in the concrete context) statements or it is made clear that they presupose some statement or other of this kind they perform a methodological function.

4. In the following review I shall use some new ideas (elaborated or suggested by me), namely:

- The existence of a trend toward methodologisation of science, as well as of the opposite trend toward a scientification of M.[2]
- The comprehension of M mainly as heuristics.[3]
- Correlation between scientific situations and efficient (relevant) M-s.[1]
- The consideration of the sciences as a set of moduls.
- The clarification of the dynamics of sciences through the prisma of dominants of scientific research (or dominant trends of growth).[1]
- The overlapping of the domains of algorithmic procedures, heuristics and creativity.[1]

5. In a specific form these problems were also posed in the domain of AI. Explicitely one speaks of M in a narrow sense - as related to the methods (only), and implicitely it is extended to the whole range of methodological problems.

Among the premises for the construction of computer programme for general intellect McCarthy and Hayes postulate: "We must undertake to construct rather comprehensive philosophical system, contrary to the present tendency to study problems separately and not try to put the results together."[4]

As a specific methodological problem Ringle singles out the explanatory status of investigative simulation. Among the epistemological problems are the necessity of simplification and the danger of oversimplification in the simulation or modeling of objects, the relation between programme and (statement of) theory etc.[5]

According to (the statement of) McCarthy and Hayes, a computer programme capable of acting intelligently must have a general representation of the world in terms of which its inputs are interpreted. Designing such a programme requires commitments about what knowledge is and how it is obtained. Thus some of the major traditional problems of philosophy arise in AI.[4]

For the clarification of these problems various approaches are used: philosophical, mathematical, biological, psychological, and in the framework of AI - from the position of some conceptions (trends) or others, namely bionic, evolutionary, linguistic (semiotic) et al.

Philosophical and methodological problems get altogether diverse answers, among which a rational selection has to be made.

6. I can begin with the question of the subject (-matter) and the content of the new branch. AI embrasses different topics, namely technology, simulation, modeling, and theory. The difference between simulation and modeling lies in the direction of movement, namely from[5] data to the model in the former case and vice versa in the latter.

Besides, one distinguishes between demonstrative and investigative simulation, having in mind an external ressemblance (only) or identity, or analogy of the internal structure of object and model, respectively.[3]

Until now AI developes mainly as technology and simulation, while the theory remains less developed, and correspondingly the related problems of a system and its substantiation are not yet put on the agenda.

The specificity of the domain is reflected in various new concepts such as scripts and plans (Schank), frames (Minsky), productions

(Newell), as well as situation, fluent, future operator, action, strategy, result of a strategy and knowledge (McCarthy, Hayes).

7. The framing of AI begins with a demarcation of related branches - cybernetics, computer science et al.

The problems of AI may be approached in two main ways: psychocentric and logocentric. It has turned out that the latter approach is more powerfull and prospecitve.

For the solution of the arising problems besides standard logic also other logics, especially philosophical logics may be used, like modal logic, logic of knowledge, logic of action etc.

Characteristic for the dynamics of AI is the elaboration of many heuristic programmes and heuristics. In the programme AM their number is more than 200, and in the programme EURISCO they are 300. This quantitative accumulation marks a new qualitative situation which allows to speak of the framing of the branch of heuretics (Lenat).[6]

The dynamics in this domain may be represented as a transition from technology to science and a sequence of dominant trends which overlap and between which there is a considerable continuity.

The basic periodization according to the dominant trends is as follows:
1. language translation,
2. design of self-organizing systems,
3. problem solving, game playing, composing music, and theorem proving using heuristic search,
4. computer representation of the world it works with, talks about, copes with, etc.[7]

As a new stage in this respect may be considered the works on simulation of discoveries in the domain of physics and chemistry by BACON (Langley, Simon, Bradshaw) and the modeling of discoveries of branches of mathematics and other scientific achievements by AM and EURISCO (Lenat).

It is natural to make parallels between AI and the framing of classical sciences (and pattern of science) like mechanics. Along these lines the contemporary stage of AI is compared with the pre-Newtonian stage of development of dynamics.

8. Essential is also the problem of criticism from a methodological point of view in this domain. This criticism was directed to the questions of the possibilities of the new branch, its character, basic statements and prospects.

Against this kind of criticism from positions which I shall qualify as conservative, they were adduced more or less cogent arguments, among which attention has to be paid to the consideration that some restrictions of AI are inherent also for man, especially the restrictions steaming from Gödel's theorem.

If mentalistic terminology is used not in a metaphorical sense but is accepted as an attitude this leads to an (idealistic) antireductionist view. We share the critique that this view is untenable, because "computers are not self-conscious and that there is no standard set ot criteria for nonmetaphorical application of such terms exept to ourselves and perhaps to intelligent animals".[11]

Notwithstanding the ample prospects of AI it remains open the problem of the potential barriers in this respect. One of them is Einstein's idea that beyond the domain of AI remains the possibility of problem's posing. Another restriction may steam from the dependence of more complicate scientific discoveries on a complex constellation of factors which cannot be simulated by means of AI.

9. As to the history of the discussion of methodological problems of AI they were stated in connection with the concrete growth of this branch and more especially with theoretical statements and conceptions. They oscillate between the extremist views of the possibilities or the restrictions of AI in general and of its single trends, the character of this branch and its prospective directions of development. The criticism evolved from radical to constructive and made more precise the validity of some propositions and claims.

These problems were posed as early as in the 50-ies in the works of Wiener, Ashby, Turing, Newell, Simon, Minsky, M. Scriven et al., thereafter (in the 60-ies) in Simon, Reitman, Putnam, Sayre, Dennett, McCarthy, Hayes. Among the more significant new publications dedicated to these problems are those of Weizenbaum, Sayre, Raphael, Boden, Sloman, Ringle et al., Lenat, Ritchie, Hanna etc.

We have all reasons to expect that the impact of M on AI will increase.

II

1. The origines and framing of the AI is not only a domain of implementation and specification of M, but the latter underlays the influence of this branch while posing new problems, modifying some conceptions, providing arguments which strengthen or weaken traditional views - especially the applicability of general scientific methods - and imposing certain improvements and changes in the methodological conceptions. As Ringle puts it, AI has something special to offer in two key areas of investigation: (a) the ontological problem of the relationship between mind and bodies, and (b) the epistemological problem of the analysis of mentalistic terms.[5]

2. The conception of M as related mainly to the dynamics of science and intimately associated with heuristics gets a strong support.M is enriched with heuristics and getting closer to heuretics (as an independent branch).

From a contemporary point of view heuristic search is adequate for modeling worlds which are observable (so heuristics can be formed), stable (so heuristics abstracted from past experiences will be useful in the future), and continuous.

Interesting is Lenat's conclusion that there must be a METHODOLOGY for answering such questions as what is the source of a heuristic's power? the origin of new heuristics? the quantitative impact of a heuristic on a search? the interactions between heuristics working toward the same ends? the useful attributes of a heuristic? He proposes to use the standard empirical inquiry paradigm which dominates AI research: test hypotheses about heuristics by constructing - and studying - computer programs such as AM and EURISCO, programs which use heuristics and which try to find new ones.[6]

To the question: "How does new heuristics originate?", Lenat answers: "By generalizing other heuristics, abstracting from data, specializing other heuristics, finding analogies to other heuristics and to processes whereby other heuristics were formed." EURISCO demonstrated that these processes themselves can be guided adequately by a corpus of heuristics, that there is no need to distinguish 'meta-heuristics' from 'object-level heuristics'.

Further on he states that EURISCO was developed as the successor system, one whose field of expertise was not mathematics or diagnosis, but rather heuretics. That is, EURISCO had a corpus of heuristics which, as they ran, gathered data about their own running, and synthesized new members of that corpus (and modified old ones).

Along with heuristics for reducing the possibilities and for a selection among them (which had to overcome the difficulties with the so called 'brute force methods' like the British Museum method), now there is opposite heuristics, which has less to do if removed.

3. The new problematics concentrated above all in the question: Can or will the computers be able to think. The positive answer of this question is conceivable in two different versions: essentialistic and functionalistic, i.e. in the sense of reductionism (or mechanicism), resp. antireductionism, or else the functionalist conception.

Interesting in this respect is Ed. Moor's table referred to by Shannon. In this table the conceptions of many specialists in the field of computer science are given. As a result, a range of attitudes is established, starting with those who believe that computers can resemble human brains and accordingly can accomplish work similar to thinking and ending with those for whom[9] the computer is something like a complicated logarithmic slide-rule.

Here belongs also the problem of the restricted possibilities of the thinking machines in comparison with man's thinking. It receives various answers too. It turns out that the limitations of the machines are inherent also to man. The only real limitation to machine intelligence, according to von Neumann, rests with man's (in) ability to precisely specify the mental processes that he wishes to duplicate.

4. AI provides the possibility for a new, neutral, so to say, posing of the mind-body problem. Putnam mapped out the analogy between the software/hardware dichotomy and the mental/physical dichotomy.

5. Alongside other contemporary scientific branches AI increases the relative weight of the funcitonalist approach and conception compared with the competing programme for an essentialistic (substantial) explanation in science.

This leads to a corresponding reaction expressed in attempts to restrict the claims and possibilities of functionalism and ballancing it by a substantial approach to the problems at issue.

6. The successes of a definite group of sciences (including AI) necessitates a greater precision of the bearing to reductionism.

Despite its non-justifiability, the reductionist conception definitely supported views of a mechanistic (neomechanicistic) nature and conditioned both a certain recreation and radical reactions against them.

7. In the new domain, against the background of the traditional use of the general methods of induction and deduction, the increased significance[6] of analogy and more generally said of traduction, may be stated.

This role is at least partially due to a corresponding posing of the problem, i.e. it is applied to appropriate cases and conditions.

8. The transition from algorithmic to heuristic approach leads also to manifestation of dialectical situations, approach and conception.

Very interesting in this respect is the representation by Newell of the problems of AI as an overcoming of a series of traditional and contemporary oppositions.[10] According to him the long lasting strife between mechanicism and teleology was settled with cybernetics. The contradiction between analog and digital (machines) created the contemporary computer science etc.

In favour of dialectics speaks the unity of inductive and deductive approaches. In connection with the programme BACON Simon points out that the history of the discovery of Black's law suggests that it was neither wholly data-driven nor wholly deduced from theoretical assumptions, but that both induction from experimental observations and deduction from notions of the conservation of extensive properties played a role in the discovery.[11]

9. In connection with AI the problem of creativity can be seen from a new angle and is posed again and given primary importance.

Based on certain statements and conceptions of creativeness (e.g., of Gestalt-psychology) AI leads to a specification of these conceptions and - in prospect - to the possibility of simulation and modeling the process.

The creative process involves REPRESENTATION of knowledge (here the main role is played by memory), CONTROL and USE of the same (associated with problem-solving and planning) and ACQUISITION of new knowledge or learning. If these processes are gradually brought about in computer's programmes SINGULARLY, typical for man's creative thinking is its CLOSE INTERACTION, even their merging.

A distinction is made between strong and weak methods."Problem solving in novel domains makes use of weak methods - problem solving techniques of quite general application whose generality is assured by the fact that they do not use or require much prior knowledge of the structure of the problem domain. Problem solving in well-understood domain uses strong methods - powerful techniques that are carefully tailored to the specific structure of the domain to which they are applied. Of course strong methods are almost always more powerful than weak methods, but they are simply not available, by definition, when entirely new territory is to be explored.

The commonest weak problem solving methods are generate-and-test, heuristic search, and means-ends analysis."[12]

These methods have a direct bearing to the situation in science ("normal", "extraordinary") and to the training of scientists (experts and novices in problem solving)."Expert problem solving in any domain is characterized by the systematic application of powerful methods, each adapted to a recognizable subdomain. The expert does not have to seek and search; he recognizes and calculates. Problem solving by novices, on the other hand, is characterized by tentativeness and uncertainty. The novice frequently does not know what to do next; he searches and tests; he uses crude and cumbersome methods because he is not familiar with the powerful tools of the expert."[12]

The experience in this domain leads to the conclusion that"the mechanisms of scientific discovery can, indeed, be subsumed as special cases of the general mechanisms of human problem solving. To be sure, there may be essential novelty hidden in those aspects of problem solving that lie outside the range of the programs. But given the evidence of behavior that we have reviewed here, bare claims that such novelties exist are not convincing. There seems to be no present reason to believe that any aspects of scientific discovery must remain indefinitely beyond the powers of heuristic search, or that the discoveries of human scientists cannot in time be explained within the information processing paradigm for problem solving."[12]

The contemporary success in simulating scientific discoveries in the domain of mathematics, physics etc. on the basis of corresponding empirical data or theory is an argument in favour of the internalistic conception of the growth of science in the sense of a preponderance of the internal 'logic' in the interaction between empirical and theoretical knowledge in comparison with the impact of external factors relative to this cycle of a societal character (which the externalism considers as playing a firstrange role).

10. Finally, concerning the prospects of AI the question arises whether a fundamental theory of intelligence (common for man and computers) is even possible within a symbolic processing model.

Already at the contemporary stage AI has a certain contribution in the general process of scientification of M. There are all reasons to expect that this role of AI in the specification and development of M will increase parallel with the progress of AI itself.

REFERENCES:

1 Polikarov, A., Methodological Problems of Science (Sofia,1983).

2 Ginev, D., Polikarov, A., On the Methodologisation of Science Filosofska Misl, No 9 (1984 in Bulg.).

3 Polikarov, A., Science and Philosophy (Sofia, 1973).

4 McCarthy, J., Hayes, P.J., Some Philosophical Problems from the Standpoint of Artificial Intelligence, in: Machine Intelligence, Vol. 4,B.Maltzer, D.Michie (eds.)(Edinburgh, 1969).

5 Ringle,M.D., in: Philosophical Perspectives in Artificial Intelligence (Atlantic Highlands, 1979).

6 Lenat, D.B., The Nature of Heuristics, Artifificial Intelligence, 19 (1982) 189.

7 Boden, M. Artificial Intelligence and Natural Man (Hassocks, Gr,Britain, 1977).

8 Nelson, R.J., Margaret Boden, Artificial Intelligence and Natural Man ..., Synthese, 43 (1980) 433.

9 Greenberg,M.(ed.) Computers and the World of the Future (Cambridge, Mass., 1962).

10 Newell, A. Intellectual Issues in History of Artificial Intelligence, (Carnegie Mellon Univ., October 1982).

11 Bradshaw, G.F., Langley, P.W., Simon, H.A., Studying Scientific Discovery by Computer Simulation, Science 222 (1983) 971.

12 Simon, H.A., Search and Reasoning in Problem Solving, Artificial Intelligence, 21 (1983), 7.

ARTIFICIAL INTELLIGENCE: Methodology, Systems, Applications
W. Bibel and B. Petkoff (Editors)
Elsevier Science Publishers B.V. (North-Holland)

ARTIFICIAL INTELLIGENCE AND COMPUTER SIMULATION OF SCIENTIFIC DISCOVERIES

Boris Petkoff

Scientific Information Centre
Bulgarian Academy of Sciences
Sofia, Bulgaria

A meta-model of scientific activity is offered, which could be incrementally described in formal terms and implemented as a Knowledge Based System (KBS) in order to intensify the scientific research and development in a specific domain. Solving problems is considered to be an epistemologically motivated acivity which accumulates knowledge in recurrsively performed inductive-deductive cycles. The present meta-model has two application aspects:
* prescriptive - as a general framework for solving problems in the area of AI. A nontrivial application in the field of high-energy physics is described.
* descriptive - as an obvious epistemological interpretation of internal scientific mechanism e.g. of Cybernetics, Computer science, Artificial Intelligence (AI) etc.

INTRODUCTION

With the systematical discovery and investigation of the objective existing natural laws began the conscious research for structural and behavioural models of the world,giving the human beings the ability to transform their intellectual faculty in technical constructions - helping them not only "to explain the world, but also to alter it" (Adam /1970/).
We observe that matter appears in enormous varieties of different realizations, qualities, shapes, and forms, transforming and changing from one into others; but we observe also many recurrent properties, many features that remain unchanged, or if changed, return under similar conditions and conclude that there must be something unchanging in nature that causes these recurrent phenomena (Weiskopf /1973/). This is the origin of the idea that matter consists of some simple and unchanging elementary constituents and this point of view is so deeply ingrained in our way of thinking, that its influence can be noticed in the three avant-garde research areas today:
* elementary particles (high-energy) physics - considering the fundamental problems of the inanimate matter;
* gene engineering (molecular biology) - considering the fundamental problems of the animate matter;
* knowledge engineering (Artificial Intelligence) - considering the fundamental problems of the mind.
It seems to be very strange that "engineering"-disciplines have to do with fundamental aspects of matter and mind, but the contemporary trends in science lead to the development of new interdisciplinary fields of scientific research, like AI, in which there are various influences from different parent disciplines.

The AI-area is a sub-field of Computer Science concerned with symbolic solving of problems, or else a sub-discipline of Cybernetics aiming at constructing machines, capable of acquiring, storing and utilizing knowledge about the real and / or abstract world, and at the same time acting automatically, on the basis of adequate built-in models of the environment, as an intelligent human being, i.e. the KBS "is clever enough to answer a wide variety of questions on the basis of this model, it can get additional information from the external world when required, and can perform such tasks in the external world as its goals demand and its physical abilities permit". (McCarty, Hayes /1969/).
As any other scientific discipline the development of AI can be considered in terms of stages (Michie /1971/):
I. "Ad-hoc-discoveries"
II. Formalization and theoretical foundation
III. Systematization and practical application
AI seems to be now in the II stage, irrespective of the developed KBS, the so called Expert Systems (ES)-(Hayes-Roth etal. (Eds., 1983)
** '65 - '70 - DENDRAL, MACSYMA, etc.*
** '70 - '75 - MYSIN, HEARSAY-II, PROSPECTOR, etc.*
** '75 - '80 - PUFF, GUIDON, SACON, HASP, CASNET, etc.*
** '80 - '85 - R1, DRILLING ADVISOR, ...etc.*
and their practical applications in the fields of medicine, chemistry, geology, physics, technology etc.
A look at the existing ES gives some idea of the diversity of the knowledge engineering ways of designing models for solving problems, i.e. there are many pragmatical approaches families of systems respectively (Bond /1981/):
** the top-down or MYSIN type*
** the model-based or CASNET type*
** the blackboard or HEARSAY type*
** the bottom-up or R1 type, etc., but no established methodology.*
AI provides operational test of human cognitive models and as far as recent AI-tendencies lead to the creation of new interdisciplinary profiles of scientific activity rather than to replacing as many as possible human activities by computers, we shall be interested in epistemological founded KBS allowing the integration of intellectual human activities with computer's program-technical skills. The research of KBS has to focus on the building of general frameworks for solving problems and on the architecture of large and complex knowledge bases, because the current systems have instrinc limitation (Guida, Tasso /1984/):
** the basic inference mechanisms (the classical / matching-conflict resolution-action / loop) and control strategies (forward, backward, mixed) are not effective enough to allow the development of real time KBS operating with very large knowledge bases;*
** the knowledge available to KBS is not well structured in terms of the enrichment stages (empirical, hypothetical, theoretical knowledge etc.) and doesn't include a general (mainly model-theoretical) description of the subject domain; therefore it is impossible to perceive the missing knowledge and to derive it according to the general principles of the inductive-deductive scientific research cycle;*
** mechanisms for validation of the KBS activity for plausibility are not available, resp. conclusions they propose may be naive or even misleading, because of the absence of generalised models for knowledge acquisition applicable regardless of possible research area;*
This work is an attempt to develop a general framework for solving scientific problems as an epistemological alternative to the current approaches. We argue that there is a level of abstraction which allows to generalize methodologically the existing experience with KBS.

EPISTEMOLOGICAL ISSUES

The dominant research technique in AI seems to be the construction of programs and this leads to the difficult problem of how to check the scientific contribution of such

production.
Unfortunately there is a "pragmatical approach", respectively a tendency in which large and complex programs are writen, some impressive printouts are produced and then papers are published specifying a performance to be attained, but how to attain it is not arguable issue. The deficiency of this style of research is that there are no well defined research problems and no well developed general principles, hence this approach is methodologically sterile (Ritchie, Hanna /1984/).
In view of the II stage of AI-development state it may be not easy to assess the exact contribution of a piece of research, but it wouldn't be unrealistic to demand that an AI project should conform to the notion of scientific investigation of the philosophy of science. Epistemological problems arise despite of the fact that there is no established AI-methodology and can be solved interactively because epistemology has a more direct relation to AI than it has to other science. According to (McCarthy /1977/) the consideration of the epistemological problems like
** what kinds of facts about the world are available,*
** how these facts can be represented, and*
** what rules permit legitimate conclusions to be drawn from these facts,*
separately from the heuristic problems like
** how to search spaces of possibilities, and*
** how to match patterns*
has many advantages:

1. AI is very difficult scientific problem, so there are advantages in finding parts of the problem that can be separately attacked.
2. A single solution of the epistemological problems can support a wide variety of heuristic approaches to a problem.
3. The same problem of what knowledge is available and what conclusions can be drawn from knowledge arises in connection with a variety of problem solving tasks.
4. Existing programs that manipulate facts in some of the domain are confined in special cases and don't face the difficulties that must be overcome to achieve intelligent behaviour.
What this means is - we should be able to use both directions:
** from specific programs to general principles, and*
** from epistemological principles to efficient programs,*
in order to develop sound theoretical patterns applicable to real-world problems.
We can consider current constellation of AI-activities in terms of the following meta-aspects (Ringle /1979/):
** AI modelling - as branch of cognitive science is primary concerned with the internal components of cognitive processes and provide a coherent and plausible model of the way people think. It moves above all from theory to object, and demand the use of the computer only in order to represent, manipulate and explore the numerous factors pertinent to a particular facet of intelligent behaviour,*
** AI simulation - concerned with similarity of appearance, i.e. of overt behaviour and can be:*
*** demonstrative - exhibiting human-like behaviour rather than capturing human thought;*
*** investigative - hypothesizing that the internal structure of the simulation is the same as the internal structure of the object modelled and the extension of the simulation can cover novel inputs for the purpose of predicting as-yet-unrealised behaviour. It moves above all from object to the theory, rather than the other way about.*
In dealing with cognitive processes, i.e. their models resp. simulation we are faced with the methodological problem typical for every "black-box" situation - the derived "theories" can be validated only indirectly by means of inference-testing, predictive power, consistency, coherence with other "theories", etc. In this connection we have to inquire for the epistemological status of the so-called AI-"theories", because it has now become commonplace

for some people from from the AI-community to speak of computer programs as statements of theories.

We would like to focus the attention of the issue that there exist many different concepts for theory in the epistemology: the "statement view", the "non-statement or structuralist view", etc. (Stegmüller /1980/). May be the "logical view" is the best concept for AI-research, because logic provide suitable languages for expressing facts about the world for epistemological investigations:

* A theory is a list of axioms and a list of consequences of the axioms;*
* A model of a theory is a collective that satisfies the axioms.*

In other words, a theory is a "formal system" (Hackstaff /1966/) whose elements and relationships are:

* Primitive symbols;*
* Sequence of symbols;*
* Formation rules, that indicate when a sequence of symbols "is a formula" (is well formed, belongs to the system)*
* Axioms, which are initial formulas;*
* Theorems, which are formulas obtained from axioms, through transformation rules;*
* Models are "interpretations" of the theory, or models are systems whose elements and relationships are in correspondence with those of the theory. (Caselles /1984/).*

AI programs are in this sense realisations of models, i.e. implementations of interpretations of theories - if they exist. AI theorists are interested in principles of knowledge and intelligence which may be used to account for concrete, physically- instantiated, time- and perspective-dependent cognition (Ringle /1979/). Given the definition of "intelligence" as the capacity of a system or organism to successfully adapt its behaviour to attain its goals, we are faced with the problem whenever or not we can ascribe intrinsic goals to systems other that our own. (Dennett /1971/) One possible approach to this problem is to be aware of the difference between ascription and discovery. Speaking in terms of ascription we make the weaker claim that for the purposes of explanation we have assessed the goals of a system according to the criteria of consistency, coherence and observational accuracy. (Ringle /1979/)

Because we are in the habit of thinking in terms of binary opositions like theory vs. experiment: the nearest counterpart to the traditional "experiment" is the application of some theory to some actual fragment of reality or data then to report the consequences. The practical investigation proceeds by implementing programs and the assessment of results from this activity, which can be scrutinized by the following (Ritchie, Hanna /1984/) criteria:

* mapping between the statical and dynamical aspects of the theory during program-interpretation of results in terms of the theory*
* consistency, versatility, reliability, cost-effectiveness, etc.*

SCIENTIFIC DISCOVERY AS PROBLEM SOLVING

The scientific enterprise is dedicated to the extension of knowledge about some real or abstract worlds. The scientific method consists according to (Wartofsky /1968/) in the following:

* Observation of the collective object of study;*
* Formulation of theory explaining the properties of the elements and the relations among them;*
* Using the theory for prediction of events referred to the collective;*
* Experimentation in order to determine whether the predictions are accurate or not; when not it proceeds to modify the theory etc.*

Usually these activities are conceived as occuring in cyclical fashion: (Petkoff/1983, 1984/)

* gathering facts by observation of natural events or by "producing" phenomena through experimentation;*
* elaborating the facts by generating some hypotheses resp. testing the hypotheses against the facts;*

** elaborating a theory from the hypotheses resp. suggesting new hypotheses on the basis of a theory;*
** inferring models and corrollaries from the theory resp. enriching a theory on the basis of particular models;*
** interpreting the facts in terms of the models, resp. matching of existing models against facts, etc.*
In some trivial cases this cycle can be incomplete, i.e. some of these components can be superfluous, but generally each of these activities can be further subdivided. Since theories encourage the acquisition of new data and vice versa - scientific discovery can enter the cycle of scientific activity at any point, although some researchers prefer to speak of theory resp. data driven process.
There are several respects in which scientific discovery can be considered as problem solving. The main difference between the two is the indefiniteness of the goals of the scientific investigations and because of that the AI-problem solving can be subsumed as special cases of the general mechanisms of the solving scientific problems, i.e. scientific discovery.
In spite of this difference it is quite possible that the solving of complex scientific problems is not qualitatively distinct from the processes that have been observed in simpler problem solving situations, because the component process, which if assembled makes the mosaic of scientific discovery, generally involves their decomposition into sets of simpler problems as mentioned above and then attacking them. (Simon, Langley, Bradshaw /1981/)
A very important component of intelligent behaviour is the capacity that enables humans and / or KBS to structure the vast ammount of facts they receive and to form a space of hypotheses for their explanation and at least to abstract a suitable theory. This is the so called data driven or inductive approach used for solving problems in novel scientific domains or in diagnostic KBS.
The problem solving techniques or "weak" methods are quite generally applicable, because they do not use or require much prior knowledge of the structure of the problem domain:
** the generate-and-test method employs one process to produce candidate problem solutions while another process tests each candidate to determine whether it meets the criteria of solution;*
** the heuristic search method generates new solution candidates by modifying candidates already tries;*
** means-ends analysis guides the search by comparing solution candidates with criteria and modifying them in order to reduce the differences, etc.*
By the data-driven approach we are faced with the inductive inference problem or the so called model inference problem (Shapiro /1981/) which can be summarized as follows:
"In a model inference problem we assume some unknown model M for a given first order language L. We distinguish two types of sentences in L: observational sentences, which correspond to descriptions of experimental results, and hypotheses, which can serve as explanations for these results. The model inference problem is - given the ability to test observational sentences for their truth in some unknown model M, find a finite set of hypothese, true in M, that imply all true observational sentences... If T is a set of sentences true in M that implies all ground atoms of L true in M then T is called an atomic-complete axiomatisation of M".
In analogy to the diagnosis situation the model inference problem can be characterized by the fact that there does not exist complete proof procedure for checking the validity of the proposed solutions. Since a finite number of facts about a model can not in general determined it uniquely among all possible models, and since a model inference algorithm always bases its conjectures on a finite number of facts, it is bound to make mistakes. Inexact reasoning in diagnostic KBS can be also described as follows: (Ganascia /1984/)
** Rules are not theorems, but empirical statements expressing inexact reasoning;*
** Data contain many redundancies and sometimes contradictions;*
** All possible reasonings are triggered simultaneously and then combined. Therefore all valid rules are set off.*

For that reasons recent work on AI has recognised the need for selection criteria incorporating measure of theory complexity and likelihood as well as a measure of the degree of fit between data and theory. (Georgeff, Wallace /1984/)
The essence of most approaches to inductive inference over a given body of data is to define some criterion for what constitutes a good or useful theory, and then to search the space of all possible theories for the one that, under this measure, best describes the data. In this sense solving the problem - generate an "acceptable" theory explaining a set of empirical observations - can be described in two steps:
** generate a hypothesis space as a countable set of theories over the space of empirical observations in which each theory has an associated probability of occurence;*
** search all over the hypothesis space - selectively guided by the defined meta-criterion for "acceptable" theory - and find one which best reflects our prior expectation about the environment, descriptions of common and important objects, and their relations.*
This is the aspect of scientific discovery in which problem solving can be considered as search. In the next step of the epistemologic converse view - the so called theory driven or deductive approach - we have to consider problem solving as reasoning. We can postulate a system of logic that allows us to deduce new statements from the theory - axioms and previously deduced statements (Simon /1983/). Given a theory, i.e. a language, a deductive apparatus and a set of axioms, knowledge is what can be expressed in it: (Aiello, Levi /1984/)
** axioms are knowledge;*
** theorems that can be derived from them are knowledge, etc.*
Facts that can not be derived within the theory, but that can be asserted about the theory are metaknowledge, which has to guide the accumulating of more and more knowledge by inference until the possible models of the theory have been found.
The last way of viewing problem solving in the theory driven branch of the inductive-deductive cycle is as constraint satisfaction. We have inferred a set of models and can postulate various subsets defined by the constrains they satisfy. Solving the problem consists in narrowing down the original set to a subset or unique model that satisfies all of the constraints provided by the empirical observations. (Simon /1983/)
At this point we are able to implement the model(s) as a computer program if the way in which our scientific discovery has been done was a traditional one, or we have generated semiautomatically resp. interactively program-realisation(s) of the model(s) if our claim was the KBS-simulation of scientific discovery.
According to (McCarthy /1977/) we can declare:
** If there is no program that could achieve the goal by making deductions allowed by the theory no matter how fast the program run, than the theory is epistemologically inadequate;*
** An epistemologically adequate theory would be considered heuristically inadequate if no program running at a reasonable speed with any representation of the facts expressed by the data could do the job.*
Especially when a theory is expressed in mathematical or logical form, theory driven discovery can make extensive use of "strong" methods associated with the mathematics or the logic, or with the subject matter of the theory itself. The discovery procedures will not be general in this case, like the "weak" methods procedures, but will be tailored and guided by the problem domain meta knowledge (Simon, Langly, Bradshaw /1981/). Problems may be posed in some natural or formal language, or by direct confrontation with the external world - the set of problem data is usually incomplete and have to be supplemented by additional information available for the problem solver. As McCarthy /1969/ has pointed out in assessing problem solving procedures we must consider not only their performance in solving problems, but also their adequacy in representing problems, because most of the information does not derive from principles of logic, but represents empirical assumptions about the

problem domain:
**A representation is called metaphysically adequate if the world could have that form without contradicting the facts of the aspect of reality that interests us. Metaphysically adequate representations are mainly useful for constructing general theories.*
** A representation is called epistemologically adequate if it can be used practically to express the facts that one actually has about the aspect of the world.*
** A representation is called heuristically adequate if the reasoning processes actually gone through in solving a problem are expressible in the language.*
Now we are prepared to describe our attempt to develop a general framework for solving scientific problems as an epistemological generalisation of the above mentioned AI-approaches. We use the word "epistemology" in this paper from AI-point of view, i.e. we must take into account what is knowable with available observational and computational facilities. (McCarthy /1977/)

BASIC PRINCIPLES (Petkoff /1984/)

I. Solving problems is a knowledge intensive activity based on the "reafference principle" (Holst, Mittelstaedt /1950/, Anochin /1958/), i.e. the problem solver acts on the basis of an internal model of the real or / and abstract worlds. The epistemological synonim of internal model will be "global knowledge".
II. The model contains multidimensional (about different domains) and multilevel (on different levels of abstraction) hierarchically organised global knowledge. All problem solving activities are conducted in the context of this global knowledge, utilizing and updating it. It can be assumed that the global knowledge is stored in some kind of a long term memory.
III. Each knowledge component consists of the following functional units:
** declarative: facts, hypothesis, theories, and models & corollaries;*
** procedural: inductive, constructive, deductive, and reductive methods;*
connected generally as shown on Fig. 1.

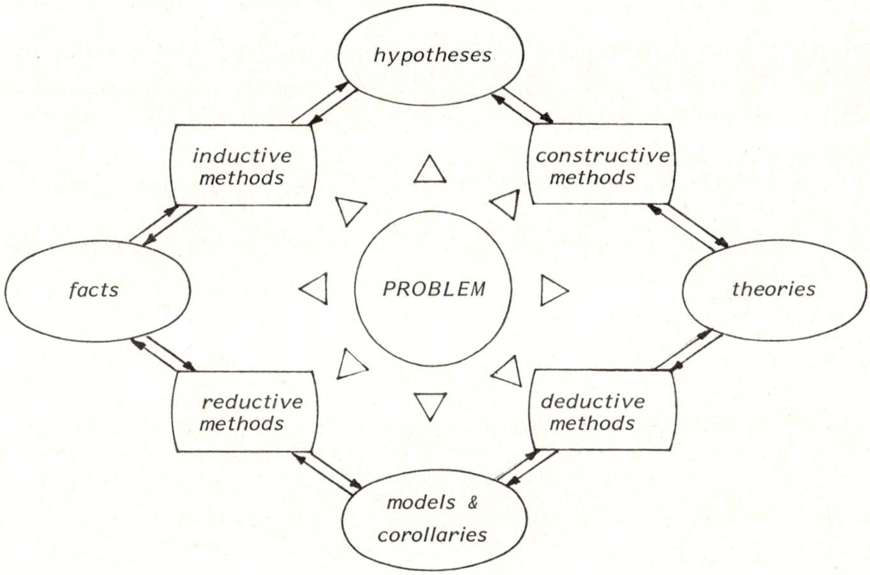

Figure 1
Basic inductive - deductive cycle

In some trivial cases this cycle can be uncomplete, i.e. some of these components can be superfluous. Facts and models are concrete knowledge while hypotheses and theories are more general. Ususally the methods are collections of declarative knowledge from other domains, i.e. the declarative / procedurale duality reflects the dialectical nature of knowledge.
IV. The basic problem solving process passess through the following phases:
1. Setting up of a local knowledge structure (organised as described in BP - III) in the short term memory by extracting the respective knowledge units, relevant to the current problems, from the global long term memory.
2. The second phase has the following interating steps:
** Explaining the facts by generating some hypotheses resp. testing the hypotheses against the facts;*
** Elaborating a theory from the hypotheses, resp. suggesting new hypotheses on the basis of a theory;*
** Inferring models and corollaries from a theory resp. enriching theory on the basis of models;*
** Interpreting the facts in terms of the models, resp. matching of existing models against the facts.*
3. Asserting that the problem at hand is solved, evaluating the resulting knowledge state.
4. When significant new knowledge is added to the local (short term) memory, it can be transferred to the global (long term) memory. If an inconsistency is detected at this local level, the global knowledge can be modified appropriately. This phase embodies the learning aspects of problem solving.
V. The overall problem solving process is a multilevel activity (divide into subproblems, solve the subproblems, solve the problem), initiating recurrsively the basic problem solving process (BP - IV). A failure to solve a particular problem at a given level may result in a higher level problem - revise the environment in such a way that the original problem can be solved.
VI. The general problem solving framework should allow the use of formal methods for asserting and proving important properties of general and specific problem solving activities.
VII. Principles I - IV are general principles with strong epistemological motivation, i.e. it is possible that some of their aspects may become unnecessary (or even obsolete) in more restricted particular problem solving situations. However this does not decrease their generality.

DOMAIN INDEPENDENT FRAMEWORK FOR PROBLEM SOLVING

The proposed general framework for solving problems will be described semiformally in a PROLOG-like style as a collection of clauses (Dimitrov, Petkoff /1984/). We believe that this approach will result in more compact, precise and clear specifications. Some acquaintance with the basic principles of PROLOG is assumed on the part of the readers.

```
1.1. solve (Problem, Args, State, Result) :-
1.2. set_up (Loc_state),
1.3. cycle (Loc_state, Loc_state1),
1.4. problem (Args, Loc_state 1, Result),
1.5. update_knowledge (Loc_state1, Result).
1.6. solve (Problem, Args, State, Result):-
1.7. revise_Knowledge(Result).
```

"solve" (1.1, 1.6) is the basic problem solving procedure, producing the Result of solving a given Problem with given arguments Args in an environment State. Following BP - IV., the procedure "set_up" (1.2) sets up a local knowledge structure Loc_state, using the local context (the parameters of "solve") and the global context (the problem solver's model of the real world - BP - I., II.).
This local structure is the starting point for the epistemological procedure "cycle" (1.3) which acquires problem-specific knowledge Loc_state1 from all possible sources - internal and external.
The next step (1.4) is to solve the given problem, using the accumulated knowledge. Here the problem is considered to be a procedure - parameter (the value of

the vaiable problem) that operates on the passed arguments Args in the constructed Loc_state 1, and produces the desired Result.
The last procedure "update_knowledge" (1.5) uses the knowledge, obtained from Loc_state and Result, to update the global knowledge base (if necessary).
The backtracking feature of PROLOG guarantees that all possible actions to solve the problem will be taken. However, if the problem cannot be solved in that environment (i.e. the first goal - 1.1 - fails), an attempt is made to revise the problem solver's global knowledge (1.6) so that the original problem can be solved and the required result produced (1.7).

```
2.1. set_up (Loc_state):-
     extract (facts, Facts),
     extract (methods_f_h, Methods_f_h),
     extract (hypotheses, Hypotheses),
     extract (methods_h_th, Methods_h_th),
     extract (theories, Theories),
     extract (methods_th_m, Methods_th_m),
     extract (models, Models)
     extract (methods_m_f, Methods_m_f).
2.2. Loc_state =[Facts, Methods_f_h, Hypotheses, Methods_h_th,
     Theories, Methods_th_m, Models, Methods_m_f].
```

"set_up" behaves as described in BP - IV. (2.1, 2.2). The local knowledge state is represented as a list of knowledge units (2.2). They are extracted from the global knowledge base in the context of the particular Problem and Args (1.1) with the help of the procedure "extract". The first argument of "extract" determines the kind of knowledge that is needed, and its second argument is a structure, containing the extracted knowledge.

```
3.1. cycle (State, State):- complete (Problem, State).
3.2. cycle (State, New_state):-
3.3. (hypoth(State,State1);
3.4. theory (State,State1);
3.5. model(State,State1);
3.6. verify(State,State1)),
3.7. cycle(State1,New_state).
```

"cycle" is a cognition procedure. The problem solver has a criterion (the predicate "complete" (3.1)) which determines whether the current local knowledge is consistent and is sufficient for the solution of the problem at hand. When the current local knowledge is not complete,, "cycle" performs one of the disjunctive cognitive activities, described in BP - IV. It builds hypotheses (3.3), or constructs theories (3.4), or produces models (3.5), or verifies thesemodels against the empirical facts (3.6). The recurrsive call of "cycle" at line 3.7 either terminates this procedure (3.1) when enough knowledge is accumulated, or tries again one of the possible actions (3.3. - 3.6.). PROLOG backtracks through all admissible states until an acceptable one is found (success) or no more are left (failure).

```
4.1. revise_knowledge(Result):-
4.2. solve(unsolvable,[Problem,Args],State,New_state),
4.3. solve(Problem,Args,New_state,Result).
```

"revise knowledge" makes an attempt to revise the problem solver's global knowledge in such a way that a new environment (New_state(4.2) + updated global knowledge) is created for the solution of the original problem. This is achieved by a recurrsive call of "solve" (4.2) with a higher level problem: the current Problem with its arguments Args cannot be solved in the given environment. On success of the first subgoal (4.2) the original Problem is tried in a revised environment (4.3). If the second goal (4.3) succeeds the desired Result is produced. Otherwise the remaining possibilities (if any) are investigated through backtracking.
Note that 4.2 produces side effects, i.e.changes the problem solver's global picture of the world. In the context of scientific research this may be a discovery, causing an evolutionary or revolutionary advance of science, depending on the current level (Petkoff /1983, 1984/).

```
5.1. hypoth(State,State1):- enough(hypotheses,Problem,State).
```

5.2. hypoth(State,New_state):-
5.3 (solve(gather_facts)[Problem,Args] , State,State1);
5.4. solve(develop_methods,[Problem,Args] , State,State1);
5.5 solve(generate_hyp,[Problems,Args] ,State,State1)),
5.6. hypoth(State1,New_state).

The goal of "hypoth" is to produce local state, containing a set of hypotheses, sufficient in the context of the original Problem. A predicate "enough" tests the current State (5.1) and terminates the procedure "hypoth" when its goal has been achieved. Otherwise, one of the three disjunctive subgoals is tried: gather new facts (5.3), or develop new inductive - deductive methods (5.4), or generate new hypotheses, consistent with the facts (5.5). Note that these activities are problem-oriented. Each time the state is updated, "hypoth" is called recurrsively, either to return the desired new state (5.1 succeeds), or to try another subgoal (5.2).

The other procedures of the cognition cycle ("theory", "model", "verify") are defined in a similar way. "Theory" constructs a theory on the basis of the generated hypotheses, using constructive methods. "Model" produces a local problem oriented model of the world, consistent with the theory. "Verify" checks whether this model is consistent with the facts.

EXPLANATION OF THE GENERAL FRAMEWORK (Petkoff /1984/)

Here a fragment of global knowledge structure in the domain of scientific research is described at three consecutive levels - strategic (metaphysical), tactic (epistemological), operative (heuristical). This distributed knowledge is the context into which scientific research problems are formulated and scientific discovery processes can be simulated. The division of the knowledge in distributed declarative and procedural units make the adequate knowledge representation and the separate attacks on the particular scientific problems possible. (Fig. 2).

I. Strategic level - methodological problems of science

(DDPW) The Domain Dependent Picture of the World integrates and generalizes the empirical and theoretical knowledge of the particular discipline in the scientific domain.

/GAIP/ The Gnoseologic Aspect of the Interval Principle determines the conceptual pattern which is used by the scientist as a filter to perceive and to partition the reality in order to find a mapping between its fragments and the created hierarchical systems of notions.

(INAB) The Intervals of Abstraction reflect the imposed from Nature constraints (which are implicit but objective), and produce a framework for the determination of the hierarchical system of notions.

/OAIP/ The Onthologic Aspect of the Interval Principle describes and determines the limit between important and subordinate properties resp. factors of the object of cognition, which have to be identified in its environment during the experiment.

(DADP) The Differentiating Ability resp. Power determines the motivated and efficient identification of the object of cognition within its environment, and at the same time this ability itself is dependent on constraints and limits, imposed from the nature of the object, out of which new cognition is not possible.

/OARP/ The Onthologic Aspect of the Relativity Principle contrives the reduction of the object properties up to a set of relevant ones, because each object of cognition has a finite number of properties in respect to a system of reference.

(CORU) The Correspondent Rules manage the mapping between the properties of the object and the intervals of abstraction.

/GARP/ The Gnoseologic Aspect of the Relativity Principle brings the results of the cognition process into line with the potential outcomes, constrained by the nature of the object of cognition, because sooner or later the limits are reached where nonrelevant becomes relevant, potential becomes actual, etc.

II. Tactical level - logical problems of science

(DRP) The Discipline Related Picture of the World is a component of the Domain Dependent Picture of the World.

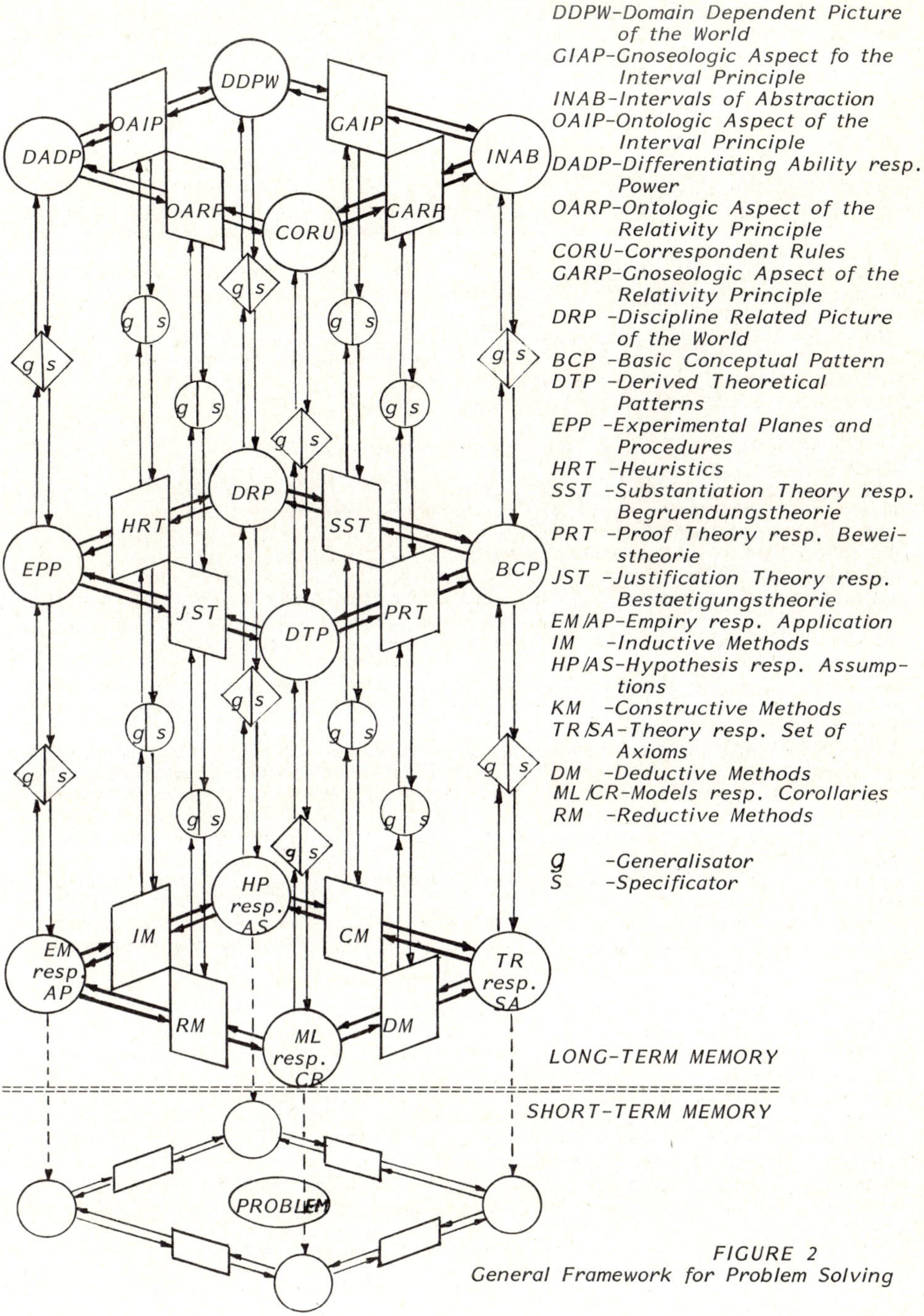

FIGURE 2
General Framework for Problem Solving

(BCP) The Basic Conceptual Pattern expresses the relations between the theoretical constructs and corresponds to the particular Discipline Related Picture of the World. (DTP) The Derived Theoretical Patterns are the inference closure of the Basic Conceptual Pattern, but sometimes these patterns are primary and can be generalized to Basic Conceptual Pattern.

(EPP) The Experimental Plans and Procedures have to isolate the disturbance and irrelevant factors.

/HRT/ The Heuristics are used to create a set of hypotheses according to the Discipline Related Picture of the World and/or to test some of these.

/SST/ The Substantiation Theory resp. Begruendungstheorie brings some of these hypotheses into line with the Basic Conceptual Pattern and/or create some new hypotheses.

/PRT/ The Proof Theory resp. Beweistheorie is used to infer many Derived Theoretical Pattern from the Basic Conceptual Pattern and/or to deduce the evidence of some theoretical patterns.

/JST/ The Justification Theory resp. Bestaetigungstheorie is used to verify the Derived Theoretical Patterns by ideal experiments and simulated measurements and/or to create some new theoretical patterns.

III. Operative level - problems of science

(EM-AP) Empiry resp. Application

/IM/ Inductive Methods are used for generating hypotheses explaining object's properties.

(HP-AS) Hypotheses resp. Assumptions

/CM/ Constructive Methods are used for elaborating theories.

(TR-SA) Theory resp. Set of Axioms

/DM/ Deductive Methods are used for infering corollaries and models

(ML-CR) Models resp. Corollaries

/RM/ Reductive Methods are used for interpreting the models.

AN EXAMPLERY APPLICATION OF THE META-MODEL (Petkoff /1984/)

This is a brief interpretation of the meta-model in the field of high-energy physics describing how it can be used as a general problem solving framework in order to receive polynomials expressing the sequence of elementary particles masses. The description is incomplete because we are at the very beginning of the development of a computerized knowledge based system in that area.

There are a lot of abstract theories based on the Quark model with state properties like: strangeness, charm, colour, etc., as an expression of general symetries. However the well-defined property mass (energy) is not of great importance for this taxonomy.

In contrast to the Quark model we have used the mass of the elementary particles as a basic property in the environment of the Quark-hypothesis - baryons and mesons are composite systems made up of fundamental particles (the so called quarks), kept together by some new field acting between the quarks whose quanta are sometimes referred to by the descriptive name "Gluons".

This is the global context. The local knowledge structure, set up by the program, is as follows:

** The empirical facts extracted from the global knowledge are sorted in a list of 79 mass values (eV) of elementary particles.*

** The hypothesis was that the sequence of the elementary particle masses satisfy one of the following laws: log, exp or polynomial.*

** No initial theory was presumed*

** No initial model was presumed*

The analysis of the elementary particle masses series has shown that a third order polynomial is a very good approximation (satisfying the χ^2 criterion) of the sequence.

The result expressed as an equational theory is: (Petkoff, Polikarov /1978/)

$$m = m_o + m_1 N^2 + m_2 N^2 + m_3 N^3$$

where N is the number of the particle and

$m_0 \approx 329,9760979$
$m_1 \approx 84,48897085$
$m_2 \approx -2,058430012$
$m_3 \approx 0,01891159258$

This theory can give rise to a model of the elementary particle with a constant that can be interpreted as a density constant and which can be used also to described the Gluone-forces.

The relation of this model to empirical knowledge in elementary particle high-energy physics is direct - the free holes on this sequence, approximated by a third order polynomial, suggest the existence of unknown elementary particles with particular masses. The discovery of such new particles will close the inductive-deductive cycle. If necessary, further iterations can be performed to develop the theory and the model.

When verified, this knowledge can be used to update the global (personal and/or scientific) knowledge in the area of high-energy physics.

EPISTEMOLOGICAL INTERPRETATION OF THE META-MODEL

On the basis of the present meta-model of scientific research and cognition one can explain the possible situations in science:

* *development of new scientific theories,*
* *genesis of new scientific disciplines*
* *arising of new scientific domains, etc.*

The three levels define a hierarchy of scientific problems whose solution determines their teleological behaviour or failure of solution makes them pass the control to the next higher level.

From a cybernetical point of view the meta-model functions as a hierarchical multiple feed-back control system. Each of the procedural knowledge units can operate as either the regulator (controller) or as the controlled unit in respect to its neighbouring units at the same or at a neighbouring level.

The science as a KBS is event-driven and accumulates knowledge as long as the knowledge acquisition process runs at the possible lowest level inside of the stability domain, defined by the next higher level:

* *If the scientific problem is solved, the knowledge acquisition process transfers to the next lowest level and the current level undertakes the control;*
* *In the case that the knowledge acquisition process is running out of the stability domain at the current level a transfer takes place to the next higher level and all or some units of the current level have to be replaced.*

The so called recursive call of a new generation of the current level reflects a qualitative new situation in the research area:

* *scientific development resp. instability at the operative level;*
* *scientific evolution resp. instability at the tactical level;*
* *scientific revolution resp. instability at the strategic level.*

The historical origin of AI resp. some of the different point of view in the scientific communities which split AI from or isolate AI within Cybernetics and its subdisciplines, Control and Computer Science could be explained in terms of critical events, but because of space-shortage we will content ourselves with a statical description.

According to Newell (1982), one could explain some important basic properties of AI research in terms of intellectual issues like

* *Symbolic vs. Continuous Systems*
* *Heuristics vs. Algoritms*
* *Interpretation vs. Compilation*

which have a perfectly objective reality, play a heuristic role in scientific activity and reflect the dialectical nature of cognition, but a taxonomy seems to be not so compelling as a framework with well defined constraints in the horizontal and vertical aspects. (Fig. 3)

"Horizontal" aspects reflect the logical structure of the scientific discovery levels, "vertical" - the relativity of the meta-knowledge levels. Generalisations increase bottom-up and couter clockwise, resp. specification increases top-down and clockwise, i.e. the knowledge processes are running in both directions.

Domain Dependent Picture of the World

CY-MM information processes analogy

CT, CS, AI } Analysis of teleological man or machine actions in discrete elements

Differentiating Ability resp. Power

CY-Information
CT-Analog signals
CS-Digital signals
AI-Facts

Discipline Related Picture of the World

CY-Teleology of dynamic systems
CT-Purpose / feedback / control
CS-Aim / algorthm / communication
AI- Goal / heuristics / intelligence

Experimental Plans and Procedures

CY-Identification of dynamic systems
CT-Identification of control loops
CS-Identification of abstract automata
AI-Identification of inference mechanisms

Hypothesis resp. Assumptions

CY-System characteristics interrelations
CT-Control, correction signals interrelations
CS-Input, state, output interrelations
AI-Search - space interrelations

Empiry resp. Application

CY-Information units
CT-Value, magnitude, quantity
CS-Data structures
AI-Symbol structures

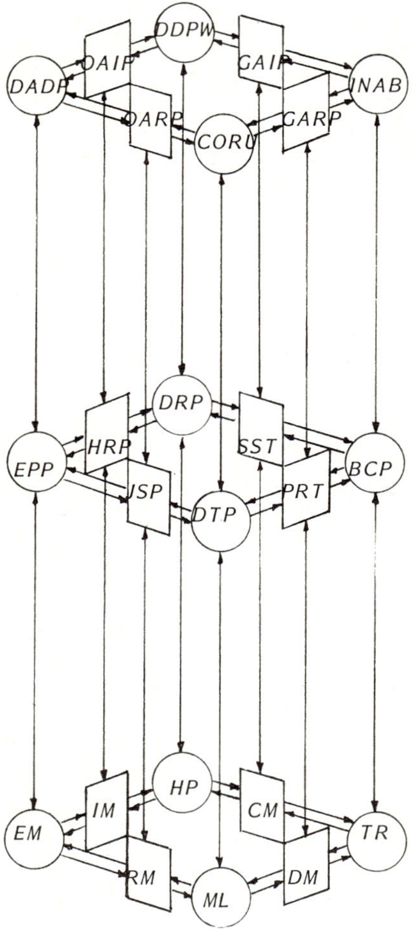

Intervals of Abstraction

CY-Dynamic System Characteristics
CT-Regulating circuit characteristics
CS-Abstract automata characteristics
AI-Inference mechanism characteristics

Correspondence Rules

CY-Mathematics, Logic

CT-Functional analysis...
CS-Boolean algebra...
AI-Logic...

Basic Conceptual Pattern

CY-Dynamic systems theory
CT-Control theory
CS-Automata theory, formal languages
AI-Semantic concepts

Derived Theoretical Patterns

CY-Hybrid, hierarchical...
CT-Linear, nonlinear...
CS-Deterministic, stochastic...
AI-Knowledge representation schemes

Theory resp. Set of Axioms

CY-VOLTERRA - equations...
CT-Differential equations...
CS-State space equations...
AI-Production systems...

Models resp. Corollaries

CY-Hybrid computer programmes
CT-Analog computer programs
CS-Digital computer programs
AI-LISP-, PROLOG-, PSI-machines programs for KBS

Figure 3

CONCLUSIONS

In this paper we offer a general framework for solving problems which is anthropomorphic, i.e. follows the general human problem solving approach, and has sound epistemological foundations. The solution proposed derives from the methodology of science and the practice of scientific research, from the theory of control system and the practical structure of knowledge employed in KBS. The present meta-model is both descriptive (reconstructive) and prescriptive (normative).

As a descriptive tool it allows to correlate meaningfully different scientific domain resp. knowledge based systems and is a basis for the development of comprehensive classification schemes.

As a prescriptive tool it emphasizes dynamic properties of each knowledge acquisition process, which is governed by the logic and methodology of certain research area and offers epistemologically motivated structuring and processing principles.

The use of rigorous mathematical and logical methods in this framework will produce important theoretical and practical results. Then the distributed knowledge base takes in consideration the complex character of the cognition process as a multi-level phenomenon and tries to satisfy the requirements of the formal reconstruction of intelligent behaviour with a powerful architecture for KBS, including parallel processing units.

A well structured knowledge base in a general framework can play a very important heuristic role for the knowledge acquiring, storing and utilizing process in KBS, because the existing powerful programing tools like flavours, windows, etc. support efficiently the parallel running problem-solving process.

REFERENCES

/1/ Adam, A., a.o., Kybernetische Modelle und Methoden,(WDV, Koeln/Opladen, 1970)

/2/ Aiello, L. and Levi, G., The Uses of Metaknowledge in AI Systems, in: O'Shea, T. (ed.) ECAI-84: Advances in AI (North Holland, Amsterdam, 1984)

/3/ Anochin, P., Physiologie und Kybernetik, in Sowietwissenschaft-Naturwissenschaftliche Beitraege 5 (Berlin, 1958)

/4/ Bond, A., Machine Intelligence (Pergamon Infotech Ltd., Maidenhead, Berkshire, 1981)

/5/ Casselles, A., A Method to Compare Theories in the Light of General Systems Theory, in: Trappl, R. (ed.) Cybernetics and System Research 2 (North Holland, Amsterdam, 1984)

/6/ Dennett, D., Inten tional Systems, Journal of Philosophy, 68 (1971)

/7/ Dimitrov, I., and Petkoff, B., A General Knowledge Based Approach to Problem Solving, in: O'Shea, T. (ed.) ECAI-84: Advances in AI (North Holland, Amsterdam, 1984)

/8/ Ganasia, J.G., Reasoning and Result in Expert Systems, in: O'Shea, T. (ed.) ECAI-84: Advances in AI (North Holland, 1984)

/9/ Georgieff, M., and Wallace, C., A General Selection of Inductive Inference, in: O'Shea, T. (ed.) ECAI-84: Advances in AI (North Holland, Amsterdam, 1984)

/10/ Guida, G., and Tasso, C., A New Approach to the Design of Expert Systems Architectures, in: Plander, I. (ed.) Artificial Intelligence and Information-Control Systems of Robots (North Holland, Amsterdam, 1984)

/11/ Hackstaff, L., Systems of Formal Logics, in: Reidel (ed.) (Dodrecht, 1971)

/12/ Hayes-Roth et al. (Eds.) Building Expert Systems, Addison-Westley (1983)

/13/ Holst, E.v., Mittlestaedt, H., Das Reafferenzprinzip, in: Landa, E.v., Holst, E.v. (eds.) Die Naturwissenschaften (Berlin, Goettingen, Heidelberg, Bd. 37, 1950)

/14/ McCarthy, J., Epistemological Problems of Artificial Intelligence (Proc. IJCAI-77)

/15/ McCarthy, J. and Hayes, P., Some Philosophical Problems from the Standpoint of AI, Machine Intelligence 4 (1969)

/16/ Michie, D., Heuristic Search, The Computer Journal 14, 1 (1971)

/17/ Newell, A. Intellectual Issues in the History of AI, Carnegie Mellon University (October 1982)
/18/ Petkoff, B., Kybernetisches Modell der wissenschaftlichen Forschung, 7th Int. Con. "Logic, Methodolgy and Philosophy of Science", Salzburg (1983)
/19/ Petkoff, B. A Cybernetic Model of Scientific Research and Cognition, in: Trappl, R. (ed.) Cybernetics and System Research 2 (North Holland, Amsterdam, 1984)
/20/ Petkoff, B. A Domain Independent Framework for Problem Solving in: Plander, I. (ed.) Artificial Intelligence and Information Control Systems of Robots (North-Holland, Amsterdam, 1984)
/21/ Petkoff, B., Policarov, A., Polynoms Approximating the Sequence of Masses of Elementary Particles, Comptes Rendus de Academie Bulgare des Sciences, Tome 31, Nr. 12 (1978)
/22/ Ringle, M., Philosophy and Artificial Intelligence, in: Ringle, M., (ed.) Philosophical Perspectives in AI (Humanities Press Inc., Atlantic Highlands, New Jersey, 1979)
/23/ Ritchie, G. and Hanna, F. AM: A Case Study in AI Methodology, Artificial Intelligence, Vol. 23, Nr. 3 (1984)
/24/ Simon, H., Search and Reasoning in Problem Solving, Artificial Intelligence, Vol. 21, Nr. 1,2 (1983)
/25/ Simon, H. et al., Scientific Discovery as Problem Solving, Synthese 47 (1981)
/26/ Shapiro, E., An Algorithm that Inferes Theories from Facts, (Proc. IJCAI-1981)
/27/ Stegmueller, W. Neue Wege der Wissenschaftsphilosophie (Springer Verlag, Berlin Heidelberg New York, 1980)
/28/ Wartofsky, M., Conceptual Foundations of Scientific Thought (MacMillan, 1968)
/29/ Weiskopf, W., What is an Elementary Particle?, in: Brown, S. (ed.) Physics 50 Years Later (Washington, 1973)

ARTIFICIAL INTELLIGENCE: Methodology, Systems, Applications
W. Bibel and B. Petkoff (Editors)
Elsevier Science Publishers B.V. (North-Holland)

UNIFIED THEORY OF KNOWLEDGE REPRESENTATION

Brian H. Mayoh
Aarhus University

In any artificially intelligent program knowledge of the external world must be represented. Many formal languages for representing knowledge have been invented and used in recent years, but there is a need for a unified theory in which one can

- prove general results that hold for many particular knowledge representation languages;
- transfer results for one knowledge representation language to other languages;
- combine knowledge represented in one language with knowledge represented in other languages.

In the first, second and last section of this paper we present a unified theory; in section 3 we indicate how the theory includes typical knowledge representation languages; in section 4 we indicate how the theory include Montague's formalisation of natural language. The motivating example in section 1 is an algebraic language for relational data bases.

The key concept of our unified theory, the concept of a gallery has a long history. Many years ago logicians generalised the study of models of first order theories to "soft model theory", the study of models of families of logics. Recently this concept of a logical family has been generalised to that of an institution [G].

Galleries are a further generalisation of institutions, in which one can have general values of expressions (terms) not just sentences with truth values.

#1 Signature, Frames, Structures and Galleries

In this section we gradually develop the concept of a gallery by introducing the concepts of signature, frame and structure. The development is motivated by the data base example in figure 1.

A particular relational data base is given by a "conceptual schema" with domains of object types and names of relations on these domains. Such a conceptual schema is an example of a sorted signature Σ where one has a set of sorts and a family Σ(S) of relation names for each set S of sorts. In figure 1 Σ(NAME,ADDRESS) and Σ(ADDRESS,PRICE,SIZE) have one element and the other families Σ(S) are empty.

Signature domains: NAME,ADDRESS,PRICE,SIZE

relations: PERSONS ⊂ NAME, × ADDRESS
HOUSES ⊂ ADDRESS × PRICE × SIZE

Two frames e1: Join (PERSONS,HOUSES)

e2: Project (PERSONS,NAME)

Two structures

m1:

PERSONS	
NAME	ADDRESS
Brian	Ry 66
Pia	Ry 66

HOUSES		
ADDRESS	PRICE	SIZE
Ry 66	750000	Stor
Alken 12	200000	Lille

$m1_{NAME} = m1_{ADDRESS} = m1_{SIZE} = WORD \quad m1_{PRICE} = INTEGER$

m2:

PERSONS	
NAME	ADDRESS
Brian	Ry 66
Pia	Bra 93

HOUSES		
ADDRESS	PRICE	SIZE
Ry 66	750000	Stor
Alken 12	200000	Lille
Bra 93	400000	Middel

$m2_{NAME} = m2_{ADDRESS} = m2_{SIZE} = WORD \quad m2_{PRICE} = INTEGER$

Evaluation

Val(e1,m1) =

NAME	ADDRESS	PRICE	SIZE
Brian	Ry 66	750000	Stor
Pia	Ry 66	750000	Stor

Val(e1,m2) =

NAME	ADDRESS	PRICE	SIZE
Brian	Ry 66	750000	Stor
Pia	Bra 93	400000	Middel

Val(e2,m1) =

NAME
Brian
Pia

= Val(e2,m2)

Figure 1: Relational Data Base Example

In the algebraic approach to relational data bases one can define new relations from old using algebraic oeprations. We can suppose that the expressions for defining new relations are given by

```
<exp> ::=  Persons | Houses |
           Union        (<exp>,<exp>) |
           Intersection (<exp>,<exp>) |
           Join         (<exp>,<exp>) |
           Project      (<exp>,<list>) |
           Select       (<exp>,<list>) |

<list> ::= NAME|ADDRESS|PRICE|SIZE|<list>,<list>
```

This grammar is an example of the definition of the Σ-frames for a signature Σ.

The contents of our data base will change when new houses are built and people buy and sell houses. At any time m we have a set m_{NAME} of names, a set $m_{ADDRESS}$ of addresses, a set m_{PRICE} of prices, a set m_{SIZE} of sizes, a relation $m_{PERSONS} \subset m_{NAME} \times m_{ADDRESS}$, and a relation $m_{HOUSES} \subset m_{ADDRESS} \times m_{PRICE} \times m_{SIZE}$. We may also have data base operations of insertion and deletion, which change the contents m of the data base to some m'. This is an example of the definition of the <u>Σ-structures</u> and <u>Σ-structure-morphisms</u> for a signature Σ.

The value of a data base expression e is a relation that depends on the contents m of the data base; it is given by the usual function for evaluating algebraic expressions in a data base. This is an example of an <u>evaluation function</u> which gives a value to each Σ-frame in each Σ-structure.

<u>Definition</u> A <u>discrete gallery</u> consists of a set SIGN of signatures, a set FRM(Σ) of Σ-frames, a category STR(Σ) of Σ-structures and an evaluation function Val_Σ:FRM(Σ) $\times$ STR(Σ) $\rightarrow$ SET for each $\Sigma \in$ SIGN.

The data base D in figure 1 is closely related to the data base D' in figure 2, because D' is given by renaming relations and domains, then adding a new relation. As figure 2 shows, this operation takes each D-frame e into a D'-frame e' and each D'-structure m' into a D-structure m, in such a way that: Val(e,m) = Val'(e',m'). This is an example of a signature morphism ϕ from Σ to Σ' generating a function FRM(ϕ):FRM(Σ) $\longrightarrow$ FRM(Σ') and a functor STR(ϕ) from STR(Σ') to STR(Σ), such that Val_Σ(e,STR(ϕ)m') = $Val_{\Sigma'}$(FRM(ϕ)e,m').

<u>Definition</u> A <u>gallery</u> consists of a category SIGN of signatures, a functor FRM from SIGN to some category of sets, a functor STR from SIGN to some category of categories, and an evaluation function Val_Σ:FRM(Σ) $\times$ STR(Σ) $\longrightarrow$ SET for each $\Sigma \in$ SIGN such that

$$Val_\Sigma(e,STR(\phi)m') = VAL_{\Sigma'}(FRM(\phi)e,m')$$

for each signature morphism ϕ from Σ to Σ', each e $\in$ FRM(Σ) and each m' $\in$ STR(Σ').

<u>Comment</u> An institution (G) is a gallery such that Val_Σ(e,m) $\in$ (true,false) for each signature Σ, each e $\in$ FRM(Σ) and each m $\in$ STR(Σ).

Signature Σ' domains: N,A,P,S

relations: $PP \subset N \times A, HH \subset A \times P \times S, VV \subset N \times S$

Two frames e1': join (PP,HH)

e2': project(PP,N)

Two structures

m1':

PP	
N	A
Brian	Ry 66
Pia	Ry 66

HH		
A	P	S
Ry 66	750000	Stor
Alken 12	200000	Lille

VV	
N	S
Brian	Stor
Pia	Stor

$m1'_N$ = INTEGER $m1'_N = m1'_A = m1'_S$ = WORD

m2:

PP	
N	A
Brian	Ry 66
Pia	Bra 93

HH		
A	P	S
Ry 66	750000	Stor
Alken 12	200000	Lille
Bra 93	400000	Middel

VV	
N	S

$m2'_P$ = INTEGER $m2'_N = m2'_A = m2'_S$ = WORD

Morphisms For Σ in figure 1, renaming gives a signature morphism φ from Σ to Σ' such that:

FRM(φ) e1 = e1',FRM(φ) e2 = e2'
STR(φ) m1' = m1,STR(φ) m2' = m2

Evaluation function

Val'(e1',m1') = Val(e1,m1), Val'(e1',m2') = Val(e1,m2)
Val'(e2',m1') = Val'(e2',m2') = Val(e2,m1) = Val(e2,m2)

Figure 2: Morhpisms of Relational Data Bases

One reason why signature morphisms are important is that they capture parametrization; one often has a formal parameter signature Σ_0, an actual parameter signature Σ_1, a parametrized signature Σ_2 and parametrization diagrams

$$\begin{array}{ccc} \Sigma_0 & \xrightarrow{\phi} & \Sigma_2 \\ \pi \downarrow & & \downarrow \\ \Sigma_1 & \longrightarrow & \Sigma_3 \end{array} \quad \Rightarrow \quad \begin{array}{ccc} FRM(\Sigma_0) & \xrightarrow{FRM(\phi)} & FRM(\Sigma_2) \\ \downarrow FRM(\pi) & & \downarrow \\ FRM(\Sigma_1) & \longrightarrow & FRM(\Sigma_3) \end{array} \quad \begin{array}{ccc} STR(\Sigma_0) & \xleftarrow{STR(\phi)} & STR(\Sigma_2) \\ \uparrow STR(\pi) & & \uparrow \\ STR(\Sigma_1) & \longleftarrow & STR(\Sigma_3) \end{array}$$

In most useful galleries the category SIGN has pushouts so Σ_3 is determined by the signature morphisms ϕ and π.

#2 Specifications and Theories

The contents of the data base D in figure 1 may vary in time but "constraints" can restrict them to a particular class M of D-structures. Two data base expressions, e_1 and e_2, may or may not satisfy the condition

$$\forall m \in M.\ Val(e_1,m) = Val(e_2,m)$$

This condition gives an equivalence relation that is the theory determined by M.

Definition Let $M \subset STR(\Sigma)$ for some signature Σ in a gallery <SIGN,FRM,STR,Val>. The theory determined by non-empty M is the equivalence relation on $FRM(\Sigma)$ with the equivalence classes

$$[e]_M = (e' \in FRM(\Sigma) \mid Val(e',m) = Val(e,m) \text{ for all } m \in M)$$

A true sentence of this theory is a frame $e \in FRM(\Sigma)$ such that $\forall m \in M.Val(e,m) = true$.

Comment If a theory has a true sentence, then one of its equivalence classes consists of all the true sentences.

Example For the data base in figure 1 "Project(join(persons, houses),name)" is equivalent to "Project(persons),name" in the theory determined by M = {m1,m2}.

Definition For any signature Σ in a gallery <SIGN,FRM,STR,Val> the theory determined by the empty subset of $STR(\Sigma)$ is the "Universal" equivalence relation with $[e]_\phi = FRM(\Sigma)$ as its only equivalence class.

The reason for the last definition is that it gives a connection between subsets of $STR(\Sigma)$ and theories with such useful properties as

$$[e]_M = \{[e]_m \mid m \in M\}$$

$$\phi \subseteq m1 \subseteq m2 \subseteq STR(\Sigma) \rightarrow [e]_{STR(\Sigma)} \subseteq [e]_{m2} \subseteq [e]_{m1} \subseteq [e]_\phi$$

This connection is a natural generalisation of the more usual Galois connection in which theories are identified with their set of true sentences.

<u>Definition</u> The <u>specification</u> determined by non-empty $E \subset FRM(\Sigma)$ in a gallery <SIGN,FRM,STR,Val> is the equivalence on $STR(\Sigma)$ with the equivalence classes

$$[m]_E = \{m' \in STR(\Sigma) \mid Val(e',m) = Val(e,m') \text{ for all } m \in M\}$$

<u>Comment</u> For each result about theories there is a dual result about specifications.

#3 Knowledge Representation Language

In this section we indicate how our unified theory captures A.I. languages for knowledge representation by looking at two examples: Sowa's conceptual structures [S] and Wolfengang's frames [W]. The representation of "a monkey eating a walnut with a spoon made out of the walnut shell" in the two languages is shown in figure 3.

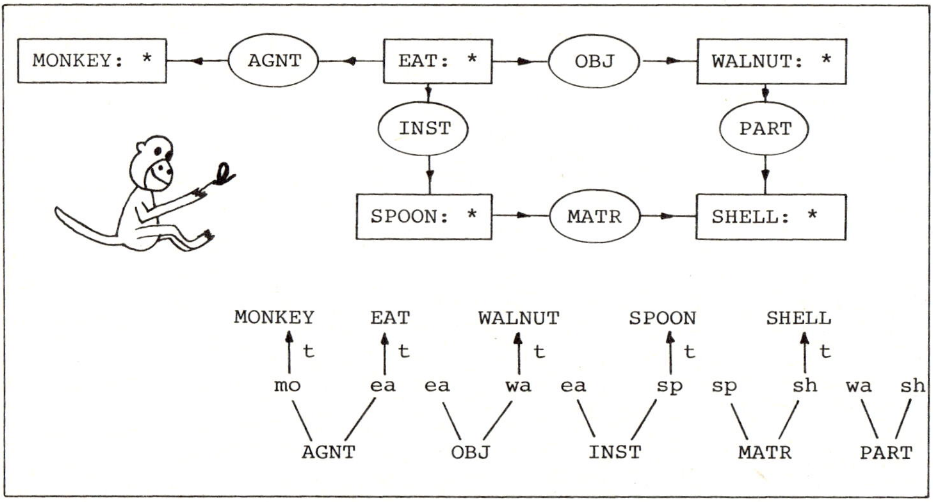

Figure 3: Two Frames with the Same Meaning

The signature Σ of a Sowa representation consists of (1) a set C of "concept types" partially ordered by "is a subconcept of" (2) a family Σ_c of individual names for each $c \in C$ (3) disjoint families $\Sigma(c_1, c_2, \ldots)$ of relation names for each sequence $(c_1, c_2, \ldots) \in C^*$.

The Σ-frames are given by

- instances of relations in the signature

- restrictions of Σ-frames in which concept types are replaced by subconcept types

- joins of frames in which matching concept types are identified.

Figure 4 shows instances of signature relations and restrictions of Σ-frames; the join of its five restrictions is the frame in figure 3. Sowa [p. 92] also allows copying and simplification of frames, but this is not necessary when frame joining is defined appropriately.

<u>Signature</u> Σ concept types		MONKEY<ANIMATE<ENTITY
		EAT<ACT
		WALNUT<SPOON<SHELL<ENTITY
	Relationnames	Σ(ACT,ANIMATE) = {AGNT}
		Σ(ACT,ENTITY) = {OBJ,INST}
		Σ(ENTITY,ENTITY) = {MATR,PART}

<u>Instance frames</u>

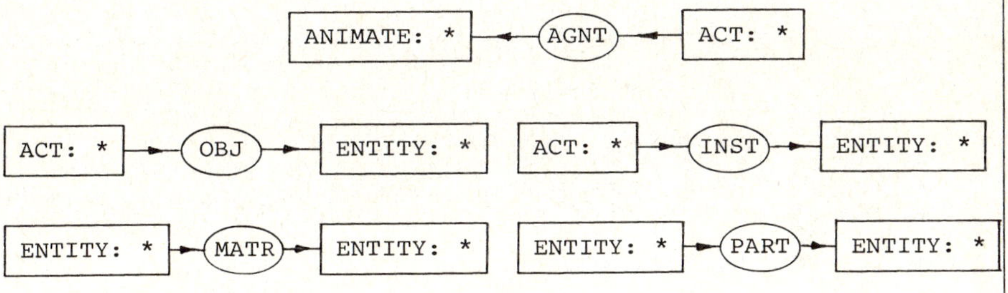

<u>Restriction frames</u>

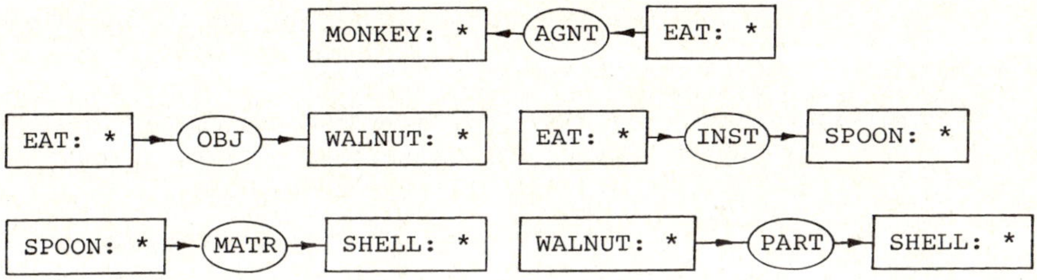

Figure 4: Sowa Representation Language

The Σ-structures are given by (1) a set m_c for each concept type c such that $c1<c2$ implies $m_{c_1} \subseteq m_{c_2}$ (2) an element $m_i \in m_c$ for each individual name $i \in \Sigma_c$ (3) a relation $m_p \subseteq m_{c_1} \times m_{c_2} \ldots$ for each $p \in \Sigma(c_1, c_2 \ldots)$.

An assignment to a Σ-frame e in a Σ-structure m gives an element of m_c to each [c: *] in e. The natural inductive definition gives either "e is true in m for the assignment a" or "e is false in m for the assignment a". We can define Val(e,m) as the set of assignments that make e true in m. When there are no *-concepts in e, there is a unique assignment a_o to e in m; if e is true in m, then Val(e,m) = $\{a_o\}$; if e is false in m then Val(e,m) is the empty set; Σ-frames without *-concepts are Σ-sentences.

Our Σ-specifications correspond to Sowa's canons, sets of canonical graphs; our Σ-structures correspond to his closed worlds; for simplicity we have ignored his open worlds and replaced his game semantics for modal and higher order logic by traditional first order semantics. We will make similar simplifications in our description of the gallery for the knowledge representation language in [W].

A signature Σ of a Wolfengangen representation consists of (1) a set C of sorts such that $c_1 \rightarrow c_2, c_1 \times c_2 \in C$ for all sorts $c_1, c_2 \in C$ (2) disjoint families Σ(c) of function names for each sort $c \in C$. The Σ-frames are given by

- instances of function names in the signature
- variables for each sort
- $\langle t_1, \ldots, t_n \rangle$ where $t_1 \ldots t_n$ are Σ-frames
- (s,t) where s is a Σ-frame of sort $c_1 \rightarrow c_2$ and t is a frame of sort c_1
- $(\lambda y.t)$ where t is a Σ-frame and y is a variable.

Figure 5 illustrates some of these ways of building new frames from old; the product of its ten frames is given in figure 3.

Signature Σ	sorts:	ENTITY,ACT,ACT → ENTITY ...	
	Functionnames:	Σ(ACT × ENTITY → 2)	= {AGNT,OBJ,INST}
		Σ(ENTITY × ENTITY → 2)	= {MATR,PART}
		Σ(ACT → 2)	= {EAT}
		Σ(ENTITY → 2)	= {MONKEY,WALNUT, SPOON,SHELL}
Frames	(MONKEY,mo),(EAT,ea),(WALNUT,wa),(SPOON,sp),(SHELL,sh) (AGNT,<ea,mo>),(OBJ,<ea,wa>),(INST,<ea,sp>) (MATR,<sp,sh>),(PART,<wa,sh>)		

Figure 5: Wolfengangen Representation Language

The Σ-structures are given by (1) a set m_c for each sort c such that $m_{c_1 \times c_2} = m_{c_1} \times m_{c_2}$ and $m_{c_1 \rightarrow c_2}$ is the set of functions from m_{c_1} to to m_{c_2} (2) an element m_i of m_c for each function name $i \in \Sigma_c$. An assignment a to a Σ-frame e in a Σ-structure m gives an element of m_c to each free variable of sort c in e. The natural inductive definition gives a function f_a for each <e,m,a>, so we can define Val(e,m) as the map taking assignment a into function f_a. When there are no free variables in e, there is unique assignment ao to e in m and Val(e,m) is essentially f_{ao}; Σ-sentences are Σ-frames without free variables such that f_{ao} is a truth value.

#4 Natural Languages

In this section we indicate how our unified theory captures Montague grammars [P], one of the most elaborate formal theories of natural language. In this formal theory a natural language expression e has zero, one or more representations as formula in an intensional logic. The meanings of e are given by the values of its representative formula. For simplicity we only consider equational logic here, not full intensional logic.

The signature Σ of a Montague grammar consists of (1) a set C of sorts (2) a family Σ_c of variables for each sort c (3) a family $\Sigma_{c_1,c_2} \rightarrow c_0$ of function names for each non-empty sequence of sorts c_0, c_1, c_2 ... The Σ-frames are given by

- variables from the signature
- $\sigma(t_1, t_2 \ldots)$ where $\sigma \in \Sigma c_1, c_2 \ldots \rightarrow c_0$, t_1 is frame of sort c_1, t_2 is frame of sort c_2
- $t_1 = t_2$ where t_1 and t_2 are frames of the same sort.

This set of frames is unusual because a Σ-frame always has one sort, but it can have more than one sort. Figure 6 is the Montague version of figures 4 and 5.

Signature Σ	sorts:	ENTITY,ACT,ANIMATE	
	Functionsnames:	Σ(ACT,ENTITY → 2)	= {OBJ,INST}
		Σ(ACT,ANIMATE → 2)	= {AGNT,OBJ,INST}
		Σ(ENTITY,ENTITY → 2)	= {MATR,PART}
	Variables:	Σ, ANIMATE	= {mo,wa,sp,sh}
		Σ, ENTITY	= {wa,sp,sh}
		Σ, ACT	= {ea}
Frames	AGNT(ea,mo),OBJ(ea,wa),INST(ea,sp),MATR(sp,sh),PART(wa,sh)		

Figure 6: Montague Representation

There are two kinds of ambiguity in the Montague approach to natural language. A natural language expression L can be syntactically ambiguous because L can be represented by more than one Σ-frame. Even if the expression L is syntactically unambiguous, it can be semantically ambiguous because the unique representative e of L can be assigned sorts in several ways. Semantic ambiguity affects our definition of Val(e,m) - assignments in the domain of Val(e,m) may be of different sorts.

The Σ-structures are given by (1) a set m_c for each sort c (2) a function $m_f: m_{c_1} \times m_{c_2} \ldots \rightarrow m_{c_0}$ for each f in $\Sigma_{c_1,c_2 \ldots \rightarrow c_0}$. An assignment a to a Σ-frame e in a Σ-structure m gives an element of m_c to each variable of sort c in e. The natural inductive definition gives "value of e for the assignment a", so we can define Val(e,m) as the map taking assignment a into value va. When the frame e has the form $t_1=t_2$, then va is a truth value for all a - the value <u>true</u> when assignment a gives the same m-value to t_1 and t_2, the value <u>false</u> when a gives different values to t_1 and t_2.

#5 Gallery Morphisms

In this section we introduce gallery morphisms; the key to our achieving two of the three aims of the unified theory - transferring results from one representation language to another and combining knowledge represented in several languages.

Consider two galleries, G = <SIGN,FRM,STR,Val> and G' = <SIGN',FRM',STR',Val'>. One can argue for the following requirements on a morphism Ψ from G to G':

(1) a function Ψ:SIGN → SIGN'

(2) functions α_Σ: FRM'($\Psi(\Sigma)$) → FRM(Σ) for each Σ ∈ SIGN

(3) functors β_Σ: STR(Σ) → STR'($\Psi(\Sigma)$) for each Σ ∈ SIGN

(4) $Val_\Sigma(\alpha_\Sigma(e'),m) = Val'_{\Psi(\Sigma)}(e',\beta_\Sigma(m))$ for each Σ ∈ SIGN, m ∈ STR(Σ), e' ∈ FRM'($\Psi(\Sigma)$)

Figure 7 illustrates these requirements by indicating a morphism φ from the data base gallery in section 1 to the first knowledge representation gallery in section 3. The reader can check that φ satisfies the

<u>Definition</u> A gallery morphism from G to G' consists of (1) a functor Ψ from SIGN to SIGN' (2) a natural transformation α from FRM';Ψ to FRM (3) a natural transformation β from STR to STR';Ψ such that $Val_\Sigma(\alpha_\Sigma(e'),m) = Val'_{\Psi(\Sigma)}(e',\beta_\Sigma(m))$ for m ∈ STR(Σ), e' ∈ FRM'($\Psi(\Sigma)$).

<u>Motivation</u> Gallery morphisms transfer G-signatures, G-frames, G-structures, G-specifications and G-theories into G'-signatures, G'-frames, G'-structures, G'-specifications and G'-theories.

<u>Signatures</u> Σ

domains	NAME,ADDRESS,PRICE,SIZE		NAME,ADDRESS,PRICE,SIZE
relations	PERSONS$\subset$NAME$\times$ADDRESS	$\overset{\Psi}{\Rightarrow}$	$\Sigma_{NAME,ADDRESS}$={PERSONS}
	HOUSES$\subset$ADDRESS$\times$PRICE$\times$SIZE		$\Sigma_{ADDRESS,PRICE,SIZE}$={HOUSES}

<u>Frames</u>

join(PERSONS,HOUSES) $\overset{\alpha_\Sigma}{\Leftarrow}$

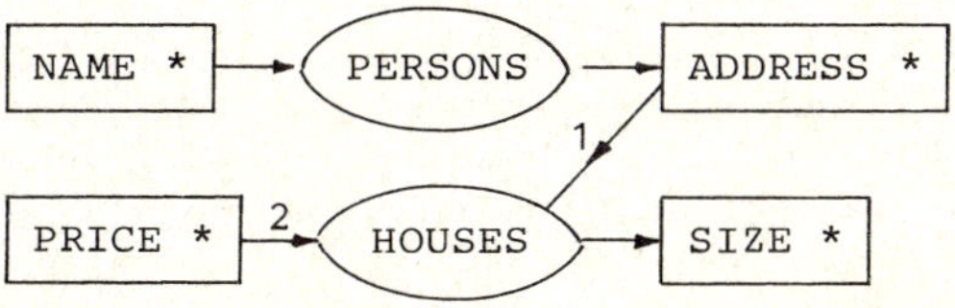

<u>Structures</u>

m_{PRICE} = Integer

m_{NAME} = $m_{ADDRESS}$ = m_{SIZE} = WORD

PERSONS	
NAME	ADDRESS
Brian	Ry 66
Pia	Ry 66

$\overset{\beta_\Sigma}{\Rightarrow}$

m'_{PRICE} = Integer

m'_{NAME} = $m'_{ADDRESS}$ = m'_{SIZE} = WORD

$m'_{PERSONS}$ = {<Brian, Ry 66>,
<Pia, Ry 66>}

m'_{HOUSES} = {<Ry 66,750000,Stor>,
<Alken 12,200000,Lille>}

HOUSES		
ADDRESS	PRICE	SIZE
Ry 66	750000	Stor
Alken 12	200000	Lille

Figure 7: A Gallery Morphism

References

[G] J.A. Goguen, R.M. Burstall: Introducing Institutions, Springer LNCS 164, pp. 221-256.

[P] B.H. Partree, ed.: Montague Grammars, Academic Press, 1976.

[S] J.F. Sowa: Conceptual Structures, Addison-Wesley, 1984.

[W] V.E. Wolfengangen: Frame theory and computations, Computers and Artificial Intelligence 3 (1984), pp. 1-30.

ARTIFICIAL INTELLIGENCE: Methodology, Systems, Applications
W. Bibel and B. Petkoff (Editors)
Elsevier Science Publishers B.V. (North-Holland)

THE HYPERNETS METHOD FOR REPRESENTING KNOWLEDGE

Ioan Georgescu

Central Institute for Management
and Informatics
Bucharest - ROMANIA

The method is based on a recursively defined structure called hypernet $H=(\mathcal{N},\mathfrak{R},p)$, where $\mathcal{N}$ is a set of objects called hypernodes, $\mathfrak{R}$ is a set of relational entities called hyperrelations, and p is a property list. The knowledge representation language HYPER is presented with full syntactic and semantic specifications. The method has been used for representing knowledge in connection with the INTEXP Domain Independent Expert System.

1. INTRODUCTION

Various knowledge representation techniques have been successfully used for AI applications. Though they are distinct as far as their conceptual insights are concerned, existing knowledge representation methods share a common characteristic: they have been devised mainly for allowing humans analyse the knowledge environment, tailor the knowledge into pieces, represent a simple model of such an artificial world, and understand what happens when using represented knowledge in reasoning processes. These requirements for human interaction during all implementation steps of intelligent systems, led to an oversimplification of knowledge representation techniques. As a consequence, it takes years of human efforts, both from the part of knowledge engineers and of domain experts, to build a knowledge base for a real application, but the major difficulties coming from the lack of flexibility in the maintenance appear soon during systems operation.

With the development of knowledge acquisition systems, the motivation for oversimplified knowledge representation methods becomes obsolete. The knowledge representation language is no more the language of the knowledge engineer, it is an intermediate systems language, the output language of the knowledge acquisition component and the input language of the knowledge base system.

There is here a new shift in paradigm, from oversimplified knowledge representation methods, to structural representation methods, adequate for the real complexity of the domain of expertise. The need for still another knowledge representation method has been generated by the requirements for coping with the structural complexity of real scientific applications, which are among the main objectives of the INTEXP Domain Independent Expert System.

2. THE HYPERNETS METHOD

A hypernet is a triple $H=(\mathcal{N},\mathfrak{R},p)$, where:

$\mathcal{N}$ is a set of recursively defined objects called hypernodes;
$\mathcal{R}$ is a set of recursively defined relational entities called hyperrelations;
p is a set of attribute-value pairs, arranged as a property list.

The concept of hypernode is related to the concept of abstract object. A hypernode is a quintuple $N=(h_n,s_n,I_n,E_n,p_n)$ where

h_n is the identifier of the hypernode;

s_n is the sort of the hypernode;

I_n is a lower level hypernet which describes the internal structure of the hypernode, in terms of component hypernodes and hyperrelations;

E_n is a set of well-formed formulae called linkage patterns, which describe the restrictive selection of component hypernodes allowed for participation like linkage point in combination with other knowledge pieces;

p_n is a property list.

For example, the concept of TOWN may be represented by a hypernode, as a composite object whose components are DISTRICTS, related to each other by ROADs. All the component districts are represented within the INTERNAL STRUCTURE of the knowledge piece, while those which are outer districts are represented within the EXTERNAL STRUCTURE (fig. 1a).

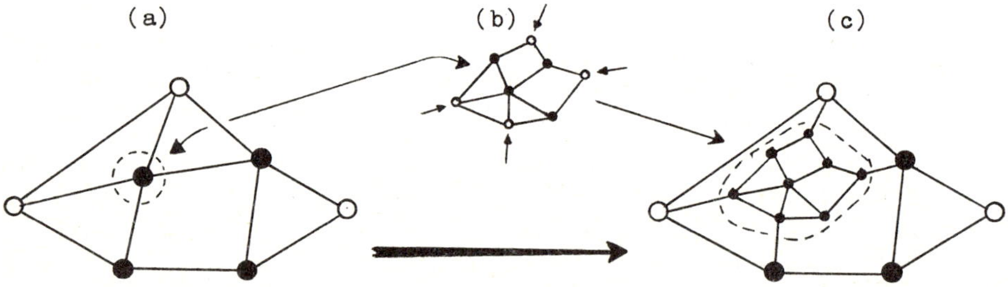

Figure 1
The refinement (c) of a hypernode TOWN (a), by replacing one of the components DISTRICT with its detailed representation (b)

By definition, the objectual component of an internal structure is also a hypernode. We may look at a DISTRICT as to an instance of the concept of PLACE, which is the same the concept of TOWN is derived from. A district has components (buildings - the ground instance for the concept of PLACE), also related to each other by ROADs. When we refine our knowledge about the town, we usually replace a primitive hypernode (the former DISTRICT) by a more detailed description of it (the representation of the real components and structure of the given district, figure 1b). The EXTERNAL STRUCTURE of the district must provide all road connections required for preserving the initial representation of the TOWN consistent with the actual refinement (figure 1c). When an instance of the concept TOWN (a town) is related to another instance of the same concept (another town) by the relation ROAD, they are linked by providing districts from the external structures of involved towns, at the endings of the connecting road (figure 2).

The concept of hyperrelation is related to the concept of relation generator, and captures the mechanism representing how relational entities with structural similarity are produced starting from a unifying concept. The basic support for such a mechanism is the concept of hole, which is a shaped structured space, a hypernode acceptor, playing within the method a similar role as the concept of place in primitive functional or relational expressions. A hyperrelation is a quintuple $R=(h_r,s_r,I_r,E_r,p_r)$ where

h_r is the identifier of the hyperrelation;

s_r is the sort of the hyperrelation, which identifies the class of the hyperrelations sharing the same structural characteristics

I_r is the internal structure defined in terms of component holes and lower level hyperrelations;

E_r is the external structure, defined in terms of linkage patterns specifying those holes of the hyperrelation which participate in composition operations;

p_r is a property list.

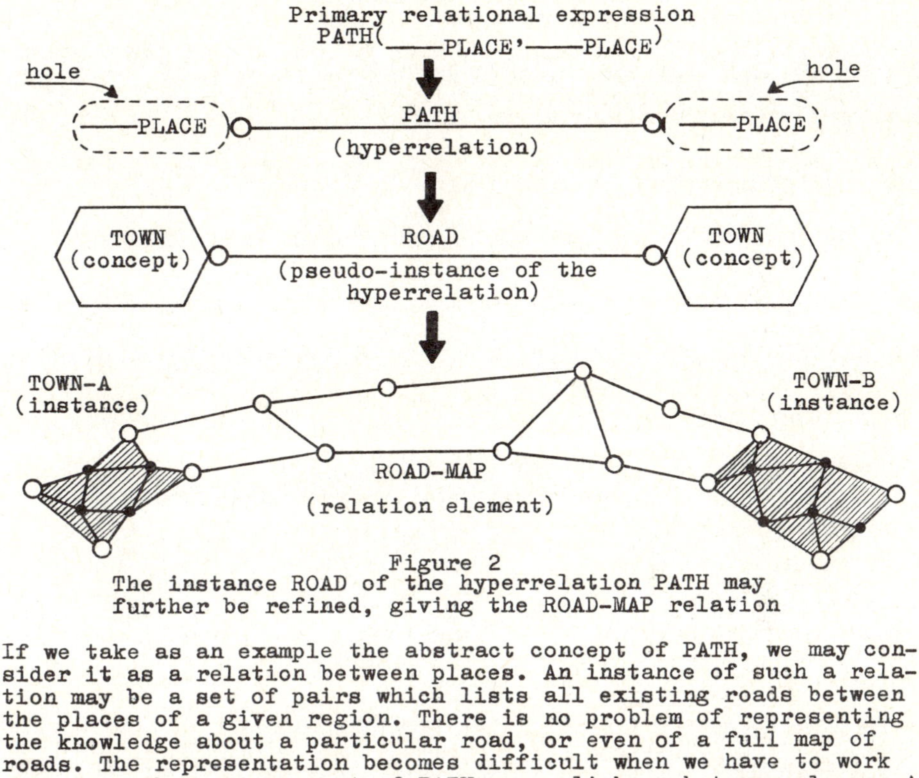

Figure 2
The instance ROAD of the hyperrelation PATH may further be refined, giving the ROAD-MAP relation

If we take as an example the abstract concept of PATH, we may consider it as a relation between places. An instance of such a relation may be a set of pairs which lists all existing roads between the places of a given region. There is no problem of representing the knowledge about a particular road, or even of a full map of roads. The representation becomes difficult when we have to work with such abstract concept of PATH, as a linkage between places. A path in a graph, or a path in a consistency proof, or even a path on a road map, all might be generated from the same abstract unifying concept we try to represent now. The binary hyperrelation

PATH(——PLACE'——PLACE)

holds between objects which satisfy the structural restrictions defined for the holes having the sort PLACE. This is true for the concept of TOWN, and the abstract concept of PATH becomes then a new hyperrelation, which generates all kinds of roads between towns, such as the road shown in Figure 2 for the ROAD-MAP between TOWN-A and TOWN-B. The initial binary relation is therefore refined, showing its real arity and structural complexity.

The basic structure of the hole is similar to the structures of the above defined entities, a quintuple $G=(h_g,s_g,I_g,E_g,p_g)$ where

- h_g is an identifier, a symbol which relates the place of a unspecified entity to the structural description of the hole; when assigned a value, its value becomes a formal variable which participates to further interpretation processes;
- s_g is the sort accepted by the hole;
- I_g is the internal structure of the hole (a prototype diagram for the hypernodes to be filled in), specified in terms of component holes and hyperrelations;
- E_g is the external structure of the hole, with linkage patterns specified in terms of component holes;
- p_g is a list of generic properties.

For example, the holes in Figure 2 have at least one linkage point in each of their external structures, and they are of the sort PLACE. Any other structural restictions may be stated within the knowledge pieces representing the holes.

At the ground level of the system, there are primitive hypernodes, hyperrelations, and holes, which have no components.

2. THE SYNTAX OF THE KNOWLEDGE REPRESENTATION LANGUAGE HYPER

2.1. Metalinguistic considerations

The formalism used for syntax definitions is BNF-IN, an extension of the Backus-Naur-Form with an indexing facility, which allows for the use of nonterminals as indexes for other nonterminal symbols.

2.2. The syntax

2.2.1. Basic entities

$$\langle\text{knowledge-base}\rangle ::= \langle\text{knowledge-piece}\rangle_{\langle\text{type}\rangle} \mid \langle\text{knowledge-base}\rangle, \langle\text{knowledge-piece}\rangle_{\langle\text{type}\rangle}$$

$$\langle\text{knowledge-piece}\rangle_{\langle\text{type}\rangle} ::= (\langle\text{type}\rangle(\langle\text{identifier}\rangle_{\langle\text{type}\rangle}((\langle\text{sort}\rangle_{\langle\text{type}\rangle}) (\langle\text{internal-structure}\rangle_{\langle\text{type}\rangle})(\langle\text{external-structure}\rangle_{\langle\text{type}\rangle}) (\langle\text{properties}\rangle_{\langle\text{type}\rangle}))))$$

$$\langle\text{type}\rangle ::= \text{HYPERNODE} \mid \text{HOLE} \mid \text{HYPERRELATION}$$

$$\langle\text{identifier}\rangle_{\text{HYPERNODE}} ::= \langle\text{name}\rangle$$

$$\langle\text{identifier}\rangle_{\text{HYPERRELATION}} ::= \langle\text{name}\rangle$$

$$\langle\text{identifier}\rangle_{\text{HOLE}} ::= \langle\text{formal-variable}\rangle ::= @\langle\text{name}\rangle$$

$$\langle\text{sort}\rangle_{\text{HYPERNODE}} ::= \langle\text{name}\rangle$$

$$\langle\text{sort}\rangle_{\text{HYPERRELATION}} ::= \langle\text{name}\rangle$$

$$\langle\text{sort}\rangle_{\text{HOLE}} ::= \langle\text{name}\rangle \mid \langle\text{formal-variable}\rangle$$

2.2.2. Basic structures

$$\langle\text{internal-structure}\rangle_{\langle\text{type}\rangle} ::= \text{INTERNAL-STRUCTURE } (\langle\text{structure-list}\rangle_{\langle\text{type}})$$

```
<structure-list>_<type> ::=<sort>_<type>(<structural-description>_<type>)|
    <structure-list>_<type>;<sort>_<type>(<structural-description>_<type>)
<structural-description>_<type> ::= (<structure>_<type>)|
    <structural-description>_<type>(<structure>_<type>)
<structure>_<type> ::= <unoriented-structure>_<type>|
                       <precedence-structure>_<type>|
                       <succedence-structure>_<type>
<unoriented-structure>_<type> ::= LINK(<ramification-list>_<type>)
<precedence-structure>_<type> ::= PRECEDE(<ramification-list>_<type>)
<succedence-structure>_<type> ::= SUCCEED(<ramification-list>_<type>)
<ramification-list>_<type> ::= (<ramification>_<type>)|
    <ramification-list>_<type>(<ramification>_<type>)
<ramification>_<type> ::= (<root-node>_<type>,<leaf-node-list>_<type>)
<root-node>_<type> ::= <node>_<type>
<leaf-node-list>_<type> ::= <node>_<type>|<leaf-node-list>_<type>,
                            <node>_<type>
<node>_HYPERNODE ::= <identifier>_HYPERNODE
<node>_HOLE ::= <formal-variable>
<node>_HYPERRELATION ::= <node>_HYPERNODE|<node>_HOLE
<external-structure>_<type> ::= EXTERNAL-STRUCTURE(<pattern-list>_<type>)
<pattern-list>_<type> ::= <sort>_<type>(<pattern-description>_<type>)|
    <pattern-list>_<type>;<sort>_<type>(<pattern-description>_<type>)
<pattern-description>_<type> ::= <connective>(<list>_<connective>,<type>)|
    <pattern-description>_<type>;<connective>(<list>_<connective>,<type>)
<connective> ::= <logical-connective>|COND
<logical-connective> ::= OR | EXCLUSIVE-OR | AND
<list>_<logical-connective>,<type> ::=<component>_<type>,<component>_<type>|
    <list>_<logical-connective>,<type>,<component>_<type>
<component>_<type> ::= <node>_<type>|<pattern-description>_<type>|
    <component>_<type>,<node>_<type>|
    <component>_<type>,<pattern-description>_<type>
<list>_COND,<type> ::= <condition>_<type>,<connection>_<type>
<condition>_<type> ::= <boolean-variable>|<pattern-description>_<type>
<connection>_<type> ::= <node>_<type>|<pattern-description_<type>
<properties>_<type> ::= PROPERTY(<attribute-list>_<type>)
<attribute-list>_<type> ::= (<attribute>_<type>,<value>)|
    <attribute-list>_<type>(<attribute>_<type>,<value>)
<attribute>_HYPERNODE ::= <name>
<attribute>_HYPERRELATION ::= <name>
<attribute>_HOLE ::= <name>|<formal-variable>
<value> ::=<number>|<symbol>
```

Note: The alphabet of the language, and the productions for non-terminal symbols <name>, <number>, and <boolean-variable>, which complete the syntax of the language, are left unspecified for they are dependent on particular implementation options.

2.3. Basic operations

<operation> ::= <instantiation>|<composition>|<decomposition>|
<abstractization>|<modification>|<deletion>|<renaming> ■

<instantiation> ::= INSTANTIATE(<instance-identifier>,
<concept-identifier>,<list>)

Semantics: A new knowledge piece named <instance-identifier> is created according to the prototype <concept-identifier>, by filling in the symbols and associated values (if any) from the <list>. ■

<composition> ::= <inclusive-composition>|<exclusive-composition>
<inclusive-composition> ::= INCLUSIVE-COMPOSE(<identifier>,
<knowledge-piece-1>,<knowledge-piece-2>)
<exclusive-composition ::= EXCLUSIVE-COMPOSE(<identifier>,
<knowledge-piece-1>,<knowledge-piece-2>)

Semantics: A new knowledge piece K is created as a result of the operation of composition, applied to the specified pieces of knowledge, <knowledge-piece-1> and <knowledge-piece-2>. The symbol specified by the <identifier> becomes the name for K. The sort of the new knowledge piece sort(K)=(sort(K1),sort(K2)), where K1 and K2 are actual names for <knowledge-piece-1> and, respectively, <knowledge-piece-2>. Let I1, I2 be the symbols standing for internal structures, and E1, E2 the symbols for external structures of K1 and K2. Then the structure of the composite result K will be

- for inclusive composition

$$I = I1 \cup I2$$

$$E = E1 \cup E2$$

- for exclusive composition

$$I = I1 \cup I2$$

$$E = (E1 \cup E2) \setminus (E1 \cap E2)$$

The property list is unpredictable, and must be specified by the user. ■

<decomposition> ::= DECOMPOSE(<knowledge-piece-1>,
<knowledge-piece-2>)

Semantics: The first operand <knowledge-piece-1> identifies the original piece of knowledge K1 which is decomposed by detaching K2, the piece specified by the second operand <knowledge-piece-2>. Following there are the results of the operation:

(i) The description of K2=(h2,s2,I2,E2,p2), if previously unspecified, where:

h2 and s2 are the identifier and the sort of K2, as specified and contained within the description of the knowledge piece K1;

I2 is an internal structure generated from the prerequisite condition of having K2 as a component of K1; if $\mathcal{I}_{K2}$ is the index set for the linkages of K2 within I1, there is a minimal star structure

$I2=(LINK(K2',\ldots,K2_i,\ldots))$, $i\in \mathcal{I}_{K2}$, with K2' an intermediate hypernode, which perfectly matches all possible configurations for K2;

E2 is an external structure for K2, generated from prerequisite linkage conditions of K2 within the internal structure of K1, where:

- if $K2 \not\in E1$, then $E2=(AND(\ldots,K2_i,\ldots))$, $i\in \mathcal{I}_{K2}$;
- if $K2 \in E1$, let E12 be the subset of linkage patterns of E1 where K2 appears; then $E2=(E12 \cup (AND(\ldots,K2_i,\ldots)))$, $i\in \mathcal{I}_{K2}$.

The property list is unpredictable.

(ii) The description of the hypernode $Kr=(hr,sr,Ir,Er,pr)$, where:

hr is an identifier, generated from the names of K1 and K2 by a standard systems procedure;

$sr=s1 \setminus s2$;

$Ir=I1 \setminus K2$;

Er is the external structure, obtained from the following alternative:

- if $K2 \not\in E1$, then $Er=E1 \cup E2$;
- if $K2 \in E1$, then $Er=(E1 \cup E2) \setminus E12$.

The property list is unpredictable.

(iii) The description of the hyperrelation $H12=(r12,s12,I12,E12,p12)$ which generates the composition process of K1 from its components K2 and Kr, where:

r12 is a generated identifier for the hyperrelation;

s12=s1, because the sort of a hyperrelation is that of the generated tuple;

$I12=(LINK(G2,\ldots,G2_i,\ldots))$, $i\in \mathcal{I}_{K2}$, where G2 is a hole matching the structure of K2, and $G2_i$ are accordingly defined by the requirements for matching the structures of $K2_i$;

$E12=(AND(G2,\ldots,G2_i,\ldots))$, $i\in \mathcal{I}_{K2}$;

p12=p1, because the properties of a hyperrelation are those of the generated tuple. ∎

<abstractization> ::= <conjunctive-abstractization>
<disjunctive-abstractization>

<conjunctive-abstractization>::= CONJ-ABSTRACT(<knowledge-piece-list>)

Semantics: Let $K_1,\ldots,K_n$ be knowledge pieces. Then the conjunctive abstractization generates a concept $K=(h,s,I,E,p)$ which abstracts all the features of the given arguments, as follows:

h is a generated identifier;

$s=\bigcap_i s_i$, $1\leqslant i\leqslant n$, is a sort resulted from the intersection of all formal expressions of individual sort;

$I=\bigcap_i I_i$, $1\leqslant i\leqslant n$, is an abstracted internal structure which represents the common structure for every individual piece of knowledge;

$E=\bigcap_i E_i$, $1\leqslant i\leqslant n$, is a similarily abstracted external structure;

$p=\bigcap_i p_i$, $1\leqslant i\leqslant n$, is the property list having only the common properties.

Semantics: This operation abstracts the class prototype for a set of previously unclassified knowledge pieces.

<disjunctive-abstractization>::=DISJ-ABSTRACT(<knowledge-piece-list>)

Semantics: This operation abstracts a new knowledge piece from its partial descriptions. All the intersections from the previous semantic description, specified for conjunctive abstractization, are therefore replaced by unions. ■

<modification> ::= MODIFY(<knowledge-piece>(<modification-list>))
<modification-list> ::= <elementary-modification>|
    <modification-list>,<elementary-modification>
<elementary-modification> ::= <insertion>|<replacement>|
    <elimination>
<insertion> ::= INSERT(<description>)
<description> ::= <sort>$_{\langle\text{type}\rangle}$|<internal-structure>$_{\langle\text{type}\rangle}$|
    <external-structure>$_{\langle\text{type}\rangle}$|<properties>$_{\langle\text{type}\rangle}$
<replacement> ::= REPLACE(<description>$_1$,<description>$_2$)
<elimination> ::= ELIMINATE(<description>)

Semantics: Insertion incorporates the specified descriptions into the body of a knowledge piece. The replacement specifies that a part of the knowledge piece, specified by <description>$_1$, is replaced by the structure described by <description>$_2$. Elimination produces, apart from the deletion of the specified description, new linkage patterns according to the resulted external structure. All modifications are subject to implicit consistency proofs. ■

<deletion> ::= DELETE(<knowledge-piece>)

Semantics: Deletes the specified knowledge piece from the knowledge base. ■

<renaming> ::= RENAME(<old-identifier>,<new-identifier>)
<old-identifier> ::= <identifier>$_{\langle\text{type}\rangle}$
<new-identifier> ::= <identifier>$_{\langle\text{type}\rangle}$

Semantics: The knowledge piece having the name <old-identifier> is renamed with the symbol specified by <new-identifier>. ■

2.4. Statements

Apart from the basic operations presented in the previous paragraph, the knowledge representation language HYPER provides statements for working with knowledge bases, or for those operations which involve more than a single access to a knowledge piece. Though that the syntactic structures of these atatements are highly dependent on the implementation options, in the following will be made an informal presentation of their semantics.

CREATE statement: provides for the creation of a new knowledge base. Working with several knowledge bases is typical for belief systems. Regular arguments for this statement are the knowledge base name, and the name of the expert the knowledge is acquired from. Optional arguments may also be provided to specify passwords, classification policy, global credibility figure associated with the source of knowledge, symbols for procedural attachment used to bypass system interpretations for knowledge base access operations.

DESTROY statement: applies to the partial or total deletion of a knowledge base. Regular arguments for this statement are the knowledge base name, and a prototype name. The execution of this statement results in the deletion of the subtree having as root node the specified prototype, and includes all its descending instances. The default option for the prototype name produces the deletion of the full content of the knowledge base, without destroying the knowledge base header record, which contains the global information specified by the original CREATE statement. This allows for starting again the knowledge acquisition process within the frame of the original, now empty, knowledge base. When there is a request for destroying the entire knowledge base, including its global information and, of course, its name, a KILL argument in the position of the prototype name will be used.

DECLARE statement: records, within the specified knowledge base, a new prototype knowledge piece. Prototypes are provided for pattern controlled class definitions. Regular arguments for this statement are the knowledge base name, and the description of the prototype according to the syntax presented in section 2.2. For special, protected or classified knowledge bases, passwords and classification keys are also needed as arguments. The statement is provided only for independent prototypes, which stand for roots in taxonomic trees. Subsequent prototypes, which describe branches within taxonomic trees, are introduced with the basic operation INSTANTIATE, as they are conceptual instances of the independent root prototype.

REFINE statement: expands the specified components of a given knowledge piece, by searching the knowledge base for detailed descriptions of corresponding pieces of knowledge. The regular arguments for refine statement are the name K of a knowledge piece to be refined, and a list of components to be searched in the knowledge base and expanded within the structure of the knowledge piece K under refinement process. For those components not found within the knowledge base, appropiate messages are issued. Errors detected when trying to match linkage patterns in refinement processes, invalidate expanded structures for those components in error. The result of a refinement statement contains only those expanded components which are consistent with the structural requirements of the knowledge piece K, and replaces the initial description of the knowledge piece K within the knowledge base. Default specification for the list of expandable components, is considered a requirement for the refinement of all the components.

SELECT statement: selects the specified knowledge base to be operated on with basic operations. A new SELECT statement unassigns the previously selected knowledge base.

TRANSFER statement: provides for the transfer of knowledge pieces between knowledge bases. Regular arguments for this statement are the identifier of the source knowledge base, the identifier of the knowledge piece to be transferred, and the identifier of the destination knowledge base. Appropiate modifiers specify the characteristics of the transfer operation: transfer with deletion of the transferred piece from the source knowledge base, transfer of a copy of the knowledge piece, transfer by broadcasting, with or without deletion from the source knowledge base.

Other statements are supplied by the knowledge representation language HYPER for useful utilities concerning knowledge base maintenance. These utilities are provided for:

- saving operations concerning various types of physical volumes which contain knowledge bases;
- extracting conceptual directories and taxonomic trees from exist-

ing knowledge bases;
- reorganizing knowledge bases;
- creating new knowledge bases by selective copying of classes and individual knowledge pieces from existing knowledge bases, according to specified taxonomic requirements;
- on-line maintenance functions.

3. THE KEY ROLE OF LINKAGE PATTERNS IN IMPLICIT CONTROL STRATEGIES

3.1. Preliminaries

According to the model for knowledge representation with hypernets, the composite structure of a knowledge entity is represented by the graph of the relationships between its components, which has been defined as the internal structure I of that entity. A restriction E has also been defined over the components of the internal structure, so that $E \subseteq I$ represents only those components of the structure with the property that they are used as linkage points when the given entity is composed or combined with other entities, resulting in knowledge pieces with higher order of complexity.

The variety of linkage patterns results from the rule

$$\langle sort\rangle_{LINKAGE\text{-}PATTERN} ::= FREE \mid DISJ \mid CONJ \mid COND$$

and the general aspect of a pattern definition may be organized by collecting together the elementary expressions which are connected by the same logical connective, as for example

$$E_{LP} = (OR(p_1,\ldots,p_j), XOR(p_{j+1},\ldots,p_k), AND(p_{k+1},\ldots,p_n))$$

with $j<k<n$, where LP is abbreviated from LINKAGE-PATTERN, XOR is abbreviated from EXCLUSIVE-OR, and p_i, $1 \leqslant i \leqslant n$, are linkage points or lower level linkage patterns. Let the above expression stand for an argument of a linkage pattern $LP=sort_{LP}(E_{LP})$. Then, for each linkage point there is assigned a boolean variable whose value is true only if the corresponding point is actually involved in a composition. Consequently, the validity of the composition controlled by this pattern is given by the truth value of E_{LP}, where OR-ed, XOR-ed and AND-ed subexpressions are connected by disjunction for free and disjunctive patterns, and by conjunction for conjunctive patterns.

3.2. Free linkage patterns

The free linkage patterns are defined for those compositions where only some of the linkage capabilities of patterns are actually used. Then, the free property of a pattern assumes for all the linkage points not actually used within the composition, that they will appear in the external structures of the generated composite knowledge piece and, therefore, they may further be used for subsequent composition processes.

Let $FREE(OR(p_1,\ldots,p_j), XOR(p_{j+1},\ldots,p_k), AND(p_{k+1},\ldots,p_n))$ be a free linkage pattern, and

$$\{p_{j_1},\ldots,p_{j_q}\} \subseteq \{p_1,\ldots,p_j\},\ \{p_{k_1},\ldots,p_{k_r}\} \subseteq \{p_{j+1},\ldots,p_k\}, \{p_{k+1},\ldots,p_n\}$$

the linkage points actually used in a composition. The linkage pattern which will be transferred to the external structure of the generated composite entity will be

$$FREE(OR((p_1,\ldots,p_j) \setminus (p_{j_1},\ldots,p_{j_q})),$$
$$XOR((p_{j+1},\ldots,p_k) \setminus (p_{k_1},\ldots,p_{k_r}))).$$

Note that all AND-ed points have to be used for a valid composition. However, in free patterns, when AND-ed subexpression is not actually used, it will appear within the resulted linkage pattern which will be transferred to the external structure of the generated composite knowledge entity. These properties are shown in Figure 3.

(a) (b) (c)

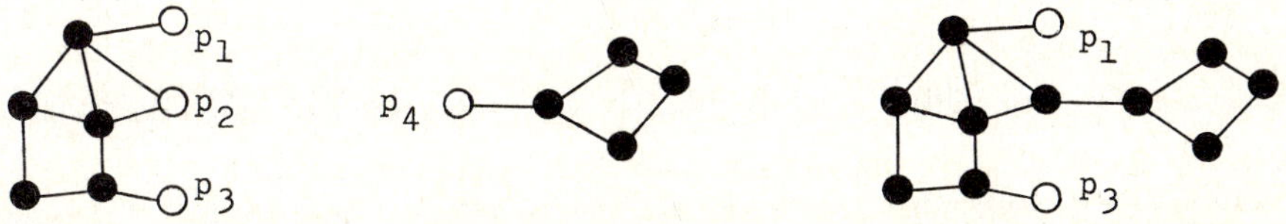

FREE(OR(p_1,p_2,p_3)) CONJ(COND(p_2,p_4)) FREE(OR(p_1,p_3))

Figure 3
Knowledge pieces (a) and (b) which participate in a composition process involving a free linkage pattern and the resulted (c) composite knowledge piece

3.3. Disjunctive linkage patterns

Disjunctive linkage patterns are similar to free patterns as the validity of the composition controlled by these patterns is concerned. They, however, are different in that disjunctive linkage patterns do not allow unused linkage points to participate in subsequent compositions. Therefore, the linkage pattern which results to be transferred to the generated composite entity is empty. These properties are shown in Figure 4.

(a) (b) (c)

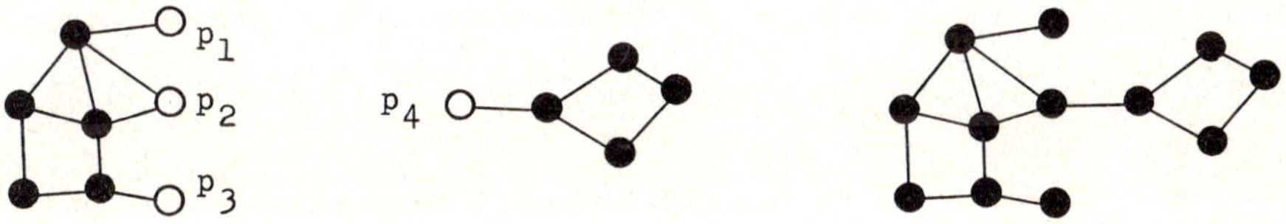

DISJ(OR(p_1,p_2,p_3)) CONJ(COND(p_2,p_4)) $E = \emptyset$

Figure 4
Connected disjunctive patterns are removed from the external structure of the generated composite entity

3.4. Conjunctive linkage patterns

Composition under the control of a conjunctive linkage pattern is valid only if all pattern subexpressions are true. There is no resulted linkage pattern to be transferred to the external structure of the generated composite knowledge entity. The conjunctive linkage pattern provides the most restrictive control information for composition processes. The properties of conjunctive patterns are shown in Figure 5.

3.5. Conditioned linkage patterns

According to the syntax presented in section 2.2, conditioned linkage patterns are used to validate a linkage pattern as a component within an external structure, when some condition is satisfied. These patterns act as IF...THEN... rules.

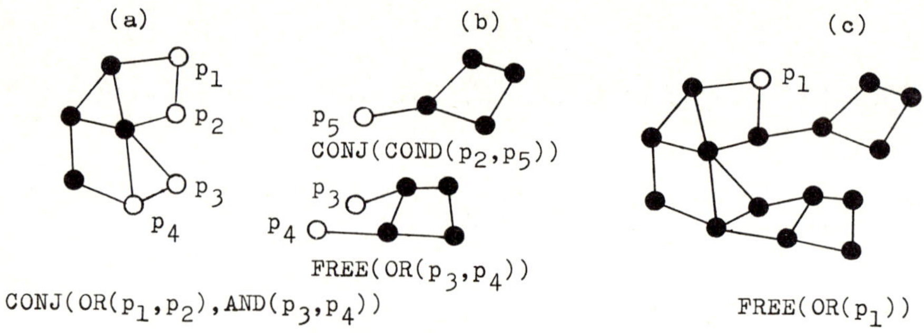

Figure 5
All the subexpressions of a conjunctive linkage pattern have to be true when connected in composition processes

There is no restriction concerning the terms and the complexity of the condition part of a conditional linkage pattern. Thus:

- the condition may be stated by another linkage pattern, whose involvement in an actual composition assigns the truth value to the condition, thus validating the pattern part for use in further composition processes;
- the condition may be stated by an expression in terms of hyperrelations, thus validating the pattern part for use only in the context of these hyperrelations;
- the condition may be stated by an expression in terms of hypernodes, which directly select those hypernodes which are allowed for composition under the control of the conditioned pattern;
- the condition may be stated by an expression in terms of other entities which are not involved inthe composition processes, but play a catalytic role for them.

4. CONCLUSIONS

The method provides a powerful mechanism for representing knowledge, and includes all the restrictions for combining knowledge about several entities into more complex constructs, such avoiding the generation of absurd objects and further trial and error rejection procedures. Because of some hardware restrictions, the method has been partly implemented within INTEXP system [4], but has proved a higher efficiency than other knowledge representation methods.

REFERENCES

[1]. Georgescu I.: Knowledge representation with hypernets, AI-FDo26 Central Institute for Management and Informatics, (1982).

[2]. Georgescu I.: A hypernet model for representing knowledge about actions, AI-FDo37, Central Institute for Management and Informatics, (1983).

[3]. Georgescu I.: Compositional capabilities of hypernets for knowledge representation, AI-FDo35, Central Institute for Management and Informatics, (1983).

[4]. Georgescu I., Hotăran A., Predescu R., Vlasiu M., Petrescu F., Nicolăiţă D., Nagy A.: INTEXP: A Domain Independent Expert System, this volume.

ARTIFICIAL INTELLIGENCE: Methodology, Systems, Applications
W. Bibel and B. Petkoff (Editors)
Elsevier Science Publishers B.V. (North-Holland)

Reducing design complexity, or: Why does AI work?

Erik Tengvald

Department of Computer and Information Science
Linköping University
S-581 83 Linköping
Sweden

We believe that AI is both a hard science, like physics, and a soft science like psychology or the managerial sciences. In this paper, we will confine ourselves to an argument for the notion that AI is a soft science. The argument will be conducted in two steps. First we will introduce a measure, design complexity, and argue that the main concern of AI is to minimize what the measure measures. In the second step, we argue that the measure must partly be based on considerations of designer psychology. Consequently, AI must also be a soft science.

Foreword

This paper is first and foremost a philosophical paper. We will attempt to address the question of what AI is. We believe AI to be a very special kind of science. More precisely, we believe that AI is both a hard science, like physics, and a soft science like psychology or the managerial sciences.

More precisely, we see a much greater need for using many levels of hardness or softness in the languages (formalisations) of the science. The range must span a spectrum from hard mathematics almost to the softness of a novel.

Because of these beliefs, we consider the discussion of what AI is to be a very important discussion. Most people now beginning to use AI methodology come, as we do, from the hard sciences. Because of this, they may have a tendency to underestimate the soft side of AI methodology. This can lead to problems in understanding an important part of current AI practice, and possibly also theory.

Incidentally, we have noted that it is often difficult to explain what AI is for industrialists interested in its use. It may be that the reason for these problems depends not only on an unfamiliarity with the AI concepts but also on the underlying philosophy of the science.

In this paper, we will confine ourselves to an argument for the notion that AI is a soft science. We have ourselves long ago accepted that it is a hard science, and we also believe that our audience does not contend this point.

We will try to argue for the softness of AI using as hard methods as possible. Since the paper is addressed to the hard science community, this type of argument should have the greatest chance of success.

Introduction

The argument for the centrality of the design complexity concept will be modelled on algorithm theory, which indeed is a hard branch of computer science. In algorithm theory, one algorithm is considered better than another if its time complexity is less. In the same manner, we will argue that one AI-design is better than another if its design complexity is less.

What, then, is design complexity? Well, we are not quite sure. For the current discussion, it suffices to approximate it with design cost, just as time complexity can be approximated with execution cost.

The second step of the argument will be as follows. Designs are made by humans. Consequently, design complexity estimates must partly be based on human psychology. Thus the science itself must at least to some extent be a soft science.

Finally, to give the reader a better idea of what we mean by design complexity, we will go through a practical example of design complexity reasoning. The example will consist of a comparison of multiple and single inheritance from the design complexity viewpoint.

The hard view of AI-system building: An argument for the centrality of the design complexity concept

The hard view of system building is based on the idea that the end product of system design is not the system as such, but its behaviour, i.e the system is viewed as an implementation of a string-to- string function, the details of which are of no consequence for the user. Two AI systems are equal if their behaviours are equal. We consider this viewpoint to be truly hard; in fact, it is basically the same as the view of algorithm theory.

We will argue that AI's main concern is with design complexity (design cost) and not with time complexity (execution cost). More precisely, AI concentrates on suppressing design complexity. Time complexity is disregarded as long as it does not become too disturbing.

The entire process starting from nothing to the end product, behaviour, can be illustrated as follows:

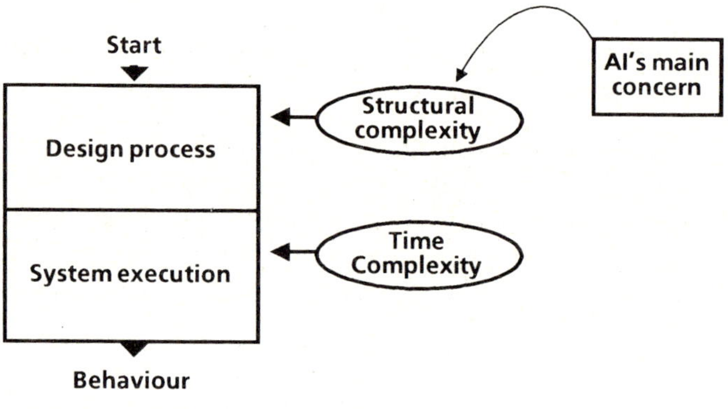

The hard view of system building

To support the argument for the centrality of the design complexity concept, we only have to use the basic method of all hard natural sciences, that of observing nature.

We will see that the currently central AI methods are, in fact, concerned with suppressing design complexity and not time complexity.

The methods of AI

In this section, we will go through each of the central AI methods. The idea is to show that our thinking is applicable in the major cases.

Search based methods

In blind search, the idea is to throw the computer straight at the exponential complexity barrier, thus reducing design complexity by freeing the designer of the tedious work of specifying most of the control knowledge <Nilson80>. As we now know from practice, this method is unusable since time complexity issues will almost immediately become very disturbing.

The workable searchbased methods are based on informed generators and/or early pruning <Winston84>.The argument that these methods reduce design complexity is best performed by contrasting them with the "ordinary" (as opposed to AI) method of programming. An oversimplified description is the following: in ordinary programming the designer starts out with one correct execution path and then extends it to more executions by padding on if-tests. In the searchbased AI methods, the designer starts with very many paths (blind recursive search) and then deletes most of them by informing the generators or adding early prune-tests. Experience shows that there are cases where it is simpler for the designer to use the searchbased AI approach than ordinary programming. In such cases, the searchbased methods reduce design complexity.

Expert system methods

Many expert systems are based on search. However, we believe that expert system research has supplemented the searchbased methods with qualitatively different methods <Hayes-Roth83>. We call these methods the expert system methods.

There are two such expert system methods which we believe are very important. We call them the expert language and the systemware methods.

An idealisation of the ***expert language*** method can be illustrated as follows:

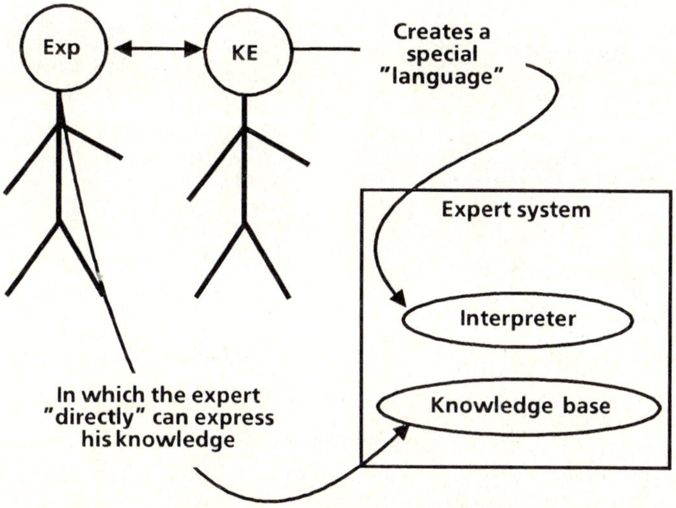

The expert language method

Using intense questioning and discussion with the expert, the knowledge engineer creates a special programming "language" in which the expert can "directly" express his knowledge. We have placed "language" in quotes since it is to be interpreted very widely; a more correct term would perhaps be programmable structure.

Usually, the expert will also have to do some, though little, programming. "Directly" is to be interpreted in an approximate sense.

In practice, the situation is not as tidy. There are usually many iterations of expert-knowledge engineer discussions, followed by total or partial reimplementations of the expert language interpreter, before the design becomes usable. Furthermore, the expert needs help to formulate his knowledge in the expert language, at least at the beginning of the design process.

The way in which the method suppresses design complexity is almost immediate. Compare the expert language method with ordinary programming. We understand that the expert language method reduces the need for communication between the expert ("future user") and the knowledge engineer (programmer). More precisely, the expert no longer needs to communicate the knowledge of the domain to the knowledge engineer. It is sufficient if he only communicates the proper ***form*** of the domain knowledge. Since the form knowledge is more abstract than the domain knowledge, the total amount of communication needed becomes less.

Many expert systems are based on search formalisms. Consequently, it may be interesting to try to understand why the expert language method does not necessarily bog down in exponential search.The hard-style argument explaining why the systems do not necessarily bog down is as follows:

The expert has a preformed concept structure. The concept consists of abstractions for reducing the time complexity of the recursive search. Time complexity is reduced since the expert abstraction structure is such that the least commitment principle <Stefik80> is, to a high extent, followed implicitely. (Otherwise the expert would not be an expert).

The ***systemware*** method can be understood by first noting that building AI-systems means that one tries to build up a type of theory for part of the reality, and then contrasting AI-system building with old style theory building without the benefit of computers. We illustrate this as follows:

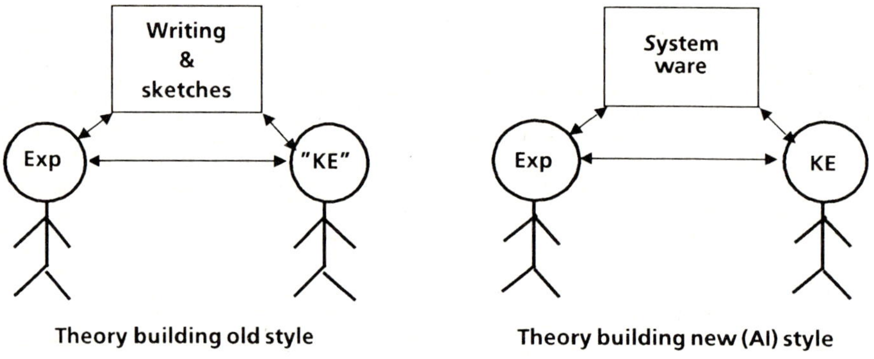

The systemware method

The KE in quotes, in the old style picture, is to be understood as a formalistically inclined worker, for example a mathematician.

That the systemware can be used to suppress design complexity can be understood using the following argument: the increased efficiency of theory formation is a result of the systemware's ability to create at least short arguments which make the human-to-human discussion more concrete and usually also more formal (sharper). The systemware takes over part of the ***design*** work.

More precisely, the systemware method can help with:*Discussion*, or communication between expert and knowledge engineer and *Remembering*, or communication with the former selves of the expert and knowledge engineer. This helps the expert and knowledge engineer to *Debug*, i.e. to communicate with reality.

To make the suppression of design complexity possible, the systemware has to meet certain requirements. We will not go into the details of these requirements here. The interested reader is referred to <Tengvald84>. However, we will mention what we believe to be the most important requirement, namely that the systemware has an adequate visibility-system.

A visibility-system is software which presents the details of the systemware to the user in a clear and concise manner. The visibility-system should extend to transient structures built when the system runs. Without a visibility-system, the designer and knowledge engineer are forced to make non-trivial arguments to understand what the system is doing. This results in an increase in the design complexity reducing, or even overwhelming, the benefits of the systemware method.

In conjunction with this discussion, it might be profitable to contrast the views of at least academic though not necessarily practical software engineering, with the AI-view, when considering possibly the most central concept in computer science, namely: the bug.

Some kinds of academic software engineering view the bug as an enemy <Gries81>. To avoid bugs, it is recommended that large investments be made in designer work, increasing the design complexity, in paper specifications. In AI, bugs are instead viewed as friends; we are trying to build a theory for part of the reality. The bugs do not reside in the program but in our own conception of the evolving theory.

Instead of wasting designer work on paper specifications, AI uses systemware method software, which makes the bugs in our theory visible. The clean program bugs are almost always so simple that they are killed off-hand. Similar ideas have been expounded in the rapid prototyping and Lisp-programming literature <Sandewall78>. Here we have the explanation behind the AI urge to start programming early.

The softness argument

In this section, we will argue for the idea that AI is also a soft science. In short, we will observe that design complexity is a measure of what is happening inside the designer head and not, as time complexity, a measure of what is happening inside the computer. This observation immediately supports our main point that AI is also a soft science.

The softness of the searchbased methods is well hidden. In fact, there is one truly hard method, namely blind recursive search. Blind recursive search is, however, unusable because of its exponential time complexity, and we do not consider it to be a method, except perhaps for toy problems.

As we noted above, the workable searchbased methods are built on the use of informed generators and/or early pruning. The argument that these methods are also soft is as follows: We are concerned with building a system describing part of nature. While doing this, the designer will try to match informed generators or early prune structures that he knows about over the part of nature in question. As we see, the design process goes on in the designer head, not in the computer. The science which describes the design process also has to be soft.

Incidentally, we may note that ordinary programming concerned with building systems describing part of nature is similar to AI in that many of the important problems in ordinary programming are also soft. <Jonesjö84>

There should be no problem in understanding that the expert language method is also soft. The real work is performed by discussions among humans. In fact, the central problem to solve is what representations or, more precisely, what editable presentations the expert finds natural and easy to use. This is clearly a human engineering problem.

Neither should there be any problem in understanding that the systemware method is also soft. The most important part of the systemware is the visibility system, which makes it possible for the expert and knowledge engineer to "see" how the system reasons. How to design a visibility system is clearly a human engineering problem.

A practical example

Theories are of no use if they cannot be applied in practical use. They are interesting only if they can help us understand the nitty gritty details of reality. In this section, we will try to apply our theory to a practical example, namely, why multiple inheritance generally is better than single inheritance from the design complexity viewpoint. Note that we will disregard time complexity issues. Because of space limitations our discussion will be very brief.

More precisely, we will try to provide different measures which could be parts of design complexity. Incidentally, this might dispel some of the clouds surrounding this concept. The discussion will proceed using two examples. As we proceed, we will build up a richer understanding of what design complexity is, and why it is generally less in the case of multiple inheritance.

The first example is the ubiquitous amfibian example:

Multiple inheritance

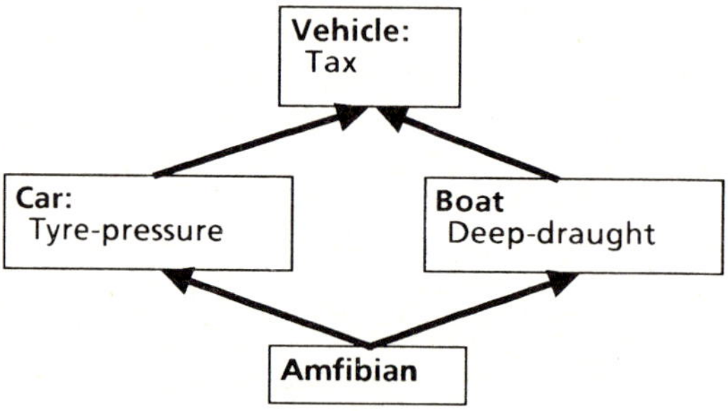

Single inheritance

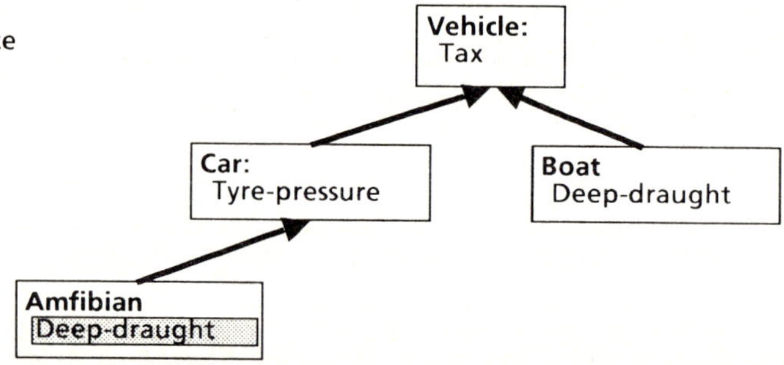

As we see, the designer is forced to write deep-draught once extra in the single inheritance system, which results in extra key strokes. In the multiple inheritance scheme, the designer has to set up an extra isa-link but this can be seen as an investment which will provide the key stroke benefit for all future boat-slots. In domains where there are more slots than concepts, multiple inheritance is consequently preferable. The example chosen is symmetric, so by moving amfibian under boat, we obtain the same problem but with the Tyre-pressure property.

One possible partial measure of design complexity is consequently the number of keystrokes. The reader may find this measure ridiculous, although it is quite reasonable, see for example <Lenat82 pg 235 §§ 1>.

However, the situation is more complicated, as can be seen from the following example:

Multiple inheritance

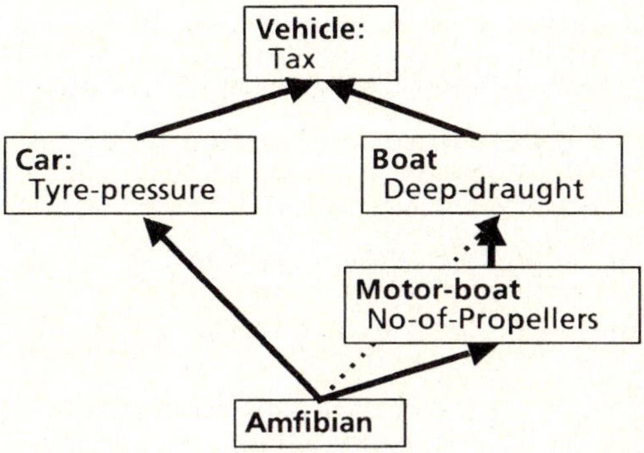

Single inheritance

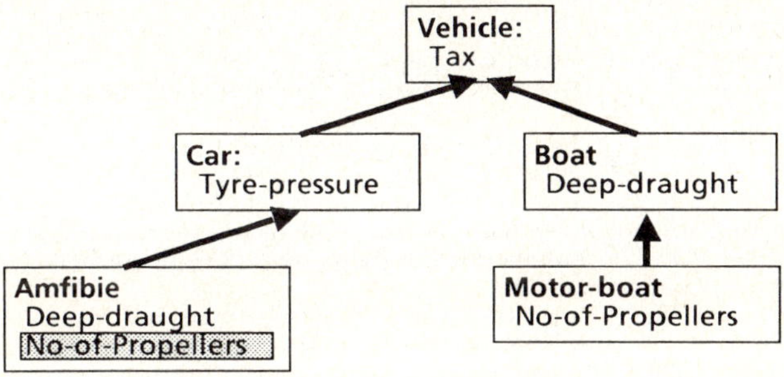

In the multiple inheritance case, the user is forced to redirect the isa-link from amfibian to motor-boat since all amfibians of the current domain use motor power in the water. In the single inheritance case, he has to write No-of-propellers one more time. Since redirection of isa-links is performed via a command which requires perhaps many key strokes, this example calls the first measure in question.

We need a more complex discussion: the real value of multiple inheritance is that the designer can introduce more knowledge into the systemware. This makes it possible for the systemware to help him remember a larger number of earlier decisions as to the similarity of the concepts.

One can also say that the systemware help him to scan the knowledge base finding reasonable neighborhoods in which to perform edits. We are talking of systems containing hundreds or even thousands of classes and scanning the knowledge base is a considerable part of designer work.

To sum up, we can say: in the multiple versus single inheritance case, design complexity can be seen as being composed of, at the least, three partial measures. The hard key-stroke measure, the possibly slightly softer scanning measure and the truly soft help-to-remember measure.

Conclusion

We believe that AI is both a soft and hard science. In this paper, we have strongly argued the point that AI is also a soft science. We have not bothered to argue that it is also a hard science since we believe this to be already accepted by the audience we are interested in.

Using the one or many rule of ordinary programming, it is immediately evident that there is no reason to confine oneself to two levels of softness or hardness. In fact, we believe that AI can make use of descriptions on many levels of softness/hardness, from a level close to that of a novel down to hard-core mathematics.

The idea of design complexity and an interest in suppressing it, is not necessarily important only in AI. It is possible to consider the quest for simplicity in logic and mathematics to be an interest in suppressing design complexity.

It is also quite possible that other sciences than AI might profit from using many levels of softness/hardness in their descriptions.

References

<Gries81> The science of programming, David Gries, Springer-Verlag New York Inc. (1981)

<Hayes-Roth83> Building Expert Systems, Frederick Hayes-Roth, Donald A. Watermann, Douglas B. Lenat, Addison Wesley Publishing Company Inc. (1983)

<Jonesjö84> Personal communication from Lennart Jonesjö and Östen Oskarsson, Ericsson Information Systems AB, S-581 01 Linköping Sweden.

<Lenat82> The Nature of Heuristics, Douglas B. Lenat, Artificial Intelligence **19** (1982).

<Nilsson 80> Principles of Artificial Intelligence, Nils J. Nilsson, Tioga Publishing company P.O. Box 98, Palo Alto, CA 94302, USA. (1980)

<Sandewall78> Programming in an interactive environment: The "Lisp" experience, Erik Sandewall, Computing Surveys, Vol 10 no 1, pp 35-71. (1978)

<Stefik80> Planning with constraints, Mark J. Stefik, Report No. STAN-CS-80-784, Stanford University. (1980)

<Tengvald84> The design of expert planning systems, Erik Tengvald, Linköping Studies in Science and Technology. Dissertations No 111. Linköping University S-58183 Linköping Sweden. (1984)

<Winston84> Artificial Intelligence, 2nd edition, Patrick H. Winston, Addison Wesley Publishing Company Inc. (1984)

ARTIFICIAL INTELLIGENCE: Methodology, Systems, Applications
W. Bibel and B. Petkoff (Editors)
Elsevier Science Publishers B.V. (North-Holland)

PROGRAM SYNTHESIS BY ANALOGY - A TWO-PHASED APPROACH

Klaus P. Jantke

Humboldt University
Dep. Mathematics
P.O.Box 1297
DDR - 1086 Berlin

We present a mathematical approach based on the framework of algebraic semantics. A main feature is a quite natural break to a first phase of learning analogy concepts and to a second phase of constructing objects being analogous with respect to an analogy concept learned before. The problems to be solved during the first phase are problems of learning theories from examples. During the second phase the main task is to generate models of finite sets of axioms. Thus the approach offers an algebraic framework for joining the research work of inductive inference and automated deduction for program synthesis.

INTRODUCTION

The present paper is dealt with some problems of algorithmic learning. The main emphasis is put on the incompleteness of information presented to an algorithmic learning device. This point of view seems to be very close to reality. It is well-known from experiences in human communication that in almost all cases incomplete problem descriptions are sufficient for learning objects like algorithms. The large amount of research work in inductive inference illuminates a great variety of possibilities of synthesizing objects from incomplete information. We refer to /1/ and /6/ as topical surveys in this regard.

In the present paper we investigate a certain kind of incompleteness of information to be processed: description of algorithms by analogy. The incompleteness stems from the fact that some algorithm is mainly explained by means of other algorithms declared to be analogous to the inteded one. Analogical reasoning is deemed important in everyday life. Consequently, it is within the scope of AI activities to develop methods for automatically simulating reasoning by analogy.

It is a basic feature of the present approach to offer the use of existing research work instead of creating new concepts. The author is convinced of the possibility to use a large amount of mathematical research work for considerable advances in AI applications. In particular it is offered a program for joining techniques and results from different fields like algebraic semantics (abstract data type theory), inductive inference and automated deduction. The author's paper /5/ is quite similar in spirit.

A detailed introduction into the approach proposed would require the invocation of a large number of mathematical concepts, because of the different mathematical fields involved. For the sake of readability, we will suppress almost all technical details. The reader will be directed to some topical references in this regard. Instead, we discuss an introductory example which is far from reasonable applications but can be easily visualized.

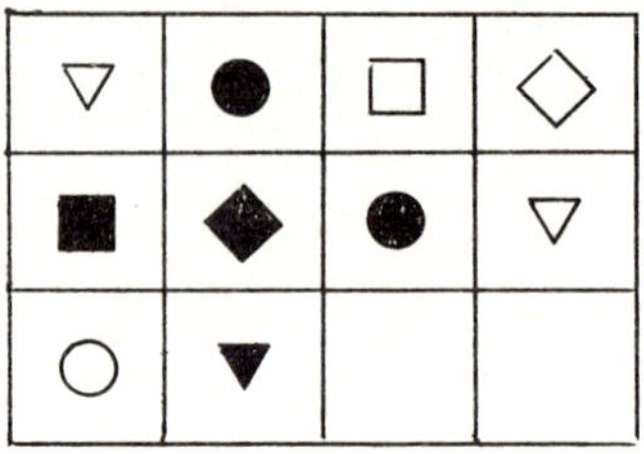

Figure 1

The first figure above shows a rectangle containing 12 cells, 10 of them being filled with some symbols from an implicitly given collection. The reader's task is to fill up the figure. Obviously, there is not enough information how to do this in the desired way. Therefore, we present to the reader the complete rectangle of figure 2 and advise him to fill up the first rectangle analogously.

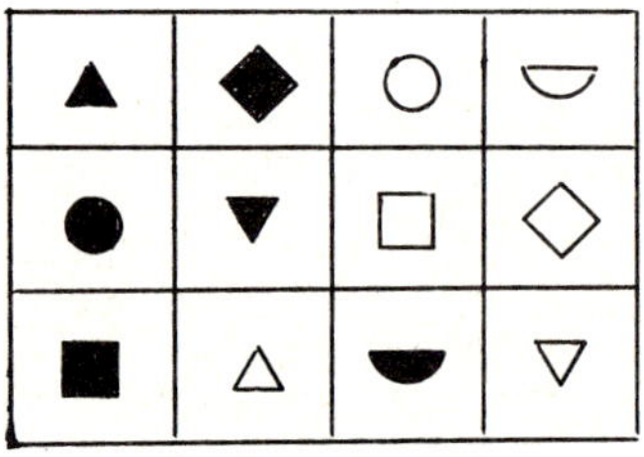

Figure 2

Now, working up the additional information provided by the second figure, someone will solve the problem by inserting the symbols ◆ resp. □ into the free cells of the first rectangle. What does encourage him to do so?

An inspection of the sample rectangle of figure 2 exhibits that there are some conditions satisfied by the sample. Consequently, one tries to fit in symbols in such a way that the first rectangle will fulfil these conditions, too. Such conditions are

(A) For every shape of symbols, there is the same number of entries of this shape in the rectangle.
(B) For every colour of symbols, there is the same number of entries of this colour in the rectangle.

(C) In each row, there are not two symbols of the same shape.
(D) In each column, there are not two symbols of the same shape.
(E) Different columns contain differently many white entries.

Obviously, the sample above satisfies the conditions (A), (B), (C), (D), and (E). Therefore, it seems to be reasonable to complete the first rectangle by fitting in ◆ and ◻ , respectively. As a result, it meets the same conditions.

Note that the recognition of the conditions above assumes some concepts like shape and colour of a symbol, row and column of a rectangle, and natural numbers for comparisons of cardinalities. The ability to detect conditions as above, i.e. to learn analogy concepts, and to generate objects meeting these conditions, i.e. to synthesize analogues, depends essentially on the collection of available concepts. This will be illuminated by means of the next sample.

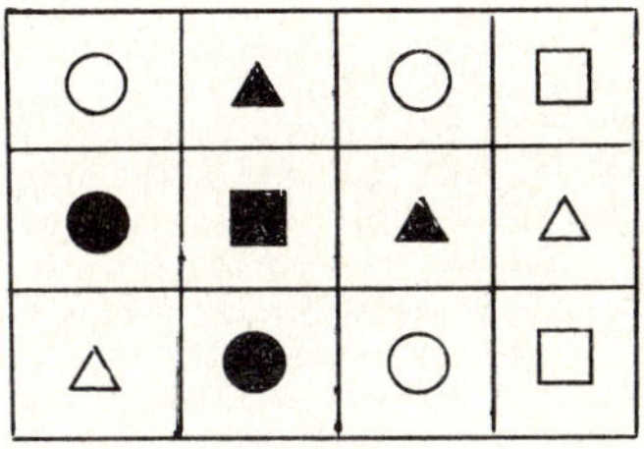

Figure 3

Assume that we provide the reader with the two samples of figure 2 and 3, resp., for completing the rectangle of figure 1 analogously. Unfortunately, the last sample does not fulfill anyone of the four axioms deduced above. Consequently, it requires a new attempt to learn the underlying analogy concept before synthesizing the desired analogue. But this seems to be quite difficult. If a particular new concept is available, namely the concept of knight moves on a chess board, it becomes considerably simple again.

(F) All cells containing symbols of the same shape can be ordered along a sequence of knight moves such that the colour of symbols in the sequence alternates.

It is left to the reader to find the six different pairs of entries for completing the rectangle of figure 1 such that it meets condition (F) representing the analogy concept learned from the two samples above.

A SKETCH OF THE FRAMEWORK

The present approach basically assumes that the objects to be synthesized by analogy are describable as algebras of some finite, heterogeneous and finitary signature. Moreover, we assume that they are finitely specifiable. Thus , in fact, we suppose the concepts of abstract data type theory and refer to the standard reference /3/ for a painless introduction.

It is well-known from the literature that all program properties of interest, structural as well as behavioral ones, can be formalized on the basis of this framework, possibly using certain techniques like conditional axioms or hidden enrichment specifications, in addition. That means that the approach proposed is suitable for investigating program synthesis problems.

Any signature **SIG** consists of a finite set **S** of sort names, a finite set **O** of operator names and an arity function **a** mapping **O** into the set S^+ of non-empty finite strings over **S**. If for any operator name f $\in$ **O** it holds **a**(f) = s for some sort name s $\in$ **S** , f is understood as the name of some constant of the sort named by s. Otherwise, the equation **a**(f) = $s_1 \ldots s_n s$ indicates that f names an n-ary function mapping the cartesian product of the respective sets into the set named by s. We write **SIG** = (**S**, **O**, **a**) , for short. Algebras of the signature **SIG** are heterogeneous algebraic structures consisting of an S-indexed family of carrier sets and having for every operator f a function of the arity indicated by **a**. Usually, one takes into account only finitely generated algebras.

Programs are viewed as finitely generated algebras of particular signatures. Besides programming language characteristics the choice of a signature reflects a) what standard functions are available and b) which program properties should be considered during the process of program synthesis by analogy. Constituents of the underlying signature have been called concepts (e.g. the concept of knight moves on a chess board) in our introductory example. Obviously, the choice of the signature may be helpful for program synthesis by analogy, but it may lead the program synthesis algorithm up the garden path, too.

Please, recall our example initially presented. The task of learning an analogy concept from given samples is understood as the task of learning axioms satisfied by the samples worked up. This approach puts a syntactical and a semantical question. The syntactical questions asks for the language of axioms. The semantical question is a more serious one, as it is always possible to deduce axioms which are trivially satisfied and do not carry any information about the samples processed. It is the question for the relation between classes of algebras and sets of axioms specifying them.

We fix any reasonable S-indexed family **X** = $\{X_s\}_{s \in S}$ of variables. On **SIG** and **X** we define well-formed terms as usual, where variables of X_s are tackled like constants of the sort s . Let us denote the class of all well-formed terms on **SIG** possibly containing variables from **X** by **T(SIG,X)**. Every term of **T(SIG,X)** is of some sort, in dependence on its outermost operator name. For two terms t and t' of the same sort we call t = t' a term equation. The set **CTE(SIG,X)** of conditional term equations is the smallest set containing all term equations on **SIG** and **X** and being closed under the construction

$$(t = t' \longrightarrow T)$$

for any conditional term equation T and arbitrary terms t , t' of the same sort. In fact, this inductive definition describes our specification language, i.e. the calculus for formalizing properties learned from samples.

The problem of choosing an appropriate semantics concept is a knotty one. Unfortunately, we have to suppress almost all discussions. The concept currently dominating all other approaches in the topical literature is the so-called initial algebra approach (cf. /3/). We stress that there are serious reasons for investigating the final algebra approach, and we direct the reader to /4/ motivating the final algebra approach from the viewpoint of certain AI problems. We confine ourselves to a brief and informal description of both semantics concepts.

A set **E** of conditional term equations from **CTE(SIG,X)** is said to specify a particular algebra **A** of the signature **SIG** under initial algebra semantics if and only if the term equations valid in **A** are exactly the equations which are logical consequences of **E** understood as a set of open first order axioms. Equivalently, if we consider the congruence of terms induced by **E** and factorize the free term algebra by this congruence relation, the resulting quotient algebra must be isomorphically to **A**.

Assume **E** and **A** as above. **E** specifies **A** under final algebra semantics if and only if the term inequalities valid in **A** are exactly the inequalities which are logical consequences of **E** provided that the concerning unit algebra is excluded. Thus an algebra specified under final algebra semantics is something like a smallest, a reduced or a minimized model.

LEARNING ANALOGY CONCEPTS

Our approach as a whole calls for any decision concerning the underlying semantics. Let us assume that we have made up our mind somehow, and we will refer to this decision by the phrase "underlying semantics" throughout the following paragraphs.

Learning an analogy concept from a set of samples boils down to the problem of deducing a finite set of axioms describing the given samples as well as possible with respect to the underlying semantics. Obviously, this assumes some signature for formulating axioms to be checked on. Such a learning process should be understood as a limiting process, in general. Shapiro's work /9/, which is devoted exactly to the problem under consideration, is a quite impressive reference in this regard.

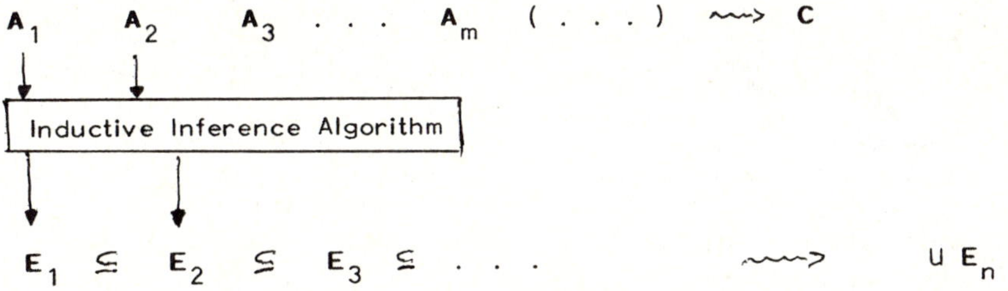

Figure 4

Figure 4 above illustrates the learning phase as a whole. The input information consists of a finite or potentially infinite sequence of sample structures $\mathbf{A}_i$ fed on step by step. The class of all samples presented is abbreviated by $\mathbf{C}$. The learning device generates growing sets of axioms $\mathbf{E}_j$ as outputs. As axioms we permit conditional term equations, only. As our introductory example suggests, there is no uniquely determined set of axioms to be deduced from a fixed set of samples. Consequently, the learning device does not work synchronized. in general, i.e. after feeding on some $\mathbf{A}_i$ there are possibly some outputs $\mathbf{E}_j, \ldots, \mathbf{E}_{j+k}$.

The inductive inference algorithm used as a learning device of our program synthesis approach is said to work correctly, if the complete set of axioms $\cup\, \mathbf{E}_n$ generated in the limit fits the class $\mathbf{C}$ of given samples as close as possible with respect to the underlying semantics. Unfortunately, there is not enough space to argue this correctness problem out. Instead, we embark on the investigation of the second phase.

SYNTHESIZING ANALOGUES

During the second phase we are dealt with problems of synthesizing programs from finite sets of first order axioms. This approach seems to be well-known from the field of so-called logic programming. In particular, there exists the very impressive system PRIZ (cf. /7/) synthesizing programs from logical specifications, which is installed in some hundred sites.

Our approach essentially generalizes those concepts, as each intermediate set of axioms is allowed to be incomplete with respect to the program to be synthesized. Nevertheless, it would be very interesting to investigate in what cases systems like PRIZ (possibly being slightly modified) successfully process incomplete specifications, too.

Please, recall our introductory example. Normally, the problem to be solved does not consist only in synthesizing some program to be declared by analogy to some given samples. Additionally, the target program is required to satisfy some additional conditions, in particular to perform some computation. We assume that these requirements are described by a finite set of axioms $\mathbf{E}_0$. With respect to the figure before we define $\mathbf{E'}_j = \mathbf{E}_0 \cup \mathbf{E}_j$.

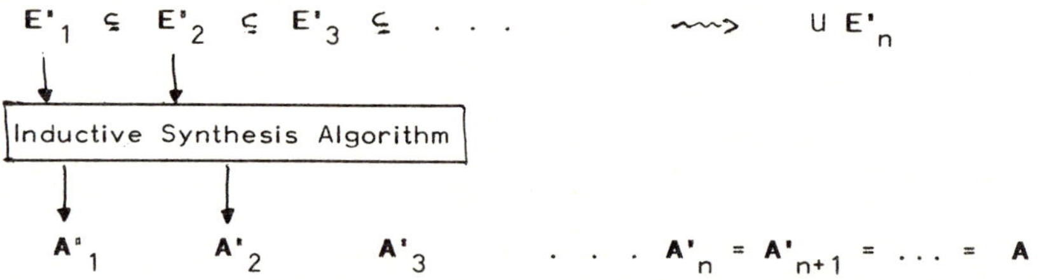

Figure 5

Figure 5 on the page before illustrates the second phase of our program synthesis approach. Each $\mathbf{A'}_k$ describes a program which is understood as an algebraic structure of the basic signature. It is a characteristics of the concept presented to require that the sequence of programs generated as hypotheses become stable after processing sufficiently comprehensive information. For a large amount of research work and results concerning learning processes of this kind, we direct the reader to the inductive inference surveys /1/ and /6/.

Instead of surveying different techniques we will sketch a particular method motivated and introduced by the author in /4/. Assume that the program **P** to be synthesized can be understood as a finite algebraic structure of the basic signature. Moreover, assume we have settled on the final algebra semantics. If the inductive learning device yields a correct logical specification of **P** in the limit with respect to the underlying semantics, i.e. the final algebra of the class of non-trivial models of $\cup\, \mathbf{E'}_n$ is isomorphically to **P** , then it applies a general program synthesis method mainly based on theorem proving as follows. **P** is build from some constituents like statements , constants occurring in operations and assignments and so on. To say it roughly and informally, the synthesis algorithm guesses these constituents, starting with terms being as simple as possible. If such a guess is wrong, it brings on the validity of some term inequality. Because of the final algebra approach, all term inequalities are provable from the complete specification $\cup\, \mathbf{E'}_n$. Unfortunately, at no intermediate stage the complete information is available. But the finite character of the classical deduction operator compensates for this. Consequently, every inequality caused by some incorrect guess is provable on the basis of some intermediate specification $\mathbf{E'}_j$. Thus each incorrect guess is rejected after some finite time. Because of the finiteness of **P** , after finitely many attemps the algorithm described guesses **P** correctly. Note that the correctness of **P** is probably not provable. The main deductive work performed by the synthesis algorithm consists in proving term inequalities (cf. /5/).

In fact, for any fixed finite, heterogeneous and finitary signature **SIG** the method described above yields a synthesis algorithm being able to synthesize any finite **SIG** - algebra **A** from any specification E_1 , E_2 , ... of **A** in the limit under final algebra semantics. This statement is the informal version of a completeness theorem for the program synthesis method introduced.

USER'S CONTROL OF PROGRAM SYNTHESIS

The author intends to implement the synthesis algorithm described in the preceding chapter. The following remarks are aimed at an explanation of the flexibility of the introduced approach. In particular, we intend to illuminate the possibilities to control the process of synthesizing programs by analogy by suitably providing information.

(1) Our introductory example exhibits the importance of the underlying signature. In fact, by specifying the signature the user provides to the program synthesis system the kind properties to be taken into account for learning analogy concepts. Thus he controls the learning phase. Moreover, by listing and characterizing the standard functions and statements for building the target program he defines the available algorithmical tools to be incorporated. Thus he controls the

synthesis phase.

(2) The choice of suitable samples essentially influences the program synthesis process. It is well-known from research work in the field of applied inductive inference (cf. 79)), that in the average case of synthesis problems a considerably small amuont of samples is sufficient for synthesizing the desired objects. Our genral approach allows to characterize informally, what does it mean to present suitable samples. The program synthesis algorithm does not "know" what program the user has in mind. Therefore, it guesses a lot of properties as explained above. Incorrect guesses are rejected by proving term inequalities. Consequently, it speeds up the program synthesis process, if all essential differences of distinguished program states or subprograms are recognizable from a small number of samples, i.e. if the information presented considerably supports the ability of proving term inequalities.

(3) A careful choice of the requirements $\mathbf{E}_0$ describing particular properties of the desired target program influences the synthesis process similarly.

A paper devoted to a detailed discussion of program synthesis of sorting algorithms is currecntly in preparation. It will provide to the reader some more insights into the effects briefly mentioned above.

CONCLUSIONS

The present paper offers a general approach to program synthesis by analogy which is intended to become the framework for further theoretical investigations and practical implementations, as well. It is a basic intent to exhibit some fields for joining algebraic, recursion - theoretic and deduction - oriented research work for the invention of intelligent programming systems. Instead of creating new approaches we should try to exploit the scientific power of existing theories and their interconnections. This is somehow the gist of this paper.

As the underlying ideas of abstract data type theory are powerful enough for investigating structural as well as behavioral program properties, the given approach seems to be considerably more expressive than the approach proposed in /8/. On the other hand, it is remarkably closer to the programming reality than the concept of /2/.

REFERENCES

/1/ Angluin, D. and Smith, C.H., Inductive inference: theory and methods, Computing Surveys, Vol. 15, No. 3, Sept.1983,237-269

/2/ Gaines, B.R. and Shaw, M.L.G., Analyzing analogy, in: Trappl, R. Ricciardi, L. and Pask, G. (eds.), Progress in Cybernetics and Systems Research IX (Hemisphere Publ. Co., New York, 1982), 379-386

/3/ Goguen, J.A., Thatcher, J.W. and Wagner, E.G., An initial algebra approach to the specification, correctness, and implementation of abstract data types, in: R.T. Yeh (ed.), Current Trends in Programming Methodology IV (Prentice-Hall, 1978), 80-149

/4/ Jantke, K.P., A generalized approach to inductive inference, in: I. Plander (ed.), Artificial Intelligence and Information-Control Systems of Robots (North-Holland, Amsterdam, 1984), 189-192

/5/ Jantke, K.P., The main proof theoretic problems in inductive inference, in: G. Wechsung (ed.), Frege Conference 1984, Proc., Series Math. Research 20 (Akademie-Verlag, Berlin, 1984), 321-330

/6/ Klette, R. and Wiehagen, R., Research in the theory of inductive inference by GDR mathematicians - a survey, Inf. Sciences 22 (1980), 149-169

/7/ Mints and Tyugu, E.H., Justification of the structural synthesis of programs, Sci. Comp. Programming 2 (1982), 215-240

/8/ Moll, R. and Ulrich, J.W. The synthesis of programs by analogy, Univ. Massachusetts at Amherst, Comp. Inf. Sci. Dep., Technical Report 79-03, 1979

/9/ Shapiro, E.Y., Iductive inference of theories from facts, Yale Univ., Dep. Comp. Sci., Research Report 192, February 1981

ARTIFICIAL INTELLIGENCE: Methodology, Systems, Applications
W. Bibel and B. Petkoff (Editors)
Elsevier Science Publishers B.V. (North-Holland)

TOWARDS A THEORY OF KNOWLEDGE REPRESENTATION SYSTEMS

Ulrich Furbach[1], Gerhard Dirlich[2], Christian Freksa[3]

[1] Hochschule der Bundeswehr München, Neubiberg
[2] Max-Planck-Institut für Psychiatrie, München
[3] Institut für Informatik, Technische Universität München

Starting from the concept of cognitive representation we develop the notion of knowledge representation systems. A knowledge representation system establishes a correspondence between two bodies of knowledge. It can be used to convert one form of knowledge into another. The implications of this concept for artificial knowledge based systems are investigated. We demonstrate the usefulness of knowledge representation systems by an application to a task in office automation, the design of a meeting scheduling system.

0 INTRODUCTION

The issue of knowledge representation has been recognized for a long time in philosophy, mathematics, physics, the social sciences, and in computer science. Knowledge representation in artificial systems so far has been understood primarily as an enterprise of inventing and realizing new representational notations (semantic nets, procedural representations, frames and scripts, parallel models of associative memory, etc.). In recent years, however, research both on artificial systems and on human cognition has led to some hotly debated controversies which demonstrated the need for a sound theoretical basis of knowledge representation (Sloman 1971, 1975; Pylyshyn 1973; Minsky 1975; Hayes 1974; Kosslyn 1975; Palmer 1978); but surprisingly, only few studies (Sloman, Hayes, Palmer) aim at establishing a general theory of knowledge representation. We regard the work presented here as a contribution to such an enterprise. We elaborate on a selected aspect of knowledge representation, specifically the relationship between two different bodies of knowledge, one being a representation of the other. Our considerations aim at a clarification of the concept of a representation system. They may contribute to an increasing understanding of certain transformation processes required in knowledge based systems to convert one representational notation into another.

1 THE NOTION OF A KNOWLEDGE REPRESENTATION SYSTEM

The task of transforming a body of knowledge from one representational notation into another is omnipresent. For instance, some well-known mathematical transformations, the conversion of Cartesian into polar coordinates in geometry and the transformation of a time series into a frequency spectrum can be regarded as a transformation of one form of knowledge into another. Important areas in artificial intelligence research, in this respect, are the conversion of iconic into propositional representations (Gelernter, 1963; Evans, 1968; Funt, 1976) and the mapping of natural language into meaning representation systems. These tasks have a common structure, namely the representational relation between two domains.

Palmer (1978) has identified five essential aspects shared by all knowledge representation systems: they contain two worlds, a represented world (World 1) and a representing world (World 2); together they provide the basis for a representation if the following entities are properly specified:

(1) what the represented world is;
(2) what the representing world is;
(3) what aspects of the represented world are being modeled;
(4) what aspects of the representing world are doing the modeling;
(5) what the correspondences between the two worlds are.

(a)

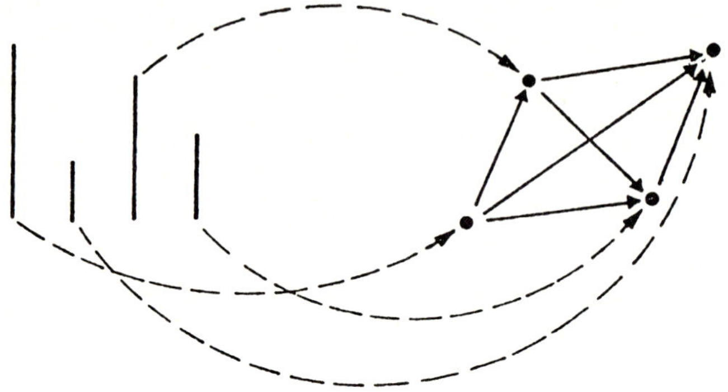

(b)

is-object (vertical-line)	is-object (dot)
	is-object (arrow)
taller-than (object1, object2)	arrow-connected (dot1,arrow, dot2)

Fig. 1: Example of a knowledge representation system
(a) left: World 1: four objects (vertical lines)
right: World 2: ten objects (four dots, six arrows)
(b) left: Reference world 1: two relations: one object defining relation, one structure defining relation
right: Reference world 2: three relations: two object defining relations, one structure defining relation
Dashed arrows define the correspondence.

An example for such a system is shown in Fig. 1a. In W1 we discern four objects, namely vertical lines. For each pair of objects we can observe relative height, i.e. the relation 'is-taller-than (object1, object2)' (1). In W2 we see ten objects: four dots and six arrows. For each pair of dots we can observe the relation 'arrow-connected (dot1, arrow, dot2)' (2). The aspects of W1 which are being modeled in W2 are the objects (the vertical lines) and the relation 'taller-than' (3). In W2 the dots and the arrows are doing the modeling (4). The correspondence between W1 and W2 is a one-to-one mapping from the lines in W1 to the dots in W2 (shown as dashed arrows in Fig. 1a), and a one-to-one mapping of 'taller-than (object1, object2) = true' in W1 to the arrows in W2 (5).

We will take this notion of a representation system as a starting point for our considerations. We aim at applying Palmer's concepts on cognitive representation to artificial systems.

1.1 COMPONENTS OF A KNOWLEDGE REPRESENTATION SYSTEM

The represented world as such is what it is; but an interpreter external to it may perceive different objects and structures in this world by applying object and structure defining processes to this world. Thus, knowledge about the represented world only becomes accessible if it is combined with a domain of object and structure generating processes, which we will call reference world R1 of the represented world W1 (Fig. 1b). An analogous consideration applies to the representing world W2: as such it is what it is; but combined with a reference world R2 containing object and structure defining processes on W2 it can be interpreted as a body of knowledge.

Two such bodies of knowledge, (W1, R1) and (W2, R2), may be related to each other in a way that (W2, R2) is a representation of (W1, R1). In order to define such a representation system, a correspondence must be established between the represented world W1 with its structure defining processes in R1 and the representing world W2 with its structure defining processes in R2.

1.2 CORRESPONDENCE BETWEEN TWO BODIES OF KNOWLEDGE

Palmer (1978) formulated the conditions for the correspondence in a representation system. However, we must reconsider these conditions in light of our refined view that the worlds W1 and W2 must be combined with their respective reference worlds R1 and R2 (Fig. 1a and b). Knowledge about aspects of the represented world must carry over into the representing world by means of the representation system. In the reference world R1 for the represented world W1 certain object and structure defining processes are assigned to these aspects. Thus, there must be processes in the reference world R2 of the representing world W2 which correspond to the processes in R1. This defines a mapping C which establishes the correspondence between the two bodies of knowledge (Fig. 1 a and b). C is necessary for (W2, R2) to be a representation of (W1, R1). Note that in the simple relational structure of Fig. 1, the mapping C is a homomorphism which ensures completeness and correctness. In the general case, however, the problem of completeness and correctness is difficult and requires further investigation. Now, we have established our notion (W1 ,R1 ,W2 ,R2 ,C) of a knowledge representation system.

2 ELEMENTS OF A THEORY OF KNOWLEDGE REPRESENTATION

We now can relate our notion of a knowledge representation system to Palmer's five aspects:

(1&2) 'what the represented (representing) world is' is given by the represented (representing) world, and by its reference world specifying interpretation processes on it, i.e. the represented (representing) body of knowledge;

(3&4) 'what aspects of the represented (representing) world are being modeled' is given by the processes in the corresponding reference world;

(5) 'what the correspondences between the two worlds are' is defined explicitly by the mapping C from the represented to the representing body of knowledge.

In the following sections we will derive further propositions on knowledge representation systems.

2.1 RELATIVITY OF OBJECTS AND STRUCTURE

The pair structure of a body of knowledge (W, R) completely determines which types of objects and which relations in W are defined. This relativity of structure in the world W provides great plasticity of representation systems: we may, for instance, conceive systems in which objects in one body of knowledge may correspond either to objects or to relations in the other body of knowledge; conversely, relations in one body of knowledge may correspond to either relations or objects in the other body of knowledge. An example for a system where objects in W1 are mapped onto relations on W2 and vice versa is the above mentioned time-series to frequency-spectrum transformation. This potential of representation systems opens ways for tailoring highly problem specific representation systems.

2.2 THE BOUNDARY BETWEEN A WORLD AND ITS REFERENCE WORLD

We conceive the reference world as a set of processes which are accessible for investigations of their properties with respect to the representation system. Processes in the reference world merely define the structure of the world to which they are assigned; however, they do not modify this world as such. In contrast to this situation we may be interested in the results generated by the processes of the reference world: we may want to add their results as new objects to the world. Such a situation is discussed in section 3. Furthermore, we may be interested in treating processes as objects in the world. In the latter case, in terms of the notion developed here, we must shift them from the reference world into the world. Obviously, such process-objects in the world would not be open for "inspection" any more. They could, however, still be triggered to yield their results.

In the example of Fig. 1, the process 'arrow-connected' can be shifted from R2 into W2 after the knowledge about the relational structure in W2 has been incorporated into the process, the relation 'is-object (arrow)' can be deleted from R2 and the arrows can be deleted from W2. Now, the arrows in W2 are replaced by a process which contains the knowledge required to decide whether two dots are arrow-connected, or not. Since this process is now part of W2, it can create an arrow each time it notes that two dots are arrow-connected.

The shift of a process from the reference world R into the related world W described here models a distinction between declarative and procedural representations of knowledge: a declarative representation may be converted into a procedural one by shifting appropriate processes from the reference world into the world W (Freksa et al. 1984).

2.3 INTRINSIC AND EXTRINSIC REPRESENTATION OF WORLD ASPECTS

In order to introduce another aspect of representation systems we modify the example from figure 1 once again. The body of knowledge (W1, R1) stays the same, while in W2 only seven objects are defined now: four dots and three arrows. The relation 'taller-than' of W1 is now modeled by the relation 'chains-to' (Fig.2), where the argument 'arrow' is replaced by the set '(arrows)'. The relation 'taller-than' in R1, as well as the corresponding relation 'chains-to' in R2 hold for all six pairs of vertical lines in W1 and the dots in W2, respectively. 'taller-than' is a transitive relation (A 'taller-than' B and B 'taller-than' C implies A 'taller-than' C); thus we may expect the corresponding relation to have the same property. There are representing worlds which provide relations that share the property of transitivity with 'taller-than'. 'heavier-than' would be such a relation, and 'chains-to' is also one of them. This is an <u>intrinsic</u> form of representing properties of relations. Intrinsic means, that a given property is inherent both in the represented relation and in the corresponding representing relation. The relation 'taller-than' has a second inherent property, namely asymmetry (A 'taller-than' B implies not(B 'taller-than' C)). 'heavier-than' shares this property with 'taller-than' but 'chains-to' does not. The relation 'chains-to' is not inherently asymmetric, this property is only maintained by excluding symmetric chains from the representing world. This is an <u>extrinsic</u> form of representation.

In the representation system depicted in Fig. 1, the transitivity of the relation 'taller-than' is represented extrinsically because the corresponding relation 'arrow-connected' is not a transitive relation. The transitive closure was therefore included in the representing world of Fig. 1 explicitly. The above

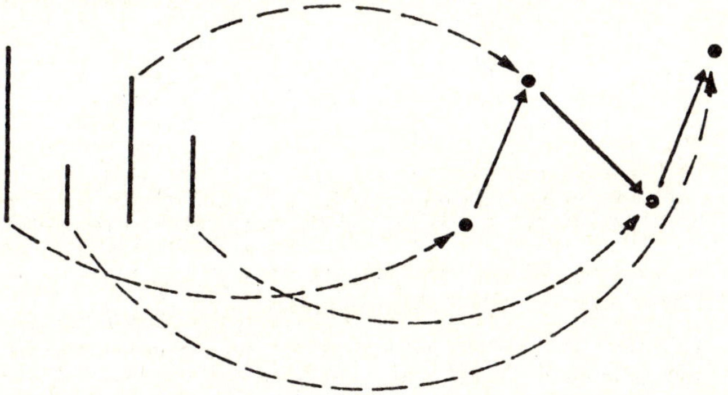

is-object (vertical-line)
taller-than (object1, object2)

is-object (dot)
is-object (arrow)
chains-to (dot1, {arrows}, dot2)

Fig. 2: Modified example

examples show that even in representing a single relation both forms can be used; one property can be represented extrinsically, while another can be represented intrinsically.

If all properties of all represented relations are represented intrinsically we have an analogical representation system (Freksa et al. 1984). This is a very special kind of system. In computing systems, we typically have mixed representation systems with intrinsic and extrinsic components (Dirlich et al. 1983).

3 AN APPLICATION TO OFFICE AUTOMATION

We will apply the concepts developed above to a task in the design of office automation systems: the conception of an algorithm for scheduling meetings. The purpose of the scheduling algorithm is to check if all candidate-participants are available for an intended meeting. A meeting is an event that takes place at a certain time-interval, in a certain room and unites certain persons. These facts about meetings can be captured by a body of knowledge containing time-intervals, rooms and persons as objects and a structure defining relation for 'meeting'. Thus, the reference world R1, i.e., the interpretation of an observer looking at the real world W1, contains three object and one structure defining relations:

is-object (person)
is-object (room)
is-object (time-interval)

meeting (time-interval, room,
set of (person))

We assume that the relation 'meeting' is defined operationally by the following process:

meeting (t, r, P) holds iff
"The observer can verify that during time-interval t all candidate-participants (set P) are in room r."

For two meetings held at the same time-interval t, meeting (t, r1, P1) and meeting (t, r2, P2), the following property Q holds:

Q: $r1 \neq r2 \longrightarrow P1 \cap P2 = \emptyset$ and $r1 = r2 \longrightarrow P1 = P2$

In other words, a person cannot be at the same time in two different rooms, and at the same time the same room cannot be used by different sets of persons for a meeting.

The representation of knowledge conceived here is based on facts about meetings in the real world. In particular, the 'unique-location property' of persons is mirrored by the property Q in the representation. Besides this approach other representations can be constructed. We describe here a representation which is based on the fact that each person has a calendar in which he notes scheduled meetings. The respective body of knowledge has a reference world R2, i.e. an interpretation by an observer looking at the the real world W2, consisting of four object defining relations:

is-object (person) is-object (time-interval)
is-object (room-nr) is-object (calendar).

- Note, rooms are no more interpreted as objects, instead there are new objects of the kind 'room-number' and of the kind 'calendar'!

Futhermore there are two structure defining relations:

entry (calendar, person, time-interval, room-nr)
scheduled-meeting (time-interval, room-nr, P)
where
P = {person | entry (calendar, person, time-interval, room-nr)}

Thus, 'scheduled-meeting' is a relation between time-interval t, room-nr r and a set of persons P. But in contrast to the relation 'meeting' in reference world R1, the elements of P are no longer given by the physical presence of the participants in room r at time t, but by entries of room-numbers rn in their calendars. This representation is based on the fact that persons have calendars and that entries in these calendars define scheduled meetings.

Now, we can construct from the two representations described here a knowledge representation system of the kind presented in section 1. This requires a definition of the correspondence between the two bodies of interrelated knowledge. The correspondence can be defined here by mapping the objects of the kind 'room' and the relation 'meeting' in R1 onto the objects of the kind 'room-nr' and the relation 'scheduled-meeting' in R2 respectively. The structures of the related bodies of knowledge are essentially determined by two differing sets of facts, namely facts about meetings in the first case and facts about calendars in the second. We want to focus on the differences between the two representations and discuss an interesting difference in the representation of the property Q defined above:

In R1 property Q is inherent to the relation 'meeting'. In contrast, it is not necessarily inherent to the relation 'scheduled-meeting' in R2: if the relation 'entry' is unique in its last argument, i.e. if for each triple (calendar, person, time-interval) there is at most one room-nr, such that entry (calendar, person, time-interval, room-nr) holds, the relation scheduled-meeting has the property Q. In this case Q is represented intrinsically. If, however, it is possible to enter more than one room-number into a person's calendar for a given time-interval, the property Q does not hold. Consequently, it then has to be represented extrinsically. This means that procedures for consistency checks are required which ensure that scheduled meetings in (W2, R2) have the same property Q as the meetings in (W1, R1).

Maes (1984) describes a calendar management system, part of which is a scheduling algorithm for meetings in an office environment. This system uses a representation of meetings which corresponds to the representation (W2, R2) described above. Therein, the property Q is represented extrinsically and thus the algorithm has to perform consistency checks. More precisely, each time a scheduled meeting is to be defined the algorithm has to check the personal calendars of the candidate participants. This clearly increases the complexity of the algorithm.

In the following we will demonstrate, that a representation like the first one described above, (W1, R1), has advantages over the second one, (W2, R2), with respect to office automation systems. In several steps we modify the body of knowledge (W2, R2) in such a way that the 'unique-location property' is intrinsically represented as in (W1, R1). In R2 the set of participants P of a scheduled meeting was defined through the relation 'entry', which makes use of the object 'calendar', i.e.:

$$P = \{\text{person} \mid \text{entry (calendar, person, time-interval, room-nr)}\}$$

Let us substitute the object defining relation is-object (calendar) by:
is-object (schedule-table),

such that for each time interval there exists one schedule-table in world W2 and let us introduce person-names by a new object-defining relation:
is-object(person-name).

Furthermore, we modify the relation 'entry' accordingly to:
entry (schedule-table, time-interval, person-name, room-nr)

such that for each time-interval we have a table in which the correspondence between person names and room numbers is marked. The relation 'scheduled-meeting' is then given by:

scheduled-meeting (time-interval, room-nr, P)
where

$$P = \{\text{person-name} \mid \text{entry (table, time-interval, person-name, room-nr)}\}.$$

Again, we have to examine the definition of 'entry' to decide whether the property Q is represented intrinsically or not.

The schedule-table assigned to each time-interval is a model of all the meetings held at this time-interval. It is like a board with a slot for each room number and one token for each person-name. Then entry (table, t, p, r) holds if slot r of board t contains the token for person-name p. It now is impossible to define a meeting which does not have property Q. In a computer implementation schedule-table can be defined as a matrix, in which rows are labeled with person names and columns with room numbers. In this case entry (table, t, p, r) holds if the matrix for t contains an entry in (p, r). Now, it is possible to have a row containing two entries, which corresponds to "one person is in more than one room at the same time". Property Q must here be represented extrinsically by adding processes for consistency checks.

In contrast to the representation based on calendars, (W2, R2), where Q had to be represented extrinsically too, it is now easier to check if a meeting can be scheduled. The scheduling algorithm only has to inspect one single matrix and to check if the tokens of all the candidate-participants are available.

Let us conclude the dicussion of this example with yet another analysis within our notion of a representation system. The relation 'scheduled-meeting' is part of the reference world R2. Thus this relation has to be given operationally, say by a computer program. If we shift this relation from the reference world R2 into the world W2 itself it can be triggered, i.e. we can invoke the program 'scheduled-meeting'. Its computation will result in a new element of the relation between tables, room numbers and persons which is the intended result of the scheduling algorithm.

4 CONCLUSION

The present paper clarifies the notion of a knowledge representation system. A proper definition of a body of knowledge requires the distinction of a world per se and its associated reference world which defines the objects and structure under consideration. In a representation system two bodies of knowledge have to be related by a mapping which establishes a correspondence. Certain properties of this mapping were clarified within the framework developed here.

In our view, representation systems have great plasticity by the uniform treatment of objects and relations. This is a useful property in the design of problem specific knowledge based systems.

Some of the issues in knowledge representation such as the procedural-declarative and the analogical-propositional distinction were reconsidered from a representation-theoretical point of view. In light of this, these issues do not appear as controversies, but as concepts, which define differing approaches for the design of knowledge representation systems.

Representation systems appear to be useful components in knowledge based systems: by specifying an appropriate representation system reasoning may become easier in the represented world than in the representing world. Separation of representation from reasoning should be considered as a design method.

ACKNOWLEDGEMENTS

We thank Peter Haddawy for critical comments on a draft of this paper.

REFERENCES

DIRLICH, G., FREKSA, C., FURBACH, U. (1983). A central problem in representing human knowledge in artificial systems: the transformation of intrinsic into extrinsic representations. 5th Cognitive Science Conference, Rochester, New York.

EVANS, T.G. (1968). A program for the solution of a class of geometric-analogy intelligence-test questions. In: Minsky, M. (ed.) Semantic information processing. Cambridge, Mass.: MIT Press.

FREKSA, C., FURBACH, U., DIRLICH, G. (1984). Cognition and representation. In: LAUBSCH, J. (ed.) GWAI-84. Heidelberg: Springer.

GELERNTER, H.L. (1963). Realization of a geometry-theorem proving machine. In: Feigenbaum, E.A. and Feldman, J. (ed.) Computers and Thought, New York: McGraw-Hill.

HAYES, P.J. (1974). Some problems and non-problems in representation theory. Proc. AISB Summer Conf., Sussex pp. 63-79.

KOSSLYN, S.M. (1975). Information representation in visual images. Cognitive Psychology, 7, 341-370.

MAES, P. (1984). Goals in knowledge-based office systems. In: LAUBSCH, J. (ed.) GWAI-84. Heidelberg: Springer.

MINSKY, M. (1975). A framework for representing knowledge. In: Winston, P. (ed.) The psychology of computer vision. New York: McGraw-Hill.

PALMER, S.E. (1978). Fundamental aspects of cognitive representation. In: Rosch, E. & Lloyd, B.B. (eds.) Cognition and categorization. Hillsdale: Lawrence Erlbaum.

PYLYSHYN, Z.W. (1973). What the mind's eye tells the mind's brain: a critique of mental imagery. Psych. Bull. 80, 1-24.

SLOMAN, A. (1971). Interactions between philosophy and AI: the role of intuition and non-logical reasoning in intelligence. Artificial Intelligence 2, 209-225.

SLOMAN, A. (1975). Afterthoughts on analogical representations. TINLAP-1, 178-182.

ARTIFICIAL INTELLIGENCE: Methodology, Systems, Applications
W. Bibel and B. Petkoff (Editors)
Elsevier Science Publishers B.V. (North-Holland)

FROM LOGIC TO LOGIC PROGRAMMING

Michel de Rougemont

European Computer-Industry Research Center
Arabellastr. 17
8000 Munchen 81
West-Germany

Abstract

We will interpret recent results of Logic on finite structures in the context of Logic-Programming, and contrast the practical method based on these results with Prolog, from the point of view of the Time complexity.

Basic to the theory is the notion of an Inductive query, and more generally of a program as an Induction hypothesis. The fundamental result is the equivalence between the class of Inductive queries and the class P, of problems computable in polynomial time. We will then take particular examples and contrast this method, where the complexity of an Inductive query is always polynomial, with the Prolog method where the complexity is exponential.

The semantics of these two approaches are radically different: the prolog-method is based on the semantic of the exhaustive search, whereas the inductive approach introduces a different semantic, called Intensional.

Introduction

We refer to Logic-Programming as the use of logical definitions on which some computational process is based. A classical method associated to some subset of First-Order Logic, is Prolog [1], which uses a particular method to compute relations.

The Prolog method, as most other methods used in similar contexts implicitely uses the fact the computation takes place on an infinite structure like the integers, and that programs can always be represented by functions and relations on such a structure. In the context of data-bases, the same implicit hypothesis is made, and often basic theorems of Logic (such as Completeness, Soundness...) are presented as a foundation for these methods.

If one only considers finite structures, such basic theorems of Logic fail. As an example, the set of valid formulas on finite models is not recursively enumerable, as it has been first observed by [10].(See [3] for an extensive comparaison).

The practical reality is made however only of finite structures, and in this paper we will mention a different method to compute functions and relations which will implicitely use the hypothesis of **finiteness.** That method is based on Inductive definability, and on general results of Logic on finite structures. On infinite structures it does not yield any notion of effectiveness, as to be Inductive is equivalent to be Π^1_1.

The method can also be presented as a calculus, or as a programming language, and in this sense could also be considered as a Logic-programming concept.

We will then compare this method with the Prolog method, as the Time complexity associated to the computation process will be our primary measure. We will in effect contrast a Polynomial Time complexity associated in a fundamental way to the Inductive method, with an exponential time complexity associated to the prolog method, using specific simple examples. We will then make general remarks on the different semantics.

In the first section we will review the basic definitions necessary to define the central notion of an Inductive query, and mention the main results. In the second section we will give examples. In the third section, we will compare the two methods, and in the fourth section we will compare the semantics .

I. Inductive queries

We will approach Logic on finite structures from the Inductive definability point's of view, on a class K of finite structures. The main definition is that of an Inductive query [7] following the theory of Inductive definability [5]. This notion can then be refined with the notion of a recursive query [6], and presented as a practical calculus.

We will first sketch the formalism, and mention theoretical results. We will then give simple examples that will be used to contrast this method with Prolog from the Complexity's point of view.

Assume a finite relational structure U,i.e.

$$U = \langle D \, , R_1, \ldots R_k \rangle$$

where D is a finite domain, $R_1 \ldots R_k$ are relations on D. The signature of the structure is the sequence $\langle a_1 \ldots a_k \rangle$ if each R_i is of arity a_i. We will only consider this special case, although the theory generalizes when one uses functions and Functionals, i.e. functions taking as arguments variables ranging over D and over the set of partial functions from D to D.

We then consider the class K of all finite structures U, that have identical signature.

Definition : A relational **query** R on a class K is a function which associates for each structure U of K a relation on R(x) on U. If the arity of the relation is null, we talk about boolean queries.

We then write $[R(x)]^U$ to denote the relation R(x) on a particular structure U.

Examples

1. Assume the class of finite graphs, of finite structures U=⟨D,E⟩ where D is a finite domain and E a binary relation on D, the edge relation. Examples of queries are :

   1a. DEGREE2 ⟨ = ⟩ The graph is of degree 2

   1b. CON ⟨ = ⟩ The graph is disconnected

   1c. DEGREE2(x) ⟨ = ⟩ x is of degree 2

   1d. TC(x,y) ⟨ = ⟩ There is a path from x to y, i.e. there are $x_1 \ldots x_k$ such that $xEx_1, x_1Ex_2 \ldots . x_kEy$.

   1e. HAM ⟨ = ⟩ The graph is Hamiltonian

   The queries 1a,1b,1e are boolean, i.e. true or false for a given graph, whereas 1c. is unary, and 1d is binary.

2. Consider now the class of graphs with successor, i.e. with an additional binary relation SUCC defining a successor relation on D. It is the binary representation of 1-1 function from D-{0} into D-{last} where 0 and last are two particular distinguished elements. We can then consider all the previous queries on graphs as queries on graphs with successor. In addition we can consider the following:

2a. EVENDEGREE $<=>$ the graph is of even degree

2b. EVENDEGREE(x) $<=>$ x is of even degree

We will now formalize the notion of an Inductive query on K, i.e. a query such that there exists an inductive definition I (an algorithm) such that for each structure U the inductive definition defines R(x). We then write:

$$[R(x)]^U <=> [I]^U$$

To a structure U, we associate the standard first-order language L with identity, where $x_1, y_1, x_2, y_2 \ldots$ are standard (first-order) variables ranging over D, and $S_1, S_2 \ldots$ are relation variables of arity 0,1,2... over D, sometimes called second-order variables. Assume the notion of S occuring positively in F(x,S) where F is a first-order formula (5).

We will now consider S-positive Formulas with parameters $y_1, \ldots y_1$, i.e. formulas

$$F(x_1 \ldots x_d, S; y_1 \ldots y_k)$$

where S is a d-ary relation. The parameters $y_1 \ldots y_k$ are kept constant in the recursions, that we shall use and are refered to as the global variables or data, as opposed to $x_1 \ldots x_d$ which refer to the local or recursion variables.

Definition : A d-system S, or a system of dimension d is a sequence of $(S_1, S_2 \ldots S_k)$-positive Formulas $F_1 \ldots F_m$ with the same parameters such that each F_i has l_i recursion variables and each S_i is l_i-ary with $0 \leq l_i \leq d$. We will write:

$$S = [F_1 \ldots F_m]$$

We can view a d-system as :

$$F_1(x_{11} \ldots x_{1l_1}, S_1 \ldots S_m; y_1 \ldots y_k)$$

$$F_2(x_{21} \ldots x_{2l_2}, S_1 \ldots S_m; y_1 \ldots y_k)$$

.... ..

.... ..

$$F_m(x_{m1} \ldots x_{ml_m}, S_1 \ldots S_m; y_1 \ldots y_k)$$

For each system S, and each structure U, we define the **simultaneous** finite stages of each F_i as follows: assuming the system has no parameters in order to simplify notations we define :

$F_i^o(x_{i1}\ldots x_{i1})=F_i(x_{i1}\ldots x_{i1},\emptyset\ldots\emptyset)$ where $\emptyset$ is the empty relation.

$F_i^p(x_{i1}\ldots x_{i1})=F_i(x_{i1}\ldots x_{i1},F_1^{p-1}\ldots F_m^{p-1})$

As we only consider finite structures, we know that for a constant A, there will be a $p < A.n^d$, called the closure ordinal such that:

$$F_1^p(\bar{x}) <=> F_1^{p-1}(\bar{x}) <=> F_1^{\infty}(\bar{x})$$

Definition : A query R is **inductive of dimension d** on a class K, if there exists a d-system $S=[F_1, F_2\ldots F_m]$ such that for any structure U of K:

$$[R(\bar{x})]^U <=> U \models F_1^{\infty}(\bar{x})$$

Similarly, we will say that a query is inductive if it is inductive of dimension d for some d.

The following observation has been made by many researchers working with different formalisms [3,4,7,9,11] :

Fact 1 : A query is inductive iff it is computable in polynomial time.

This observation is taken as a foundation, and can actually be refined in several ways [6,7], as there is a direct relationship between the dimension of the induction and the time complexity.

II. Examples

We will treat typical examples, that are similar to those appearing in the data-base litterature in the context of recursion. We will just give the Inductive system, that is intuitively easier to follow than the recursive one. We assume the reader familiar with the Prolog method.

1. Brother defined recursively from father.

Let us assume, we have a given class of structures with one explicitly defined binary relation, Father(x,y). Intuitively Father(x,y) iff x is the father of y, but let us suppose that each individual x can have more than one father y.

We can then define Inductively the relation Brother(x,y), where intuitively Brother(x,y) iff x is the brother of y as follows:

> Induction hypothesis : Either x and y have the same father, or they are brother at stage n if there is a z such that x is the brother of z and z is the brother of y at stage n-1.
>
> This will be represented by the following inductive system:
>
> $F_1(x,y,S) <=> \exists z(\text{Father}(z,x) \ \& \ \text{Father}(z,y)) \text{ OR } \exists u(S(x,u) \ \& \ S(u,y))$

It is then easy to verify that $F_1^{\infty}(x,y) <=> \text{Brother}(x,y)$.

Another possible definition, a bit easier to follow, is the following, using the notion of a system:

$F_1(x,y,S_2,S_3) <=> S_2(x,y) \text{ OR } S_3(x,y)$

$F_2(x,y) <=> \exists z(\text{father}(z,x)\&\text{father}(z,y))$

$F_3(x,y,S_1) <=> \exists u(S_1(x,u) \ \& \ S_1(u,y))$

A few explanations might be necessary to follow these notations. We slightly simplified the general notations of the previous section, in the sense that if a given Functional does not depend on the relational variables $S_1, S_2 \ldots S_m$, we do not write them as arguments. For example the definition of the second Functional F_2 shows no depency with any S_i. For clarity, we just write $F_2(x,y)$ instead of $F_2(x,y,S_1,S_2,S_3)$.

With this notation, one verifies that $F_1^{\infty}(x,y) < = > Brother(x,y)$. One clearly see that F_2 corresponds to the first "rule" (We are brother if we have the same father), and F_3 corresponds to the second "rule" (We are brother if there exists an element u such that we are both brother with u). The first Functional F_1 simply takes the disjunction of these two.

This last notation is easier to use, in case of more complex recursive definitions, and is certainly recommended for practical applications.

2. Brother defined recursively from Father and Mother.

In the previous example, the difficulty of answering a boolean query, say Brother(a,b) lay in the fact that father was not assumed to be a function. In that case, the recursive rule (rule 2), introduced the difficulty.

A more realistic example is that of a similar recursive definition, with Mother and Father, where this time we assume that each individual has at most one father and one mother. The possibility that some individuals have only one father and no mother, while some other have one mother but no father, will force the use of the recursive rule, as before.

$$F_1(x,y,S_2,S_3,S_4) = > S_2(x,y) \text{ OR } S_3(x,y) \text{ OR } S_4(x,y)$$

$$F_2(x,y, \ldots) < = > \exists z(father(z,x) \& father(z,y))$$

$$F_3(x,y, \ldots) < = > \exists z(mother(z,x) \& mother(z,y))$$

$$F_4(x,y,S_1,) < = > \exists u(S_1(x,u) \& S_1(u,y))$$

In order to obtain this new system, we just added another rule ("We are brother if we have the same Mother "). In this special case, we just had to add one more Functional to the previous system. In a more complex situation, we may have to change the system, in order to add more information in an inductive manner.

As in the previous example, we would verify (by Induction) that

$F_1^{\infty}(x,y) < = > Brother(x,y)$.

3. A more complex recursion.

We now want to give an example where Father and Mother are also defined recursively: Assume we are given a Table where all births are registered, in the sense that a line of the table defines the location, name of the father, name of the mother, name of the child, time and date of the birth. Formally speaking we have a relation Births(x,y,u,z,t) where x is the location, y is the father's name, u is the mother's name, z is the child's name and t is the date and time.

Consider the following system:

$F_1(x,y,S_2,S_3,S_4) <=> S_2(x,y) \text{ OR } S_3(x,y) \text{ OR } S_4(x,y)$

$F_2(x,y,S_5) <=> \exists z(S_5(z,x) \& S_5(z,y))$

$F_3(x,y,S_6) <=> \exists z(S_6(z,x) \& S_6(z,y))$

$F_4(x,y,S_1) <=> \exists u(S_1(x,u) \& S_1(u,y))$

$F_5(x,y) <=> \exists u \exists v \exists w \exists t\, Births(u,x,v,y,t)$

$F_6(x,y) <=> \exists u \exists v \exists w \exists t\, Births(u,v,x,y,t)$

We simply took the previous system, replaced father(x,y) by $S_5(x,y)$ in the second Function, and added the Functional F_5 defining father. In the same way, we replaced mother(x,y) by $S_6(x,y)$, and added the Functional F_6 defining it. Notice that semantically, F_5 defines a particular projection of the relation Births. Other projections, taking into account unknown variables for example, would be also reasonable, although semantically different.

From the Inductive point's of view, there is no fundamental difference between this system and the previous one, as father and mother would be defined at the first stage of the Induction. From the recursive point's of view, there is a difference as the computation of father will require a number of stages growing polynomially as a function of the data. At each stage, Father, Mother and Brother would actually be computed simultaneously, although a classical machine would only simulate this concurrency.

3. The simple case of transitive closure.

Let us now consider one of the simplest example, the definition of the transitive closure TC(x,y) , in a graph. Call E the binary relation defining the edges, and consider the following system.

$F_1(x,y,S) <=> x = y \text{ OR } \exists z(xEz \& S(z,y)))$

We will then verify that $TC(x,y) <=> F_1^{\infty}(x,y)$.

There is a practical method, which given an Inductive system, and more generally a recursive system will simulate the stages of the system. The method separates the cases of boolean queries from the cases of open queries. For open queries, it simulates the stages bottom-up in the recursion, using specific data-structures techniques to avoid duplications. In case of boolean queries, it simulates the system top-down. Both techniques are actually interrelated as in order to compute a boolean query, one may have to compute an open query, and vice-versa.

The important point is the fact that any computation will be polynomially bounded. The dimension of the system is actually a key-parameter in the time complexity, as it distinguishes linear, quadratic ... time complexities. The theory of lower-bounds on the dimension is developped in (8).

III. Inductive definitions and Prolog

We will illustrate the difference between the inductive method, and the Prolog method, following the simple previous examples. When we talk about complexity, we mean the time complexity.

Fact 2 : Prolog programs are of exponential complexity.

Fact 3 : Inductive programs are of polynomial complexity.

The three examples above use a similar type of recursion, and the arguments would almost be identical. For simplicity, let us reason with the simplest example, i.e. the transitive closure.

Let us assume we have a boolean query TC(a,b). The Prolog program will actually generate all the paths starting from the point a in the graph, looking for an extremity b. It is possible to create graphs with n points such that the number of such paths is exponential in n. In case there is a path from a to b, the prolog program may find it efficiently, if the good "choices" are made. In the worst-case however, the program will try all the paths and the query will be answered in exponential time. If there were no paths between a and b, we would only be able to answer that query after all paths had been generated, and the complexity would still be exponential.

Note however that we measure the worst-case complexity. It is quite possible that in most practical cases, the number of paths from a point a would not be exponential, and in these cases a finer analysis would be needed. Nevertheless, the systematic generation of all paths does not seem to be a very efficient method, and this is a well-known observation. At this point, enter the notions of a strategy, and of compilation.

A strategy is classically conceived as a method which will instruct a prolog interpreter as to which rule to apply at any given time. It is quite possible that this will make the average complexity better, but we argue that it will not change the worst-case analysis.

Suppose we represent such a strategy by a function, that will define at any given "time" which rule to use. In the case of the transitive closure, as we only have one rule, we are not likely to gain any information from such a function. If we have more than one rule, the gain is not quite clear. In our analysis, the question will simply be whether this function is recursive, i.e. an Inductive function query.

If it is not, then indeed the combinatorial explosion could apparently be tamed, but it has simply be shifted to the computation of that strategy. If it is recursive, there is still no evidence, that the all computation will be polynomially bounded, i.e. an Induction.

In the "Compilation" approach [2], a compiler is supposed to transform a given prolog program into an "efficient" one, although no particular notion of efficiency is mentioned. If we take as notion of efficiency, the property of being computable in polynomial time, the existence of such a compiler would solve the most outstanding conjectures of Computer science.

Any NP-algorithm can be presented as a set of rules in a prolog program. Such a compiler would turn then this NP-algorithm into a P-algorithm, an unlikely event! If the resulting program were iterative, such a compiler would transform then any NP-algorithm into a LOGSPACE-algorithm, as the class of iterative queries is equivalent to LOGSPACE (6), an even more unlikely event !!

The method of [2] only works in some very special cases, and even in these cases, there is no evidence that the resulting program is simpler.

IV. On different Semantics

With both methods, we start with logical definitions associated with queries, but the computational processes are different: the semantics are different. In the Inductive case, the semantic is based on the stages of an induction, as the time-complexity is directly related to the closure ordinal. In the Prolog method, we have a set of rules and only one Induction hypothesis which is : apply a rule if you can (decided by resolution), otherwise backtrack. Therefore all the Prolog programs have the same basic Induction hypothesis!!

As we already mentioned, such Induction hypothesis is likely to force exhaustive searchs in case of recursive definitions. For that reason, we will call the semantic of that method the semantic of the exhaustive search. Any method using this Induction hypothesis will inevitably use a similar exhaustive search. In most practical Lisp applications to expert systems, a similar Induction hypothesis is used, defining therefore a semantic similar to the prolog semantic.

On structures without ordering, like graphs, we can actually prove that some queries are not Inductive, and therefore separate these two semantics ( ). On structures with ordering, i.e. the case in practice, we can't at this point make the separation, as it is equivalent to the most outstanding conjectures of Computer Science.

Conclusion

We used the notion of an Inductive query [7], to present a calculus for Logic-programming. We then contrasted this method with Prolog, from the time-complexity point's of view.

An Inductive query is always computable in polynomial time, whereas a Prolog query is computable in exponential time, even in the case of very sinmple recursions. The semantics associated to the two methods are different: the Prolog semantics is based on the exhaustive search, whereas the Inductive semantic follows the stages of an Induction.

References

[1]. W. Clocksin,C. Mellish : Programming in Prolog. Springer-Verlag 1981.
[2]. L. Henschen, S. Naqvi : On compiling queries in recursive First-order data-bases. JACM vol. 31, 1984, p. 47-85.
[3]. Y. Gurevich : Toward Logic tailored for Computational Complexity. University of Michigan report, 1984.
[4]. N. Immerman : Relational queries computable in polynomial time. SIGACT 1982, p. 147-152.
[5]. Y. Moschovakis : Elementary Induction on Abstract Structures, North-Holland, 1974.
[6]. Y. Moschovakis : Abstract Recursion as a Foundation for the theory of algorithms, Unpublished Notes, 1984.
[7]. M. de Rougemont : Second-Order and Inductive definability on finite structures, Ph.D. thesis UCLA, 1983.
[8]. M. de Rougemont : Uniform definability on finite structures with successor, SIGACT 1984, p. 409-417.
[9]. V. Sazonov : Polynomial Computability and Recursivity on finite domains. EIK 16, 1980, p. 319-323.
[10] B. Trakhtenbrot : Impossibility of an Algorithm for the decision problem on finite classes. Doklady 70, 1950, p. 569-572.
[11] M. Vardi : Complexity of relational query languages. SIGACT 1982, p. 137-146.

SYSTEMS

ARTIFICIAL INTELLIGENCE: Methodology, Systems, Applications
W. Bibel and B. Petkoff (Editors)
Elsevier Science Publishers B.V. (North-Holland)

FP2 : FUNCTIONAL PARALLEL PROGRAMMING BASED ON TERM SUBSTITUTION

Philippe Jorrand

LIFIA
Laboratoire d'Informatique Fondamentale
et d'Intelligence Artificielle
IMAG
GRENOBLE FRANCE

Most systems can be modeled in terms of interconnected units which communicate information among each other: computer hardware and software, telecommunication networks, robotized assembly lines, office automation networks, etc. Before sending out a piece of information (or before performing an action on its environment) every unit has to compute it as a function of previously received information. Distinct units may process information independently of each other and can behave in parallel.

Yet, few language designs have focused on communication, functions and parallelism as the basic notions for system construction. Von Neumann architecture still influences language design [Ada 80], in spite of major proposals for other principles, like Backus' Functional Programming [Backus 78] and Milner's Calculus of Communicating Systems [Milner 80].

The purpose of this paper is to present FP2 (Functional Parallel Programming), a language where communication, functions and parallelism are consistent notions: its design is simple and its formal semantics are rigorously defined. This is made possible by a systematic use of terms and term substitutions for representing the basic notions of the language.

I. INTRODUCTION

FP2 is a language where systems can be described, and programmed, in terms of networks of communicating processes. A process is able to receive and to send messages through ports which are owned by it. Messages are values, in the usual sense of programming, and they have types. Selected pairs of ports may be linked by directed connectors, thus allowing messages to flow from a port to another port. The description of every process involves both the functions applied by the process to the messages it receives in order to compute the messages it sends, and the ordering among communications on connectors attached to that process, with sequencing, non determinism and parallelism.

Values are typed and types are term algebras. Values are represented by terms in these algebras and functions are defined by equations, by case on the constructors of their argument types. Processes are non deterministic state transition systems defined by rules where predicates describe under which conditions a given set of communications may occur. When a rule is applied, its set of communications all occur, thus reflecting actual parallelism, and a new state is established. Predicates and states are represented by terms and rule applicability is represented by pattern matching.

This work was conducted with support from CNRS,from INPG and from ADI.
Address: LIFIA, IMAG, BP 68, 38402 SAINT MARTIN D'HERES Cedex, FRANCE

In this language, functional programming, algebraic data types, communicating processes, parallelism and non determinism nicely fit together. This is due to the uniform use of terms for representing values, function applications, predicates, states and messages and, as a consequence, to the uniform use of term substitutions defined by pattern matching and unification for representing parameter passing, state changes and message communication.

This paper presents FP2, mainly by means of a series of examples. More complete and more formal descriptions of the language can be found in [Pereira 84] and [Cisneros 84] and an implementation of its communicating process part is presented in [Arkaxhiu 84].

Section II is devoted to the functional part of FP2. Basic function and type definitions are due to [Bert 83a and Bert 83b]. On top of this basis, the language allows combinations of functions into functional forms by means of functional operators. These operators are typed versions of those of FP [Backus 78] and their formal semantics are simple: functional forms are evaluated and they result into basic function definitions.

Section III introduces communication, non determinism, and parallelism in FP2. It presents basic process definitions and shows how processes can be combined into process forms by means of process operators. These operators, based upon [Jorrand 82], have the same sort of formal semantics as functional operators: process forms are evaluated and they result into basic process definitions. This approach to process operators is distinct from algebraic approaches, where process forms are not considered as expressions which can be evaluated into more elementary process descriptions [Milner 80, Austry and Boudol 84, Brookes 83, Hoare 83 and many others].

II. FUNCTIONAL PROGRAMMING IN FP2

Values are represented by terms and FP2 operates on values by applying functions to terms. There are two kinds of functions: constructors and operations. Terms containing operation applications should always be reduceable to terms containing only constructors. The reductions corresponding to a given operation are defined by equations.

Terms are typed and every function has a domain and a range, both of which are types (cartesian products of types are types). Thus, terms of a given type are all results of applying functions ranging in that type. Formally, types are term algebras and, with the equational definition of operations, every term is congruent to a term containing only constructors. The language provides means of defining types and operations and both of these definitions may be generic, with formal type parameters.

In addition to this reasonably classical basis for functions and types, FP2 also allows definitions of operations built by combining other functions into functional forms similar to those of FP [Backus 78].

II.1. Type definitions, operations and genericity

A type definition presents a term algebra. It provides:

- the name t of the type;
- the names, domains and ranges (necessarily t) of the constructors of t;
- the names, domains and ranges of operations involving t;
- the names and types of variables used in the equations of t;
- equations defining the congruence classes of the algebra of t.

The left and right members of equations are separated by "==" signs. Equations shoud be written in such a way that terms containing operation applications can be reduced to terms containing only constructors: this is an important question which has been studied in a number of places, especially in connection with algebraic data types [Guttag and Horning 78] and with terms rewriting systems [Boudol 83, Dershowitz 83]. It will not be discussed here.

An example is the type "Nat" of Natural integers (assuming that the type Bool of Booleans is defined with constructors "true" and "false", and with operations "or", "and" and "not"):

```
type Nat
     cons            0 : -> Nat
                  succ : Nat -> Nat
     opns     add, mul : (Nat,Nat) -> Nat
               eq, leq : (Nat,Nat) -> Bool
                     1 : -> Nat
     vars         m, n : Nat
     eqns              add(0,n)   ==  n
                add(succ(m),n)    ==  succ(add(m,n))
                       mul(0,n)   ==  0
                mul(succ(m),n)    ==  add(mul(m,n),n)
                       leq(0,m)   ==  true
                leq(succ(m),0)    ==  false
          leq(succ(m),succ(n))    ==  leq(m,n)
                        eq(m,n)   ==  and(leq(m,n),leq(n,m))
                              1   ==  succ(0)
end
```

Operations may thus be defined within type definitions. But once a type is defined, additional operations on it may be defined separately. Such operation definitions, called "basic op definitions", provide:

- the names, domains and ranges of the new operations;
- the names and types of variables used in the equations;
- equations defining to which congruence classes the new terms belong.

For example, new operations on Nat can be introduced by:

```
op
     opns  up, down : (Nat,Nat) -> Nat
     vars      m, n : Nat
     eqns    up(m,n)   ==  cond(leq(m,n),n,m)
           down(m,n)   ==  cond(leq(m,n),m,n)
end
```

The operation "cond" must itself be defined. The basic op definition proposed next for cond is generic. It requires that, for an application of cond, its formal type parameter t be bound to an actual type:

```
op  req  Ftype [t]
     opns  cond : (Bool,t,t) -> t
     vars  x, y : t
     eqns  cond(true,x,y)   ==  x
          cond(false,x,y)   ==  y
end
```

Instances of this generic definition of cond are created by binding the formal type t to the types of the corresponding parameters of applications of cond: in the equations for up and down, t is bound to Nat since m and n are of type Nat. As a consequence, cond(leq(succ(0),0),0,succ(0)) reduces to succ(0).

Type definitions may also be generic and instances of them can be created and named:

```
type  Seq  req  Ftype [t]
      cons    nil : -> seq[t]
             cons : (t,Seq[t]) -> Seq[t]
      opns   null : Seq[t] -> Bool
           append : (Seq[t],Seq[t]) -> Seq[t]
          reverse : Seq[t] -> Seq[t]
      vars      e : t
             u, v : Seq[t]
      eqns            null(nil)  ==  true
             null(cons(e,u))  ==  false
               append(nil,u)  ==  u
        append(cons(e,u),v)  ==  cons(e,append(u,v))
                reverse(nil)  ==  nil
         reverse(cons(e,u))  ==  append(reverse(u),cons(e,nil))
end

type  Snat   is  Seq[Nat]
type  Ssnat  is  Seq[Seq[Nat]]
```

With this notion of genericity it is also possible to restrict the family of actual types admissible by a given formal type. This is done by specifying an algebraic property that these actual types must satisfy. A precise treatment of this question falls outside the scope of this paper and can be found in [Bert 83a and Bert 83b]. Property definitions look like type definitions with less restricted forms of equations. For example, the partial order on a type t (reflexivity, antisymmetry and transitivity) is:

```
prop  Order  on  Ftype [t]
      opns  lequ, equ : (t,t) -> Bool
      vars    x, y, z : t
      eqns                    lequ(x,x)  ==  true
                               equ(x,y)  ==  and(lequ(x,y),lequ(y,x))
       and(and(lequ(x,y),lequ(y,z)),
                     not(lequ(x,z)))  ==  false
end
```

All actual types may be bound to "Ftype" formal types: "Ftype" is thus a property that all types satisfy. But not all types satisfy the property "Order". For example, the type Nat can be viewed as a partial order with its operations "eq" and "leq". That fact can be asserted by a satisfaction clause:

```
sat  Order [Nat with leq, eq]
```

Then, with the following generic definition, "up" and "down" could still apply to Nat, but also to any other type satisfying "Order":

```
op  req  Order [t with less, equal]
      opns  up, down : (t,t) -> t
      vars       x, y : t
      eqns    up(x,y)  ==  cond(less(x,y),y,x)
            down(x,y)  ==  cond(less(x,y),x,y)
end
```

Now, in up(succ(0),0), since the formal type t is bound to Nat, the formal operation less is bound to leq. This binding is established across the req clause of the definition of up and the sat clause which gives the Order property to Nat. Thus, up(succ(0),0) reduces to succ(0), as expected.

II.2. Functional operators and functional forms

FP2 provides six functional operators for combining defined functions into functional forms. These operators assume the existence of the type "Bool", of the generic operation "cond", of the generic type "Seq", and of a property "Monoid":

```
prop Monoid on Ftype [u]
     opns h : (u,u) -> u
          i : -> u
     vars x, y, z : u
     eqns h(h(x,y),z)  ==  h(x,h(y,z))
               h(x,i)  ==  x
               h(i,x)  ==  x
end
```

Let r, s, t, t1, t2, ..., tn be types. The six functional operators are:

1. Composition: if f and g are functions with f:t->r and g:r->s, then g.f is a functional form denoting an operation in t->s. If x is a term of type t, then the reduction of (g.f)(x) is the reduction of g(f(x)).

2. Condition: if p, f and g are functions with p:t->Bool, f:t->r and g:t->r, then (p->f;g) is a functional form denoting an operation in t->r. If x is a term of type t, then the reduction of (p->f;g)(x) is the reduction of cond(p(x),f(x),g(x)).

3. Tuple: if f1, f2, ..., fn are functions with fi:t->ti, then [f1,f2,...,fn] is a functional form denoting an operation in t->(t1,t2,...,tn). If x is a term of type t, then the reduction of [f1,f2,...,fn](x) is the reduction of (f1(x),f2(x),...,fn(x)).

4. Constant: if x is a term of type t, then |x| is a functional form denoting an operation in r->t, for any type r. If y is a term of any type r, then the reduction of |x|(y) is the reduction of x.

5. Map: if f is a function with f:t->r, then *f is a functional form denoting an operation in Seq[t]->Seq[r]. If x is of type Seq[t], then there are two cases: (i) if x reduces to nil then *f(x) reduces to nil, and (ii) if x reduces to cons(e,y) then the reduction of *f(x) is the reduction of cons(f(e),*f(y)).

6. Insert: if f is a function with f:(t,t)->t, then /f is a functional form denoting an operation in Seq[t]->t, provided that the property "Monoid" has been asserted for t by "sat Monoid [t with f, o]". If x is of type Seq[t], then there are two cases: (i) if x reduces to nil then /f(x) reduces to o, and (ii) if x reduces to cons(e,y) then the reduction of /f(x) is the reduction of f(e,/f(y)).

The semantics of functional operators are defined by considering that functional forms are second order expressions which can be evaluated. This is possible in FP2, where basic op definitions constitute a more elementary form of operation description: evaluating functional forms means producing basic op definitions. Let F(x) be a term where F is a functional form. The evaluation of F is guided by its syntax: dummy operation names f0, f1, ... are generated, one for each syntactical sub-form in F, where f0 is the operation for F itself. Then, basic op definitions for f0, f1, ..., with their respective names, domains, ranges, variables and equations can be mechanically produced . In fact, defining one of these functions fi is necessary only when fi corresponds to a map or insert functional operator and in the case of recursive functional forms. Finally, F(x) is replaced by f0(x) which has its reduction defined by the generated basic op definition.

For example, provided that "sat Monoid [Nat with add, 0]" has been asserted, the evaluation of /add produces:

```
op
        opns  f0 : Seq[Nat] -> Nat
        vars  v0 : Nat
              v1 : Seq[Nat]
        eqns          f0(nil)    ==  0
              f0(cons(v0,v1))    ==  add(v0,f0(v1))
end
```

A term like /add(x), where x must be of type Seq[Nat], is then replaced by f0(x) and reduces down to the sum of the elements of x. Functional forms can also be explicitly named. Nat may satisfy Monoid in more than one way, for example both with add, by "sat Monoid [Nat with add, 0]" as above and with mul, by "sat Monoid [Nat with mul, 1]". It is then possible to define:

```
op  sigma  is  /add
op     pi  is  (null -> |0| ; /mul)
op  sigpi  is  sigma . *pi
```

This produces the same basic op definition as above, with f0 replaced by sigma, plus two other basic op definitions, one for pi and one for sigpi:

```
op
        opns  pi : Seq[Nat] -> Nat
              f1 : Seq[Nat] -> Nat
        vars  v0 : Nat
              v1 : Seq[Nat]
        eqns          pi(v1)   ==  cond(null(v1),0,f1(v1))
                     f1(nil)   ==  1
             f1(cons(v0,v1))   ==  mul(v0,f1(v1))
end

op
        opns  sigpi : Seq[Seq[Nat]] -> Nat
                 f2 : Seq[Seq[Nat]] -> Seq[Nat]
        vars     v0 : Seq[Nat]
                 v1 : Seq[Seq[Nat]]
        eqns        sigpi(v1)   ==  sigma(f2(v1))
                      f2(nil)   ==  nil
              f2(cons(v0,v1))   ==  cons(pi(v0),f2(v1))
end
```

Recursive operation definitions with functional forms fit quite nicely in in that framework. For example, Fibonacci numbers can be computed by:

```
op  fib  is  (l1 -> id ; add . [fib.pred,fib.pred.pred])
```

where op l1 is leq.[id,|1|], where id is the identity function and where pred is the predecessor function. This definition produces:

```
op
        opns  fib : Nat -> Nat
        vars   v0 : Nat
        eqns  fib(v0)  ==  cond(l1(v0),id(v0),
                                add(fib(pred(v0)),fib(pred(pred(v0)))))
end
```

The laws of the algebra of functional programming can all be proved in FP2, using the fact that equations define congruence classes of terms.

III. PARALLEL PROGRAMMING IN FP2

The elementary component for organizing parallel computations in FP2 is the process. A process has ports through which messages may flow in and out. Messages are values, they are represented by functional terms, they have types and they are built and reduced according to functional programming. Messages arrive at ports or leave ports along directed connectors having their destinations or their origins attached to these ports. Each connector allows messages of a certain type. The transportation of one message along one connector is a communication. There is no such notion like the duration of a communication.

Describing a process is describing its ability to perform communications along the connectors attached to its ports. In addition to applying functions to received messages for computing sent messages, this involves also sequencing, non determinism and parallelism in the ordering among communications. Formally, a process is a transition system which can be represented by a tree: nodes represent process states, multiple branching represents non determinism and arcs are labeled by events, where an event is a set of communications occurring in parallel. This tree is in general infinite and every path from its root represents a possible sequence of events: one set after the other of communications occurring in parallel. FP2 provides means of defining processes. Basic process definitions may be generic, with formal type parameters. They may also have other kinds of parameters, like values and port names.

In addition to basic process definitions, the language allows definitions of processes built by combining other processes into process forms by means of process operators.

III.1. Basic process definitions and genericity

A basic process definition describes a transition system, with transition rules, where the events are sets of communications along typed connectors. It provides:

- the name N of the process;
- the names and message types of the connectors of N;
- the names and domains of predicates used in the rules of N;
- the names and types of variables used in the rules of N;
- rules defining the transitions of N.

Connectors are directed pairs of ports: if A and B are port names, A.B is the name of the connector from A to B. Such a connector is an internal connector as opposed to external connectors, which have a dangling end: A.- is an output connector name and -.B is an input connector name. For example, let STACK be a process. It can be pictured as:

It has an input connector -.I and an output connector O.- . The communication of a message v, where v is a functional term of type t, along a connector k of message type t is denoted by k(v). For example, if both -.I and O.- may communicate Nat's, then -.I(0) and O.-(succ(0)) denote communications. An event is composed of a set of communications k1(v1)...kn(vn), where k1,...,kn are n distinct connectors.

A predicate is a term of the form Q(u1,...,um) where Q is a predicate name and where the ui's are functional terms of the correct types for the domain of Q. A predicate without variables in the ui's is a state. Predicate names may not appear in the ui's.

Rules are composed of three parts: a predicate R(u1,...,um) called the pre-condition, an event k1(v1)...kn(vn) and a predicate S(w1,...,wp) called the post-condition. They have the general format:

```
R(u1,...,um)  k1(v1)...kn(vn)  ==>  S(w1,...,wp)
```

If ki is an internal or output connector, all variables appearing in vi must appear in R(u1,...,um) or in vj such that kj is an input connector. The same must be true for the variables in S(w1,...,wp). Since an event is a set it may be empty. In that case, the rule is an internal rule, of the form:

```
R(u1,...,um)  ==>  S(w1,...,wp)
```

Furthermore, among the rules of a process, there must be at least one initial rule, without pre-condition and without event, and where the post-condition is a state:

```
==>  S(w1,...,wp)
```

For example, let the process STACK be an unbounded stack of Nat's. It is initially empty and when a Nat arrives along -.I, it may be written into STACK. When STACK is not empty, the last arrived Nat may be read from it along O.- . Writing and reading are mutually exclusive. A basic process definition for this "Last In First Out" STACK may then be:

```
proc  STACK
      cncs    -.I : Nat
              O.- : Nat
      preds     S : Seq[Nat]
      vars      e : Nat
                v : Seq[Nat]
      rules                        ==>  S(nil)
                   S(v)   -.I(e)   ==>  S(cons(e,v))
          S(cons(e,v))    O.-(e)   ==>  S(v)
end
```

Rules in a process N describe a transition system in the following way:

0. Initially, one of the initial rules in N is chosen. This choice is non deterministic. The post-condition of the chosen rule becomes the current state of N. Then repeat steps 1, 2 and 3.

1. The current state q of N is matched against the pre-conditions of the rules: a rule with pre-condition r is said to be pre-applicable if there exist a substitution h for the variables of r such that h(r)=q. If there is no pre-applicable rule, the process is terminated.

2. Let e be the event in a pre-applicable rule and let mj be a message about to be sent accross kj, for all kj(vj) in e where kj is an input connector. That rule is said to be applicable if there exist a substitution g for the variables of all vj's, such that g(h(vj))=mj.

3. One of the applicable rules is chosen to be the applied rule. This choice is non deterministic. Let s be the post-condition of this rule. The event g(h(e)) occurs and the term g(h(s)) becomes the current state of N.

This operational view shows how rules express sequencing, non determinism and parallelism among communications: rules are applied one at a time (sequencing), the applied rule is chosen among several applicable rules (non determinism) and several communications occur within a single event (parallelism). It must be noted that internal rules can be used for describing computations. This can be seen in the following example: MAXNAT sends through C.- the maximun of two previously entered Nat's, the first one entered through -.A and the second one through -.B ("()" denotes the null arity for predicates):

```
proc  MAXNAT
      cncs  -.A, -.B, C.- : Nat
      preds  X : ()
             Y : Nat
             Z : (Nat,Nat,Nat,Nat)
      vars   m, n, p, q : Nat
      rules                          ==>  X
                      X   -.A(m)     ==>  Y(m)
                   Y(m)   -.B(n)     ==>  Z(m,n,m,n)
         Z(m,n,succ(p),succ(q))      ==>  Z(m,n,p,q)
             Z(m,n,p,0)   C.-(m)     ==>  X
             Z(m,n,0,q)   C.-(n)     ==>  X
end
```

In fact, this form of process definition could very well do without the operation definitions of the functional part of FP2. Assuming that the available functions are only constructors, it has been shown in [Pereira 84] that basic process definitions are sufficiently powerful to define any function that can be computed on a Turing machine. However, defined operations make basic process definitions much easier to write and to read. For example, a process sending out the maximum of its two input messages could also be generic, therefore requiring the property "Order" for its formal type parameter t. Using the operation "up", this is simple to write:

```
proc  GMAX  req  Order [t with less, equal]
      cncs    -.A, -.B, C.- : t
      preds    X : (), Y, Z : t
      vars   m, n : t
      rules                ==>  X
               X   -.A(m)  ==>  Y(m)
            Y(m)   -.B(n)  ==>  Z(up(m,n))
            Z(m)   C.-(m)  ==>  X
end
```

In addition to type parameters, which are introduced with a name and a required property, basic process definitions may also have value parameters introduced with a name and a required type. For example, a bounded queue of capacity k may be defined and instanciated as follows:

```
proc  BQUEUE  req  Ftype [t]
                   Nat [k]
      cncs  -.W, R.- : t
      preds          Q : (Seq[t],Seq[t],Nat)
      vars           e : t, u, v : Seq[t], n : Nat
      rules                           ==>  Q(nil,nil,k)
         Q(u,v,succ(n))    -.W(e)     ==>  Q(cons(e,u),v,n)
        Q(u,cons(e,v),n)   R.-(e)     ==>  Q(u,v,succ(n))
             Q(cons(e,u),nil,n)       ==>  Q(nil,reverse(cons(e,u)),n)
end

proc  BQUEUE4  is  BQUEUE [Nat] [succ(succ(succ(succ(0))))]
```

Value parameters also allow the definition of indexed families of processes. For that purpose, the domain of port names is syntactically defined as follows:

```
<port name>  ::=  <identifier> |
                  <port name> [ <list of natural numbers> ]
```

For example, a generic indexed family V of variables alternating write and read communications can be defined and instanciated:

```
proc  V  req  Ftype [t]
              Nat [i]
      cncs  -.W[i], R[i].- : t
      preds              E : (), F : t
      vars               v : t
      rules              ==>  E
             E  -.W[i](v)  ==>  F(v)
          F(v)  R[i].-(v)  ==>  E
end

proc  VNAT1  is  V[Nat][1]
```

The connectors of VNAT1 are named -.W[1] and R[1].-.

Finally, process definitions may be parameterized by port names, as in the following definition of a "CELL". A CELL performs four communications within a single event. In that event, it sends out the result of a simple computation performed on previously received values:

```
proc  CELL  req  Nat [c]
                 Port [X0,Y0,X1,Y1]
      cncs  -.X0, -.Y0, X1.-, Y1.- : Nat
      preds                     Q : (Nat,Nat)
      vars             x, y, u, v : Nat
      rules                                    ==>  Q(0,0)
         Q(x,y)  -.X0(u) -.Y0(v)
                 X1.-(x) Y1.-(add(y,mul(c,x)))  ==>  Q(u,v)
end

proc  CELL1  is  CELL [a] [U,Y0[i,j],X1[i,j],V]
```

Provided that a, i and j are natural numbers, the connectors of CELL1 are named -.U, -.Y0[i,j], X1[i,j].- and V.-.

III.2. Process operators and process forms

FP2 provides process operators for combining defined processes into process forms. The number and the nature of these operators are arbitrary and a given implementation of the language could take any collection of them. The important facts are: (a) all operators are built up on top of a common primitive basis and (b) process forms can all be evaluated into basic process definitions with connectors, conditions, variables and rules.

III.2.a. Primitive basis for process composition

A basic process definition is a syntactic object of the form:

```
proc  N
        cncs   k1 : t1         ...        kl : tl
        preds  p1 : l1         ...        pm : lm
        vars   v1 : u1         ...        vn : un
        rules    ==> q1        ...          ==> qp
          r1 e1 ==> s1        ...    rq eq ==> sq
end
```

Thus, it can be viewed as associating a process name N with a tuple <K,P,V,Q,R> composed of the 5 following sets:

- K={<ki,ti>|i=1..l}, represents connector definitions, where the ki's are l distinct connector names and the ti's are type names.
- P={<pi,li>|i=1..m}, represents predicate definitions, where the pi's are m distinct predicate names and the li's are (possibly empty) lists of type names.
- V={<vi,ui>|i=1..n}, represents variable definitions, where the vi's are n distinct variable names and the ui's are type names.
- Q={qi|i=1..p}, represents initial rules, where the qi's are states.
- R={<ri,ei,si>|i=1..q}, represents transition rules, where the ri's and si's are predicates and the ei's are (possibly empty) events.

Let N=<K,P,V,Q,R> and N'=<K',P',V',Q',R'> be two basic process definitions:

Primitive sum operators. Iff K and K' share no port name, the sum K+K' is the set union of K and K'. It is undefined otherwise. Analogously, P+P' is the union of P and P' iff they share no predicate name, V+V' is the union of V and V' iff they share no variable name and e+e', where e and e' are events, is the union of e and e' iff they share no connector name. The sums Q+Q' and R+R' are the corresponding set unions and are always defined.

Product of predicates. Given predicate definitions d=<p,l> and d'=<p',l'>, the product d*d' is a predicate definition <p_p',M(p,p',l,l')>, where p_p' is a predicate name and where M(p,p',l,l') is a list obtained by merging the lists l and l' in a way depending solely on p and p' and such that M(p,p',l,l')=M(p',p,l',l). Given P={di|i=1..m} and P'={d'j|j=1..m'}, the product P*P' is {di*d'j|i=1..m,j=1..m'}. Iff r=p(f) and r'=p'(f') are predicates such that the lists of functional terms f and f' share no variable name, the product r*r' is defined and is p_p'(M(p,p',f,f')).

Product of initial rules. Given Q={qi|i=1..p} and Q'={q'j|j=1..p'}, the product Q*Q' is {qi*q'j|i=1..p,j=1..p'}.

Product of transition rules. Iff R={<ri,ei,si>|i=1..q} and R'={<r'j,e'j,s'j>|j=1..q'} share no variable name and no port name, the product R*R' is defined and is {<ri*r'j,ei+e'j,si*s'j>|i=1..q,j=1..q'}.

Idle rules. Given a predicate definition <p,l> with l=(t1,..,tk), j(p) is a predicate of the form p(x1,..,xk) where the xi's are k distinct variable names and xi is of type ti. Given P={<pi,li>|i=1..m}, the set I(P)={<r,{},r>|r∈J(P)}, where J(P)={j(pi)|i=1..m}, is the set of "idle rules" on P and W(P) is a set of variable definitions necessary for I(P).

III.2.b. Process operators

Let N1=<K1,P1,V1,Q1,R1> and N2=<K2,P2,V2,Q2,R2> be basic process definitions where K1 and K2 do not share any port name. In each definition D of a process operator, N1 and N2 are such that the primitive operators applied in D are defined on their operands: this can be assumed without any loss of generality, since predicates and variables may always be renamed.

1. Interleaved composition: N1¦N2. When an event occurs in the process N1¦N2, it is either an event in N1 while N2 is idle or an event in N2 while N1 is idle:

```
N1¦N2 = <K,P,V,Q,R>

where  K = K1+K2
       P = P1*P2
       V = V1+V2+W(P1)+W(P2)
       Q = Q1*Q2
       R = R1*I(P2)+I(P1)*R2
```

2. Synchronous composition: N1¦¦¦N2. When an event occurs in N1¦¦¦N2, it is an event in N1 together with an event in N2:

```
N1¦¦¦N2 = <K,P,V,Q,R>

where  K = K1+K2
       P = P1*P2
       V = V1+V2
       Q = Q1*Q2
       R = R1*R2
```

3. Parallel composition: N1¦¦N2. When an event occurs in N1¦¦N2, it is an event in N1 while N2 is idle, or an event in N2 while N1 is idle, or an event in N1 together with an event in N2:

```
N1¦¦N2 = <K,P,V,Q,R>

where  K = K1+K2
       P = P1*P2
       V = V1+V2+W(P1)+W(P2)
       Q = Q1*Q2
       R = R1*I(P2)+I(P1)*R2+R1*R2
```

4. Uncontrolable choice: N1?N2. At initialization, the process N1?N2 chooses non deterministically to behave always like N1 while leaving N2 idle, or to behave always like N2 while leaving N1 idle:

```
N1?N2 = <K,P,V,Q,R>

where  K = K1+K2
       P = P1+P2
       V = V1+V2
       Q = Q1+Q2
       R = R1+R2
```

5. <u>Controlable choice: N1!N2</u>. After initialization, the first event to occur in N1!N2 may be either an event in N1 while N2 is idle or an event in N2 while N1 is idle. If that event contains input or output communications, the choice may be controled by the environment of N1!N2. After that event has occured, N1!N2 continues to behave like N1 while leaving N2 idle if it was an event in N1, or continues to behave like N2 while leaving N1 idle if it was an event in N2:

```
N1!N2 = <K,P,V,Q,R>

where  K = K1+K2                          given  P'  = {<T,()>,<T1,()>,<T2,()>}
       P = (P1*P2)*P'                            Q'  = {T}
       V = V1+V2                                 R'1 = {<T,{},T1>,<T1,{},T1>}
       Q = (Q1*Q2)*Q'                            R'2 = {<T,{},T2>,<T2,{},T2>}
       R = (R1*I(P2))*R'1+(I(P1)*R2)*R'2
```

6. <u>Connection: N1+A.B</u>. If A.- is an output connector of type t in N1 and if -.B is an input connector of the same type in N1, then A.B is an internal connector of type t in N1+A.B. N1+A.B behaves like N1 and, in addition, when an event involving both A.- and -.B may occur in N1, a new event involving A.B may occur in N1+A.B, where the message sent from A arrives at B:

```
N1+A.B = <K,P,V,Q,R>

where  K = K1+K'   given  K' = {<A.B,t>}
       P = P1             R' = { g(<r,e-{A.-(u),-.B(v)}+{A.B(u)},s>)
       V = V1                                        |    <r,e,s> ∈ R1
       Q = Q1                                        and  A.-(u)  ∈ e
       R = R1+R'                                     and  -.B(v)  ∈ e
                                                     and  g = mgu(u,v) }

                   with   mgu(u,v) = most general unifier of u and v.
```

7. <u>Hiding: N1-k</u>. If k is a connector of type t in N1, the connectors of N1-k are all the connectors of N1, except k which is "hidden". If k is an external connector, no event involving k may occur in N1-k, since the environment cannot "see" k any longer. If k is an internal connector, events involving k in N1 may still occur but, in N1-K, they do not mention k any longer:

```
N1-k = <K,P,V,Q,R>

where  K = K1-K'   given  K'  = {<k,t>}
       P = P1             R'  = { <r,e,s> | <r,e,s> ∈ R1
       V = V1                                and e involves k }
       Q = Q1             R'' = { <r,e-{k(u)},s> | <r,e,s> ∈ R1
       R = R1-R'+R'                              and  k(u) ∈ e
                                                 and  k is internal }
```

8. <u>Trigger: e->N1</u>. If e is an event, the first event to occur in e->N1 may occur only together with e. After that, e->N1 behaves like N1. Thus, e->N1 is N1 triggered by e:

```
e->N1 = <K,P,V,Q,R>

where  K = K1+K'   given  K' = {a set of connector
       P = P1*P'                   definitions necessary for e}
       V = V1             P' = {<T,()>,<T1,()>}
       Q = Q1*Q'          Q' = {T}
       R = R1*R'          R' = {<T,e,T1>,<T1,{},T1>}
```

9. <u>Control: e=>N1</u>. If e is an event, e=>N1 behaves like N1, but every event occurs together with e. Thus, e=>N1 is N1 controled by e:

```
e=>N1 = <K,P,V,Q,R>

where  K = K1+K'    given  K' = {a set of connector
       P = P1*P'                definitions necessary for e}
       V = V1              P' = {<T,()>}
       Q = Q1*Q'           Q' = {T}
       R = R1*R'           R' = {<T,e,T>}
```

10. <u>Time-out: N1.n:N2</u>. If n is a natural integer, then N1.n:N2 behaves like N1 for at most n successive events. If N1 is terminated before n events have occured in it, then N1.n:N2 is also terminated. If N1 is not terminated at that time, then N1.n:N2 stops behaving like N1 and starts behaving like N2:

```
N1.n:N2 = <K,P,V,Q,R>

where  K = K1+K2            given  P' = {<T<(Nat)>}
       P = P1*P'+P2                V' = {<v,Nat>}
       V = V1+V'+V''+V2            V''= W(P1)
       Q = Q1*Q'                   Q' = {T(n)}
       R = R1*R'+R''+R2            R' = {<T(succ(v)),{},T(v)>}
                                   R''= { <p*T(0),{},q> |   p ∈ J(P1)
                                                    and q ∈ Q2   }
```

III.2.c. <u>Process forms</u>

Process forms appear in the context of process definitions:

<u>proc</u> <process name> <u>is</u> <process form>

A process form is an expression in which the operators are process operators and the operands are processes, connectors, events or natural integers. Evaluating a process form results in basic process definitions.

In principle, the evaluation of a process form N is guided by its syntax: dummy names n0, n1, ..., are generated, one for each syntactical sub-form in N, where n0 is the name corresponding to N itself. Then, basic process definitions for n0, n1, ..., with their respective names, connectors, predicates, variables and rules can be mechanically produced by applying the definitions of the operators.

In practice, this evaluation can be greatly optimized and most intermediate basic process definitions (especially those resulting from compositions) can be avoided, as shown in [Arkaxhiu 84].

For writing the examples in this section and showing the results of process form evaluations, the folowing conventions are used:

- Process forms written "N ⊕ A.B", where N is a process form and A.B is an internal connector, are expanded to "N + A.B - A.- - -.B - A.B".

- No predicate name written by a user may contain the character "_".

- The list M(p,p',l,l'), where p and p' are predicate names and l and l' are lists (of types or of terms), is written as if it was append(l,l').

1. Maxima of sequences of Nat's. In this first example, values of type Nat are read in sequentially and they are considered as forming a series of sequences separated by 0's. At the end of each sequence, the maximum of that sequence is sent out. This is acheived by a process SMAX constructed as a network of more elementary processes. The process GMAX and the following definitions are used in that construction:

```
proc  REG
      cncs  -.W, R.- : Nat
      preds        V : Nat
      vars      r, s : Nat
      rules              ==>  V(0)
          V(r)  -.W(s)   ==>  V(s)
          V(r)  R.-(r)   ==>  V(0)
end

type  Signal
      cons  buzz, ring : -> Signal
end

proc  BZZZ
      cncs  -.K, L.- : Nat, S.- : Signal
      conds        P : ()
      vars         p : Nat
      rules                              ==>  P
        P  -.K(0) L.-(0) S.-(buzz)       ==>  P
        P  -.K(succ(p)) L.-(succ(p))     ==>  P
end

proc  GATE  req  Ftype [t]
      cncs  -.M, N.- : t, -.T : Signal
      conds        Q : ()
      vars         q : t
      rules                            ==>  Q
        Q  -.M(q) N.-(q) -.T(buzz)  ==> Q
end
```

Then, the process SMAX can be constructed as follows:

```
proc  SMAX  is
           (GMAX[Nat] || REG @ C.W + R.B - -.B - R.B)
            ||  (BZZZ || GATE[Nat] @ S.T)  @ L.A @ R.M
```

The resulting basic process definition is remarkably short:

```
proc  SMAX
      cncs  -.K, N.- : Nat
      preds  X_V_P_Q : Nat, Y_V_P_Q, Z_V_P_Q : (Nat,Nat)
      vars   p, m, r : Nat
      rules                          ==>  X_V_P_Q(0)
        X_V_P_Q(p)  -.K(succ(p))     ==>  Y_V_P_Q(succ(p),r)
        Y_V_P_Q(m,r)                 ==>  Z_V_P_Q(up(m,r),0)
        Z_V_P_Q(m,r)                 ==>  X_V_P_Q(m)
        X_V_P_Q(r)  -.K(0) N.-(r)   ==>  Y_V_P_Q(0,0)
end
```

2. Construction of a queue. In addition to process operators, process forms may also use if..then..else..fi conditionals. It is then possible to write recursive definitions, like the following construction of a bounded queue BQ built as a chain of variables of the indexed family V:

```
proc  BQ  req  Ftype [t]
               Nat [k]
          is   if  eq(k,1)
                   then  V[t][1]
                   else  BQ[t][pred(k)]
                           || V[t][k] @ R[pred(k)].W[k]
               fi

proc  BQ4  is  BQ[Nat][(succ(succ(succ(succ(0))))]
```

The instanciation can be pictured as:

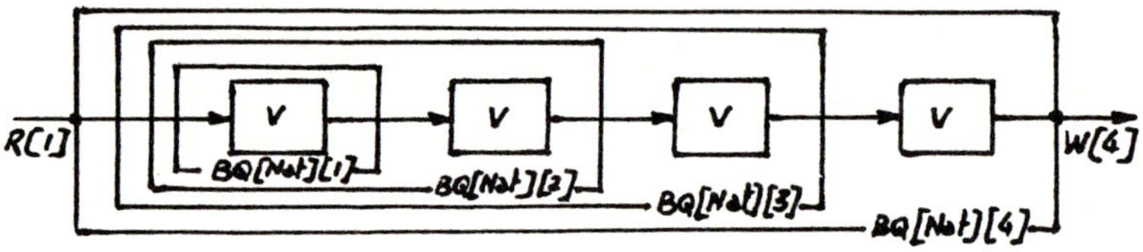

3. Systolic arrays. Recursive process constructions like the queue BQ can be generalized to systolic arrays [Kung 81]. The following example of systolic array has been first described in FP2 by [Cisneros 84].

Let A and B be two n*n matrices. Given a series X0...Xi... of vectors with n components, the problem is to compute a series Y1...Yi... of vectors with n components such that Yi = AXi + BX(i-1). This computation can be performed by a systolic array SYSTOL using 2n*n CELL processes.

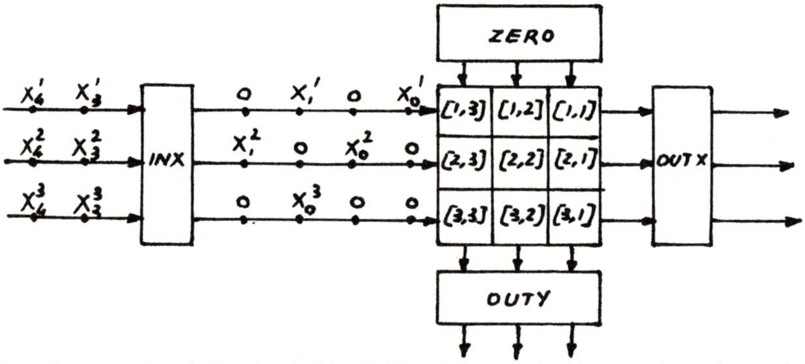

The Xi vectors arrive into the left of the system and they get out unchanged from the right, while the computed results, the Yi vectors, leave from the bottom. The processes INX, OUTX, ZERO and OUTY are interface processes: INX inserts one vector of 0's after each Xi vector and delays the j'th component of vector Xi so that it arrives into SYSTOL at the same time (i.e. within the same event) as the 1st component of vector X(i+j-1). Symmetrically, OUTX and OUTY re-establish the synchrony among the components of each Xi vector and of each Yi vector respectively. ZERO repeatedly sends vectors of 0's into the top of SYSTOL. The FP2 description of these interface processes is left to the reader.

Surrounded by its interfaces, the process SYSTOL is a n*n array of orthogonally connected processes of the family MOD, each containing 2 CELL's. MOD[i,j] is positioned at row i, column j of SYSTOL and is defined by:

```
proc  MOD  req  Nat [i,j]
           is   CELL [b(i,j)] [U,X1[i,j],YO[i,j],V] ||
                CELL [a(i,j)] [XO[i,j],Z,W,Y1[i,j]]  @ V.W @ Z.U
```

where a(i,j) and b(i,j) are elements of the matrices A and B respectively. Finally, SYSTOL is constructed as follows:

```
proc  SYSTOL  req  Nat [n]
              is   ARRAY [n,n,n]

proc  ARRAY   req  Nat [i,j,k]
              is   if  eq(i,1)
                   then  if  eq(j,1)
                         then  MOD [1,1]
                         else  MOD [i,j] || ARRAY [k,pred(j),k]
                                          @ X1[i,j].XO[i,pred(j)]
                         fi
                   else  if  eq(j,1)
                         then  MOD [i,j] || ARRAY [pred(i),j,k]
                                          @ Y1[pred(i),j].YO[i,j]
                         else  MOD [i,j] || ARRAY [pred(i),j,k]
                                          @ Y1[pred(i),j].YO[i,j]
                                          @ X1[i,j].XO[i,pred(j)]
                         fi
                   fi
```

REFERENCES

[Ada 80]
"Reference manual for the ADA programming language"
United States Department of Defense (1980)

[Arkaxhiu 84]
Arkaxhiu, E.
"Un environnement et un langage graphique pour la specification de processus paralleles communicants"
These, LIFIA, Institut National Polytechnique de Grenoble (1984)

[Austry and Boudol 84]
Austry, D. and Boudol, G.
"Algebre de processus et synchronisation"
Theoretical Computer Science (to appear)

[Backus 78]
Backus, J. W.
"Can programming be liberated from the von Neumann style? A functional style and its algebra of programs"
Comm. ACM, Vol. 21, No. 8 (1978)

[Bert 83a]
Bert, D.
"Refinements of generic specifications with algebraic tools"
IFIP 83, North Holland (1983)

[Bert 83b]
Bert, D.
"Manuel de reference de LPG"
Research Report 408, LIFIA, IMAG (1983)

[Boudol 83]
Boudol, G.
"Computational semantics of terms rewriting systems"
Research Report 192, INRIA (1983)

[Brookes 83]
Brookes, S.D.
"A model for communicating sequential processes"
Thesis, Carnegie-Mellon University (1983)

[Cisneros 84]
Cisneros, M.
"Programmation parallele et programmation fonctionnelle: propositions pour un langage"
These, LIFIA, Institut National Polytechnique de Grenoble (1984)

[Dershowitz 83]
Dershowitz, N.
"Computing with rewrite systems"
Research Report ATR-83(8478)-1, Aerospace Corporation (1983)

[Guttag and Horning 78]
Guttag, J.V. and Horning, J.J.
"The algebraic specification of abstract data types"
Acta Informatica (1978)

[Hoare 83]
Hoare, C.A.R.
"Notes on communicating processes"
Technical Monograph PRG-33, Oxford University (1983)

[Jorrand 82]
Jorrand, Ph.
"Specification of communicating processes and process implementation correctness"
Lecture Notes in Computer Science, No.137 (1982)

[Kung 81]
Kung, H.T.
"Why systolic architectures?"
Research Report, Carnegie-Mellon University, CMU-CS-81-148 (1981)

[Milner 80]
Milner, R.
"A calculus of communicating processes"
Lecture Notes in Computer Science, No. 92 (1980)

[Pereira 84]
Pereira, J.M.
"Processus communicants: un langage et ses modeles. Problemes d'analyse"
These, LIFIA, Institut National Polytechnique de Grenoble (1984)

ARTIFICIAL INTELLIGENCE: Methodology, Systems, Applications
W. Bibel and B. Petkoff (Editors)
Elsevier Science Publishers B.V. (North-Holland)

PROGRAM SYNTHESIS THROUGH PROBLEM SPLITTING: A METHOD FOR SUBPROBLEM CHARACTERIZATION

R. Brena (*) - R. Caferra (*) - B. Fronhoefer (**)
C. Gresse (***) - P. Jacquet (*) - M-L. Potet (*)

(*) LIFIA-IMAG - BP 68 F-38402 St Martin d'Heres Cedex - France
(**) Institut fuer Informatik - TUM Postfach 202420 D-8000 Muenchen 2-Germany
(***) LRI - Bat 490 Universite Paris Sud- 91405 Orsay Cedex - France

ABSTRACT:
A possible extension of a system called CATY for assisted program construction is presented. In contrast to the partial specification of a problem, i.e. essentially information about the types of input and output data, requested now by CATY, we propose to start with a complete specification stating explicitly the relation between input and output. From the partial specification, CATY creates program schemes and imparts to the programmer the partial specifications of the subproblems for which he must then write respective programs. The way in which propagation of the additional information provided by our extension yields complete specifications of the subproblems -which means an improvement of assistance for the programmer- is exemplified by two programming tasks.

1.- INTRODUCTION

The last two decades have been various attempts towards the mechanization of programming; the most ambitious among them aimed at complete automation of the synthesis of a program from a high level specification, e.g. [BIB 84], [MAN 79]. In presence of the tremendous difficulties, in particular occurring with the latter approaches, automatic program synthesis has been judged, by some researchers, to be out of reach. They rather proposed systems for assisted program construction which explicitly requires the participation of the user in the course of program construction.

One of these systems, called CATY, [GRE 84] is the focus of our paper. It is based on the observation that a program's structure is quite often the "reflection" of the structure of its input and output data. Therefore this system requests as input the so-called profile of a programming task, i.e. the name of the program and the types of the input and output data. Using this information, CATY proposes several decomposition schemes for the input and output variables and the user has to decide for one of them. Subsequently the system builds a corresponding recursive program scheme. It may contain several subproblems, the profile of which are passed on to the user, who has to write respective programs. Since a profile does not specify a problem uniquely, the user must find out the meaning of these subproblems.

While for automatic program synthesis a complete specification of the programming task is absolutely required in advance, a partial specification may be a sufficient starting point for assisted program construction. With CATY, for instance, a program's profile suffices, as can be seen from the forgoing sketch of this system. Thus the quandary of problem specification has acquired a new dimension: besides the choice of the specification formalism, the extent of specification has come under discussion.

Ours is a contribution thereto. During an attempt to learn about the CATY system, the question turned up whether CATY could benefit from a complete specification stating explicitly the relation between input and output data. Our study shows that a complete specification of the subproblems can be obtained by propagating the completed initial specification along the program scheme. As a side-effect we realized that the propagated formulae may serve as well for the decision on the adequacy of certain decomposition schemes for the programming task at hand.

Extending CATY in this way will be exemplified in the sequel by two problems which are considered difficult to handle for automatic program synthesis systems, namely sorting a list of integers and decomposing an integer into its prime factors.

2-EXAMPLES

2.1-SORTING A LIST OF INTEGERS

The problem specification requested by CATY is the folowing:

```
(r : list-int) <-- SORT (l : list-int)
```

It says that SORT is a function which maps a list l of integers into a list r of integers.

A. We want to discuss first the synthesis of a respective program by means of a decomposition of the input variable l. The following decomposition scheme is used:

```
if null(l) then l=nil
            else l=car(l).cdr(l)
```

where car(l) is of the type integer and cdr(l) of the type list-int. Here null, car and cdr have the same meaning as the respective LISP-functions. nil and "." are constructors of the type list.
Having made this decision, CATY proposes the subsequent program scheme containing a recursive call to the function being defined:

```
if null(l) then r:=SP1(nil)
           else
             l1:=car(l);
             l2:=cdr(l);
             r1:=SORT(l2);
             r:=SP2(l1,r1)
fi
```

Note that two new subproblems, SP1 and SP2, have been created. It is now the task of the programmer to find an informal but complete specification of these problems which enables him to write the respective programs.

PROPOSED EXTENSION: The extension proposed by us requires the relation between input and output to be made explicit. Thus we obtain as new initial specification for the sorting problem:

```
. (r : list-int) <-- SORT (l : list-int)
. ORD(r) and PERM(l,r)
```

ORD(r) means that r is an ordered list. It is defined by:

```
- ORD(nil)=true
- ORD(a.l)=((x in l) ==> (x>=a)) and ORD(l)
```

PERM(l1,l2) means that l2 is a permutation of l1 and is defined by:

```
- PERM(nil,nil)=true
- PERM(nil,a.l)=false
- PERM(a.l,r)=if (a in r) then PERM(l,eliminate(a,r))
                          else false
```

with:
```
eliminate(x,y.l)=if (x=y) then l
                          else y.eliminate(x,l)
```

Propagating this completed program specification through the program scheme proposed by CATY, we obtain immediately the program and the assertions:

```
if null(l) then r:=SP1(nil)  {l=nil} - - - - - - - - - - -(1)
           else              {l=car(l).cdr(l)}- - - - - - (2)
             l1:=car(l);     {l1=car(l)} - - - - - - - - -(3)
             l2:=cdr(l);     {l2=cdr(l)} - - - - - - - - -(4)
             r1:=SORT(l2);   {ORD(r1) and PERM(l1,r1)}- - (5)
             r:=SP2(l1,r1)
fi
```

and of course r must verify: ORD(r) and PERM(l,r) - - - - (6).
This program shall allow the computation of the function SORT in the two cases (null(l) and l=car(l).cdr(l)).

SOLUTION OF SP1:
In the case null(l), which corresponds to the formula (1), we can deduce from (6) that SP1(nil) must fulfill ORD(r) and PERM(nil,r). As a straightforward consequence of the definition of these predicates we deduce that r must be equal to nil, i.e. SP1(nil)=nil.

SOLUTION OF SP2:
In the other case the assertion (6) must be valid under the hypotheses (2), (3), (4) and (5). In order to find a specification for SP2 in this situation, the original specification must be transformed to a couple of conditions imposed on l1, r1 and r, i.e. the output variable and the arguments of SP2. This will be achieved by stepwise elimination of the other variables.

-Elimination of l:
from (2), (3) and (4) we deduce l=l1.l2 and get:
ORD(r) and PERM(l1.l2,r) - - - - - - - - - - - - - - - (6').

-Elimination of l2:
Using the property:

```
      PERM(a.l1,l) and PERM(l1,l2) ==> PERM(a.l2,l) - -(a)
```

and with PERM(l2,r1) (5) we can deduce:

```
      ORD(r) and PERM(l1.r1,r) - - - - - - - - - - -(6")
```

Thus we have achieved a transformation of (6) in which only occur l1, r1 and r.
The following specification of SP2 can be given now:

```
. (r : list-int) <-- SP2 (l1 : integer; r1 : list-int)
. ORD(r) and PERM(l1.r1,r) and ORD(r1)
```

SP2 corresponds to the function which inserts an element into an ordered list.

Its specification is assembled out of:

- . its profile
- . assertion (6")
- . the hypotheses on l1 and r1, i.e. ORD(r1).

B. Another way which we will take now is by means of a decomposition of the output variable r. Using the same decomposition scheme as above, CATY proposes the following program scheme:

```
if SP0(l) then r:=nil
          else
            r1:=SP1(l);
            l1:=SP2(l,r1);
            r2:=SORT(l1);
            r:=r1.r2
fi
```

Three new subproblems have been created, where SP0 is the condition on l such that SORT(l)=nil, while SP1 and SP2 bring about a partition of l in two parts. With CATY it is now the task of the programmer to provide programs for these subproblems.

PROPOSED EXTENSION: Propagating the completed problem specification through the program scheme, we obtain:

```
if SP0(l) then r:=nil        {r=nil} - - - - - - - - - - (1)
          else
            r1:=SP1(l);
            l1:=SP2(l,r1);
            r2:=SORT(l1);    {ORD(r2) and PERM(l1,r2)} - (2)
            r:=r1.r2         { r=r1.r2 } - - - - - - - - (3)
fi
r must verify: ORD(r) and PERM(l,r) - - - - - - - - - - (4)
```

SOLUTION OF SP0:
Since (4) must be true under the hypothesis (1), SP0 is defined by ORD(nil) and PERM(l,nil). With the definition of ORD and PERM we conclude that l equals nil, and therefore SP0(l) becomes (l=nil).

SOLUTION OF SP1 AND SP2:
In order to obtain a specification of SP1 and SP2 the formula (4) must be transformed so that only the variables l, l1 and r1 still occur. The assertions (2) and (3) can be used.

-Elimination of r:
from (3) we deduce: ORD(r1.r2) and PERM(l,r1.r2) - - - - (4')

-Elimination of r2:

```
Using:  . (PERM(a.l1,l) and PERM(l1,l2)) ==> PERM(a.l2,l) (a)
        . PERM(l1,r2)  (2)
        . PERM(l1,l2) ==> PERM(l2,l1) - - - - - - - - - - (b)
            (*commutativity of PERM*)
```

we can rewite PERM(l,r1.r2) to PERM(l,r1.l1).

```
Using:  . ORD(r2)  (2)
        . ORD(a.l)=((x in l) ==> (x>=a)) and ORD(l)
             (*definition of ORD*)
```

ORD(r1.r2) can be transformed to (x in r2) ==> (x>=r1).

From the property:

```
    PERM(l1,l2) ==> ((x in l1) <==> (x in l2)) - - - - - - (c)
```

and with PERM(l1,r2) (2), we obtain (x in r2) <==> (x in l1)
and finally,

```
        ((x in l1) ==> (x>=r1)) and PERM(l,r1.l1) - - - - (4")
```

We have achieved a transformation of the assertion (4) to a formula in which only the variables l, l1, and r1 occur. It correspond to a decomposition of l in the two terms l1 and r1. The following specifications for SP1 and SP2 can be given:

```
  . (r1 : integer) <-- SP1(l : list-int)
  . (l1 : list-int) <-- SP2(l : list-int; r1 : integer)
  . ((x in l1) ==> (x>=r1)) and PERM(l,r1.l1)
```

With this specification our program scheme corresponds to the selection sort algorithm; the function SP1 selects the smallest element of a list while SP2 builds the rest of this list.

In order to treat this example, we used the properties (a), (b) and (c) which are analoguous to the properties used by Clark and Darlington [CLA 78] for the synthesis of their sorting algorithms. The main difference between the two approaches lies in the way how recursion is introduced. With CATY the recursive calls are an immediate result of the proposed decomposition scheme for lists, while in [CLA 78] the following auxiliary property must be known:

```
    ((x=y) and PERM(l1,l2)) ==> PERM(x.l1,y.l2)
```

which allows PERM(x.l1,y.l2) to be replaced by the stronger assertion (x=y) and PERM(l1,l2).
It can be remarked, however, that this recursive property of PERM is based on a decomposition scheme which is analoguous to the one used by CATY. Since with CATY the recursivity of a program results directly from the inductive definition of the manipulated data, it needs less auxiliary properties than in the approach of Clark and Darlington, i.e. CATY requires no knowledge of the kind of (d) in order to construct a recursive program.

2.2- DECOMPOSITION OF AN INTEGER INTO ITS PRIME FACTORS

Here the task is to write a program, called DECOMP, which takes as input an integer and computes the list of its prime factors. Exemple: DECOMP(24) = (2,2,3,2).
The problem specification according to our extension is:

```
  . (r : seq-int) <-- DECOMP(n : integer)
  . ((x in r) ==> prime(x)) and (prod(r)=n)
```

where prime(n) means that n is a prime number and the function prod is defined by:

```
  - prod(nil) = 1
  - prod(m.l) = m * prod(l)
```

A. We choose at first a decomposition of the input variable n into (n-1)+1 together with n=1 as the basis case (DECOMP of 0 shall be considered undefined).
We come to the following program scheme augmented by assertions:

```
if n = 1 then r:=SP1(1)    {n=1} - - - - - - - - - - -(1)
         else              {n=(n-1)+1} - - - - - - - -(2)
           n1:=n-1;        {n1=n-1} - - - - - - - - - (3)
           n2:=1;          {n2=1}- - - - - - - - - - -(4)
           r1:=DECOMP(n1); {((x in r1)==>prime(x))
                                and prod(r1) = n1} - - (5)
           r:=SP2(r1,n2)
fi
```

where r must verify:

```
{((x in r) ==> prime(x)) and prod(r) = n} - -(6)
```

SOLUTION OF SP1:
Since (6) must be true under the hypothesis (1), SP1(1) can be specified by ((x in r) ==>prime(x)) and (prod(r)=1). From the definition of prod follows that r equals nil and therefore SP1(1)=nil.

SOLUTION OF SP2:
In order to obtain a specification of SP2 from the assertion (6) we start by eliminating the variable n which does not occur among the variables of this subproblem. The assertions (2), (3), (4) and (5) will be used.

-Elimination of n:
We deduce from (2), (3) and (4) that n=n1+n2 and get finally:

```
((x in r) ==> prime(x)) and (prod(r)=n1+n2) - - - -(6')
```

-Elimination of n1:
Using (5), n1 can be replaced by prod(r1) and we obtain:

```
((x in r) ==> prime(x)) and (prod(r)=prod(r1)+n2) - (6")
```

This formula contains only variables of SP2. This allows to come to a specification of SP2:

```
. (r : seq-int) <-- SP2(r1 : seq-int; n2 : integer)
. ((x in r1) ==> prime(x)) and ((x in r) ==> prime(x))
                and (prod(r)=prod(r1) + n2)
```

Part of the obtained specification is an instance of the relation between input and output of the original problem (substitute n by prod(r1)+n2). Lacking a property which allows its simplification, we can say that the subproblem is as difficult as the original one. We consider this fact conclusive to reject the chosen decomposition scheme as unsuccessful.

B. Now we proceed by decomposing the output list r according to the same decomposition scheme as already employed with the sorting problem. We obtain the following program scheme augmented by the respective assertions:

```
if SP0(n) then r:=nil        {r=nil} - - - - - - - - - - (1)
          else
            r1:=SP1(n);
            n1:=SP2(n,r1);
            r2:=DECOMP(n1); {((x in r2)==>prime(x))
                              and prod(r2)=n1} - - - -(2)
            r:=r1.r2         {r=r1.r2} - - - - - - - - - (3)
fi
```

Here r must verify ((x in r)==>prime(x)) and prod(r)=n (4)

SOLUTION OF SP0:
Using (1) the assertion (4) can be transformed to ((x in nil) ==> prime(x)) and (prod(nil)=n). Now n=1 can be deduced from the definition of prod and the fact that (x in nil) is always false. Thus SP0(n) will be replaced by (n=1).

SOLUTION OF SP1 and SP2:
The assertion (4) must be transformed to a formula in which occur only the variables r1, n1 and n.

-Elimination of r:
Using (3) we obtain

```
((x in r1.r2) ==> prime(x)) and prod(r1.r2)=n- - - -(4')
```

-Elimination of r2:

Here we need the property:

```
((x in l) ==> P(x)) ==> ((P(car(l))) and ((x in cdr(l))==>P(x)))
```

where P is an arbitrary predicate.

From it and from the definition of prod we deduce:

```
prime(r1) and ((x in r2) ==> prime(x)) and r1*prod(r2)=n - (4'')
```

By means of (2) it can be transformed to:

```
prime(r1) and r1*n1=n - - - - - - - - - - - - - - - - - - - -(4''')
```

In this assertion occur only the variables n, r1 and n1. We can deduce from it the following specification of SP1 and SP2:

```
. (r1 : integer) <-- SP1(n : integer)
. (n1 : integer) <-- SP2(n : integer; r1 : integer)
. prime(r1) and r1 * n1 = n
```

The function SP1 determines an arbitrary prime divisor of n and SP2 computes the quotient of n and this divisor.

3-CONCLUSION

Let us recall that the programmer is supported by CATY essentially in the two following ways:

-At first, information about the structure of the input and output data conveyed by the problem specification is used by CATY to propose possible decomposition schemes and to establish corresponding program schemes.
-These contain new subproblems for which the programmer must write respective programs. CATY assists by providing him with their profiles, i.e. the types of input and output data.

With the extension proposed in this paper CATY still remains a system for assisted program construction, but the assistance offered to the programmer is increased:

-Instead of imparting only the profile of a subproblem, the system now provides the programmer with a complete specification. This relieves him from inspecting each subproblem in the context of the program scheme, thus allowing him to start programming directly from the subproblem specification. This facilitates the programmer's job and is expected to be especially rewarding in the construction of large programs.
-Furthermore, propagation of the completed problem specification can reveal the futility of a program scheme as, for instance, in the case of our second example. Even if no conclusive evidence for discarding a program scheme is produced, at least a priority queue could be set up.

We do not want to conceal the fact that in order to convert these theoretical accomplishments into practice, several additional problems will be encountered. Among the most important is the question of how to automate the simplification of the propagated formulae so that specifications for the subproblems are obtained. As can be seen from our examples, attempting to eliminate certain variables may serve as heuristics, but the detection of propitious auxiliary properties needed for simplification, still remains cumbersome.

Finally, we think that extended CATY may serve as ground work on which a future bridge between automation and assistance in program synthesis might be erected. It should now be possible to incorporate research results from the domain of automatic programming which will be apt to control and enhance the performace of the system. On the other hand, by forbearing the objective to convert to automation the complete synthesis process, we will escape the major drawbacks of these systems, where imperfection is equivalent to failure and nonsuccess.

REFERENCES:

[BIB 84] W.BIBEL - K.M.HORNIG
"Lops - A system based on a strategical approach to program synthesis"
in "Automatic Program Construction Techniques"
(A.BIERMANN, G.GUIHO, Y.KODRATOFF, eds.)
MacMillan, New-York, 1984, pp. 69-89.

[CLA 78] K-L. CLARK - J.DARLINGTON
"Algorithm classification through synthesis"
The Computer Journal, vol.23,1, June 1978, pp.61-65.

[GRE 84] C.GRESSE
"Contribution a la programmation automatique. CATY: un systeme de construction assistee de programmes"
These d'Etat. Universite de Paris-Sud. March 1984.

[MAN 79] Z.MANNA - R.WALDINGER
"Synthesis: dreams ==> programs"
IEEE Trans.Softw.Eng.,SE-5, 4 (July 1979), pp.294-328.

ARTIFICIAL INTELLIGENCE: Methodology, Systems, Applications
W. Bibel and B. Petkoff (Editors)
Elsevier Science Publishers B.V. (North-Holland)

AN IMPLEMENTATION OF A THEOREM PROVER BASED ON THE CONNECTION METHOD*)

Elmar Eder

Institut für Informatik
Technische Universität München
Postfach 202420
D-8000 München 2

A simple version of a theorem prover for full first order logic (not restricted to clausal logic) has been implemented in TLC-LISP on a 64KByte desk top computer. It consists of two separate parts. The first part is a preprocessing module for non-normal form formulas transforming the input formula to its definitional form, a formula in clausal form which is different from the normal form used in other approaches. The second part of the system is a theorem prover for normal form formulas which is based on the connection method. It incorporates factorization, avoidance of circuits, elimination of useless clauses and weak unification to improve efficiency.

1. INTRODUCTION

Most theorem provers implemented so far use the resolution principle as their basic inference rule. Since the resolution rule can be formulated in a natural way only for clausal logic these theorem provers can treat only normal form formulas in a direct manner. Non-normal form formulas have to be transformed to normal form at the expense of a disruption of the internal structure of the formula and a possibly vast (exponential) explosion of the length of the formula. This disruption is a disadvantage for a proof search guided by heuristics, and the explosion of the length of the formula gives rise to an even larger increase of the size of the search space.

Our implementation is different in two major ways. First, it uses the **connection method** instead of the resolution principle. Second, it transforms, in a preprocessing step, the (non-normal form) input formula to its **definitional form** instead of its normal form. The definitional form is a formula in clausal form which does not suffer from the disadvantages of normal form mentionned above. Although the connection method can treat non-normal form formulas in a direct and natural way, the transformation to definitional form has two advantages. It allows for an easier comprehension by the user and for a modular program. Modularization is necessary because otherwise the program would not fit in the memory.

This paper is devided into four sections. In section 2 we give a short description of the general structure of the system which consists of a preprocessing module and the main part of the system.

---

*) Work supported by the Deutsche Forschungsgemeinschaft

In section 3 the definitional form is introduced and the preprocessing module is described. It is the task of the preprocessing module to determine the definitional form of the input formula. The idea behind the definitional form is to introduce, for each subformula of the input formula, a new literal which serves as an abbreviation of this subformula. Then a set of formulas is constructed which give the definitions for these abbreviations. These formulas can be obtained in clausal form and the theorem we want to prove from these clauses is the abbreviation of the input formula which is just a unit clause.

In section 4 the main part of the system is described which is a theorem prover for normal form formulas based on the connection method. It is implemented as a tree search procedure. In addition to the basic indispensable features of the connection method such features as factorization, avoidance of circuits and elimination of useless clauses are incorporated to reduce the size of the search space. A uniform treatment of connections, factorization and circuits made a compact implementation possible. The concept of weak unification is used to reduce the amount of time needed for unification.

2. THE OVERALL FLOW OF CONTROL OF THE PROGRAM

Our system consists of two components. The first component - the preprocessor - reads the input formula and converts it to a special kind of normal form, called

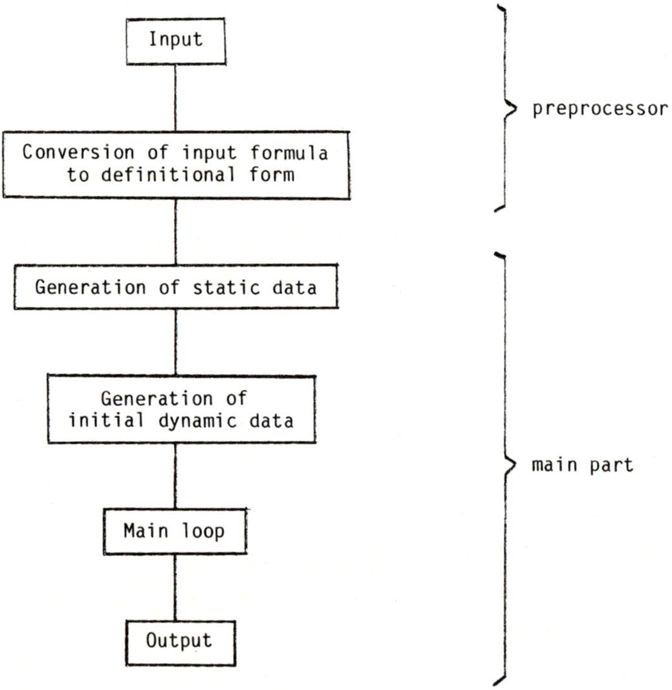

Figure 1

the definitional form. The second component - the main part of the system - is a theorem prover which searches for a proof of the definitional form. It consists of four modules "generation of static data", "generation of initial dynamic data", "main loop" and "output". These two parts together give the flow of control of the program shown in figure 1.

3. CONVERSION OF INPUT FORMULA TO DEFINITIONAL FORM

Usually the input formula F is converted to its normal form $F^{\sim}$ by first skolemizing the formula and then transforming it to an equivalent normal form formula by, e.g., using the distributive law for 'and' and 'or'. This is inefficient because it leads to an exponential explosion of the length of the formula, and it is unnatural because it destroys the internal structure of the formula.

Since the connection method can deal with arbitrary formulas of first order logic, a conversion to normal form is not necessary. There is, however, a different kind of normal form F', called the **definitional form** of F, which does not suffer from these drawbacks*). Moreover, every connection proof of F can be simulated by a connection proof of F'. The correspondence is so close that it seems even plausible that, in a later implementation, it will not be possible to tell whether the theorem prover proves F or F' with the connection method. This justifies the use of F' for obtaining proofs as well as for getting more insight into the connection method in the case of non-normal form formulas.

F' is also a normal form formula which is valid iff F is valid. In contrast to $F^{\sim}$, however, F' is constructed in such a way that to each subformula of F correspond one or more clauses of F'. This gives a close connection between the formula tree of F and the clauses of F'. So the internal structure of F is still visible in F'. Moreover, the number of literals of F' grows only linearly with the number of subformulas of F (which is smaller than the length of F).

We shall first give the definition of F' and then show the construction of F' with an example. F' is constructed in two steps. The first step is the construction of a formula F* which is valid iff F is valid. F* is not yet in normal form but very close to normal form. In a second step, F* is transformed to its normal form F' in the usual way by skolemization and by using the rules of semantic equivalence of propositional logic. It follows that F is valid iff F' is valid.

Before giving the definition of F* let us make a remark concerning the syntactic structure of formulas of first order logic. Each non-atomic formula G has the form

$$X(G1,\dots,Gn)$$

where G1, ..., Gn are the immediate subformulas of G and either X is a propositional connective of arity n or, X is a quantifier together with a list of variables (in this case n=1). In both cases we have

(1) $$\forall x1\dots xk\ (G \longleftrightarrow X(G1,\dots,Gn))$$

where x1, ..., xk are those variables occurring in G which are not bound by quantifiers of G.

---

*) This hint was given to us by Dr. Gregory Minc from Leningrad

Now, the idea in the construction of F^* is to introduce a new predicate symbol P of arity k for each subformula G of F and to build the atomic formula $L[G]$ defined as $P(x1,\ldots,xk)$ where P and k are as above. If G is a non-atomic subformula of F then we replace $G, G1, \ldots, Gn$ by $L[G], L[G1], \ldots, L[Gn]$ in (1) to obtain the formula $D[G]$ defined as

$$D[G] = \forall x1 \ldots xk\ (L[G] \leftrightarrow X(L[G1],\ldots,L[Gn])). \tag{2}$$

If G is an atomic subformula of F then we define

$$D[G] = \forall x1 \ldots xk\ (L[G] \leftrightarrow G). \tag{3}$$

We can consider $D[G]$ as an axiom defining the predicate which is denoted by the predicate symbol P. Let us denote by A the conjunction of all formulas $D[G]$ where G is a subformula of F. Then, for every subformula G of F, the following formula is valid

$$A \rightarrow (L[G] \leftrightarrow G).$$

The proof by induction on the complexity of G is straightforward.

Now, we define F^* as

$$F^* = A \rightarrow L[F].$$

It is easy to see that F is valid iff F^* is valid. F' is then obtained from F^* by various simplifications and transformation to normal form. Since F^* is already very close to normal form this transformation does not give rise to an exponential explosion or to major changes in the structure of the formula.

Example: As an example let us denote by F the (valid) formula

$$\exists x\ (R(x) \leftrightarrow \forall y\ R(y)).$$

In order to construct F^* we first consider all subformulas of F, namely

$G0 = F$
$G1 = R(x) \leftrightarrow \forall y\ R(y)$
$G2 = R(x)$
$G3 = \forall y\ R(y)$
$G4 = R(y)$

We introduce new predicate symbols $P0, \ldots, P4$ with arities $0, 1, 1, 0, 1$, respectively (corresponding to the number of free variables of $G0, \ldots, G4$), and build the literals

$L[G0] = P0$
$L[G1] = P1(x)$
$L[G2] = P2(x)$
$L[G3] = P3$
$L[G4] = P4(y)$

The next step is to establish the definitions $D[G0], \ldots, D[G4]$ of $P0, \ldots, P4$.

$D[G0] = P0 \leftrightarrow \exists x\ P1(x)$
$D[G1] = \forall x\ (P1(x) \leftrightarrow (P2(x) \leftrightarrow P3))$
$D[G2] = \forall x\ (P2(x) \leftrightarrow R(x))$
$D[G3] = P3 \leftrightarrow \forall y\ P4(y)$
$D[G4] = \forall y\ (P4(y) \leftrightarrow R(y))$

Now, F^* is the formula

D[G0] & D[G1] & D[G2] & D[G3] & D[G4] → P0.

The formula F* is already in such a form that it can be directly transformed to normal form without an exponential explosion of its length. In practice, however, we want the greatest possible reduction. A simple reduction in our example is to omit D[G2] and D[G4] and to replace P2(x) by R(x) and P4(y) by R(y). It is always possible to eliminate in this way all formulas D[G] from F* where G is an atomic subformula.

After transformation to normal form the number of literals is at most 6n-5 where n is the number of subformulas of F. If F contains no equivalences ('iff') or antivalences ('either-or') then the number of literals is at most 4n-3.

There are several ways to reduce F* further. For example, to prove P0, we need only the right-to-left directions of the equivalences stated in D[G0] and D[G1]. This is not true, however, for D[G3]. We have implemented a criterion which allows to decide quickly in which cases one direction of the equivalence stated in D[G] is sufficient. The decision depends on the monotonicity properties of the propositional connectives occuring in the input formula.

4. THE MAIN PART OF THE SYSTEM

Before giving an overview of the main part of the system we summarize some of the properties of the definitional form F' of a (non-normal form) formula F.

1. F' is a formula in normal form.
2. F' is valid iff F is valid.
3. F' has less than six times as many literals as F.
4. Every proof of F in the connection method (for non-normal form formulas) can be simulated step by step by a connection proof of the normal form formula F'.
5. Although F' may have more literals than F the size of the search space for connection proofs of F' is the same as the size of the search space for connection proofs of F.
6. If F is already in normal form then F' can be reduced to F by unit reduction.

These properties give us the justification to search for a connection proof of F' instead of directly searching for a connection proof of F. This is done by the main part of the system. It consists of a theorem prover for normal form formulas and is based on the connection method. This theorem prover gets the definitional form F' as its input formula which it tries to prove using a kind of tree search procedure.

During runtime a part of the search tree is kept in memory. The information needed for the proof process is divided into two parts, the static data (which do not change during runtime and which are established at the beginning of the process) and the dynamic data (which change during runtime). The dynamic data consist of global data (which do not belong to a particular node of the search tree) and sets of data for nodes of the search tree. Our implementation is done in such a way that, for each node of the search tree, only the "difference" between the data belonging to this node and the data belonging to its predecessor node are explicitly stored. This is necessary since otherwise the storage space would be quickly exhausted. Since every node has a pointer to its predecessor the necessary information can still be retrieved. Only where this retrieval would be too time-expensive, for example for the current substitution which is needed in almost every step of the proof process, the complete information is attached to the node itself.

4.1 THE CONNECTION PROOF CALCULUS

For a description of the connection method we have to refer the reader to [Bil]. Our implementation is based on a connection calculus containing, in addition to the indispensable features of the connection method, several features which have been introduced to improve efficiency.

Essential for keeping the size of the program small enough to fit in a 64KByte computer was a **uniform treatment of connections, factorization and avoidance of circuits.** Our way of doing this can be roughly explained as follows. We introduce two types of links between literals. If K and L are two literals which are unifiable then we say there is a positive link between K and L. If K and -L are unifiable then we say there is a negative link between K and L.

Now assume we want to extend the active path p through a clause c, and let S be the set of unsolved subgoals. Then it can be proved that, if a positive link between a literal of p and a literal of c or a negative link between a literal of S and a literal of c unifies then the clause c cannot contribute to the proof. Our calculus is constructed so that it allows to drop the clause c in such a case, thus avoiding circuits. Similarly, if we unify a negative link between a literal of p and a literal of c or a positive link between a literal of S and a literal of c, then we can skip this literal of c. This is the way connections and factorization are treated.

Another feature which improves efficiency is the **elimination of clauses recognized as useless.** It may happen in the course of a connection proof that there is a clause c from which no links have been established to later clauses. Of course, this is always true for the last clause. But if c is not the last clause then c cannot contribute to the proof and we may drop the clause c. Just dropping c, however, does not undo the unifications which have been made with literals of c and which are not needed any more but may prevent a success of the proof process.

In order to be able to construct quickly the **current substitution** (i.e., the mgu of all established links) after having dropped c, another substitution, the **incremental substitution** had to be introduced. The incremental substitution is the mgu of a certain subset of the set of all established links. From the stored current and incremental substitutions the new current substitution as well as the new incremental substitution can be obtained by just doing a unification. In the calculus developed for our implementation the elimination of useless clauses has been incorporated in the truncation process.

In our calculus there are three different kinds of proof steps:

1. generation of a new clause
2. unification of a new link
3. truncation

In 1. a new copy of a clause of F' is considered. It is, however, not generated explicitly. Only a new index and a pointer to the corresponding clause of F' are generated. In 2. a new positive or negative link is established and unified. In 3. the path is retracted from one or more clauses which do not contain any unsolved subgoals. At the same time any clauses which are not needed any more are dropped and the corresponding unifications are undone.

4.2 STATIC DATA

The first module of the program to be entered after the transformation to definitional form is the generation of static data. In this part of the theorem prover those data are generated which remain unchanged throughout the whole proof process. The static data consist of the matrix and the weak unifiers.

The matrix M is the set of clauses of the definitional form of the input formula. The literals of the clauses are represented simply by strings which serve as names for the literals. It is not necessary to store the literals themselves since we store the weak unifiers of all pairs of literals (see below).

If K and L are literals then the most general weak unifier (mgwu) of K and L is defined to be the most general unifier (mgu) of K and L* where L* is obtained from L by renaming the variables in L in such a way that K and L* have no common variables. For all pairs (K,L) of literals of M the mgwu of K and L or the mgwu of K and -L is stored if it exists. All unifications needed in the proof process are reduced to building the weak unifiers of all pairs of literals of F', to renaming certain variables, and to building suprema of sets of unifiers in the lattice of unifiers. This use of weak unification saves time in the unification process. We cannot go into this subject here, but we refer the reader to [Ede] where a detailed discussion of the concept of weak unification and of the lattice of unifiers is given.

For the task of unification needed in this part of the theorem prover and, later, in the main loop, the unification algorithm of Martelli and Montanari (see [M-M]) is used.

4.3 DYNAMIC DATA

The dynamic data consist of all the information concerning the history of the proof process which is still needed at the considered instant of time and is not already included in the static data. The implemented proof procedure is based on a tree search algorithm.

The dynamic data are organized in the form of a tree in which every node except the root has a pointer attached to it which points to the predecessor in the tree. This tree is essentially that part of the search tree which has already been traversed so far and where there are still open ends which may have to be resumed later in the proof search. The nodes of the tree are also called **states.** Besides this tree there are also "global" dynamic data such as a pointer to that state which is currently under consideration, called the **current state,** and a list with pointers to all open ends.

The name "state" has been chosen because each node of the search tree is a state of a potential connection proof of F'. A complete connection proof corresponds to a branch which connects the root of the search tree with a state in which there are no unsolved subgoals.

Most of the information in a node of the search tree is already contained in its predecessor node or in its **trunc-predecessor,** obtained by retracting the active path from the last clause. Therefore these redundant informations are not contained in the corresponding state in our implementation, but every state has a pointer to its predecessor and to its trunc-predecessor.

The simplest module of the whole program is the "generation of initial dynamic data" which is entered after the generation of static data. In this module the state of the dynamic data at the beginning of the proof search is established. This corresponds to that part of the search tree which consists only of its root.

After this the module "main loop" is entered. Its task is the actual proof search. In this part of the program the search tree is traversed and the dynamic data are changed accordingly. The proof search continues until either a proof has been found or the search tree has been completely traversed within certain limits (given to the system when it is started). If one of these two conditions holds then we say the termination condition is fulfilled. The module "main loop" is implemented as an iterative procedure of the form

until termination condition **do** main procedure

The main procedure expands the current state, i.e., it determines its successors and updates the dynamic data accordingly. Determining a successor of a state means to execute a proof step. The proof step can either be the generation of a new clause or the unification of a new link or a truncation.

CONCLUSION

The transformation of arbitrary formulas of first order predicate calculus to definitional form proved to be easy to implement in an efficient way. There were no severe problems concerning this transformation. In the main part of the system advanced features for improving efficiency have been implemented. But, due to the limited storage of 64 KByte, only very simple formulas can be treated and almost no experiments are possible. The heuristics module, which has been included for later porting to a bigger machine, had to remain empty. Thus the potential for improving efficiency could not be exploited.

REFERENCES

[BEF] Bibel, W.; Eder, E.; Fronhöfer, B.: Towards an Advanced Implementation of the Connection Method. IJCAI-83 Karlsruhe, August 83, (A. Bundy, ed.), Kaufmann Inc., Los Altos 1983, pp. 920-922.

[Bi1] Bibel, W.: Automated Theorem Proving. Vieweg Verlag, Wiesbaden (1982).

[Bi2] Bibel, W.: A Theoretical Bases for the Systematic Proof Method. Mathematical Foundations of Computer Science, Proceedings of the 9th Symposium MFCS'80, Rydzyna, Poland, September 1980, (P. Dembinski, ed.), LINCS 88, Springer, Berlin 1980, pp. 154-167.

[Ede] Eder, E.: Properties of Substitutions and Unifications. GWAI-83, 7th German Workshop on Artificial Intelligence, Dassel/Solling, September 1983, (B. Neumann, ed.), Informatik-Fachberichte 76, Springer, Berlin 1983, pp. 197-206.

[Fro] Fronhöfer, B.: On refinements of the Connection Method. Algebra, Combinatorics and Logic in Computer Science, (J. Demetrovics, G. Katona, A. Salomaa, eds.), Colloquia Mathematica Soc. J. Bolyai, Vol. 42, North-Holland, Amsterdam 1985

[Hue] Huet, G.: Résolution d'équations dans des langages d'ordre 1,2,..,ω. Thèse d'État, Univ. Paris VII (1976).

[M-M] Martelli, A.; Montanari, U.: An Efficient Unification Algorithm. ACM Transactions on Programming Languages and Systems, Vol. 4, 258-281 (1982).

[P-W] Paterson, M.S.; Wegman, M.N.: Linear Unification. J. of Computer and Systems Sci. 16, 158-167 (1978).

ARTIFICIAL INTELLIGENCE: Methodology, Systems, Applications
W. Bibel and B. Petkoff (Editors)
Elsevier Science Publishers B.V. (North-Holland)

INTEXP

A DOMAIN INDEPENDENT EXPERT SYSTEM

Georgescu I., Hotăran A.,
Predescu R., Vlasiu M., Petrescu F.,
Nicolăiţă D. and Nagy A.

Central Institute for Management and Informatics
Bucharest - ROMANIA

The structure and the functional features of the INTEXP (Intelligent Expert) system are described. INTEXP represents an intelligent problem solver based on both declarative and normative knowledge. It is able to combine backward and forward inferences and to explain the derived reasoning line as well as the causes of failures. Also, it can modify and yet keep consistent the knowledge it accumulates.

1. INTRODUCTION

The INTEXP system stands as a domain-independent framework for building autonomous knowledge-based problem solvers. Both declarative and procedural, as well as normative knowledge (rules), are considered as the standard categories of entities to be included into the knowledge base.

The two-folded structure of INTEXP - the cognitive system and the resolutive system - allowed the following classes of requirements to be fulfilled:

- knowledge base organization according to several domain and system specific criteria;
- knowledge accumulation (extending, modifying, and automatically maintaining the consistency of the knowledge base);
- retrieval oriented reasoning, based on inheritance or generic-type inferences;
- deductive reasoning, based on a PROLOG-like inference mechanism, providing automatic backtracking;
- circumstantial reasoning, supported by forward chaining;
- plan refinement during problem decomposition;
- reasoning path explanation or changing, according to user request.

A general view of INTEXP is presented in Figure 1.

The INTEXP system is implemented in DM-LISP, a LISP interpreter developed for Romanian manufactured, fully compatible with the PDP 11/34 systems, CORAL and I-100 minicomputer series. Instructed with appropiate knowledge, the INTEXP system was already used as a tool for building two sample expert systems in technical design.

2. THE KNOWLEDGE BASE

The basic structural unit used to represent entities within the knowledge base is called "description". Descriptions are distributed into several dictionaries corresponding to the standard categories of entities: objects, procedures, and rules.

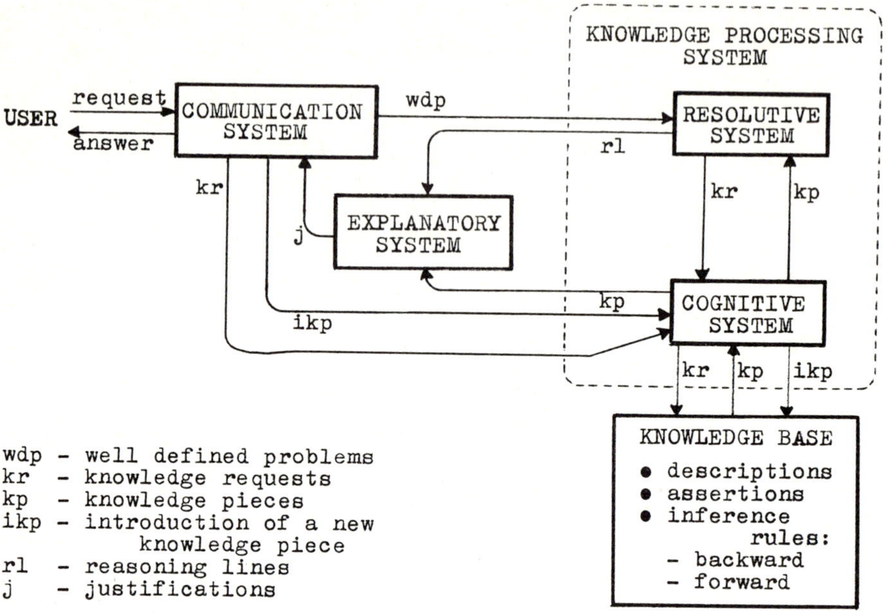

Figure 1
The general structure of the INTEXP system

The first two categories share together the following syntax:

```
(entity-name
   (GENERAL CHARACTERISTICS
      (CATEGORY              - object // procedure )
      (CLASS                 - taxonomic link )
      (SORT                  - identifies the set of admissible operators
                               acting upon the knowledge piece )
      (PROTOTYPE             - YES / NO )
      (COMPLEXITY            - atomic / complex )
   (EXTERNAL STRUCTURE       - relations connecting the entity to other
                               entities
                             - restrictive acceptance patterns avoiding
                               the generation of absurd combinations )
   (INTERNAL STRUCTURE       - relations between components )
   (PROPERTIES               - other characteristics ))
```

Entities representing instances (PROTOTYPE NO) may be subject to several descriptions, called manifestations and identified by different CLASS/SORT pairs.

The set of cognitive functions associated to the knowledge base contains:

- knowledge acquisition functions;
- functions concerning existing entities (knowledge pieces):
  - insertion of a feature in a description,
  - deletion of an entity,
  - deletion of a feature in a description,
  - modification of a description;

- functions concerning the knowledge base consistency:
    - implicit, based on taxonomic links and other relational links;
    - user-supplied, based on the automatic invocation of procedures associated with each type of process.

As far as procedures are concerned, the content of the descriptors are adapted to the necessities of pattern-directed invocation. The CATEGORY of a procedure is given by the type of the cognitive or resolutive process that may automatically invoke it. A procedure may have more than one body, depending on the differing nature of its actors. The EXTERNAL STRUCTURE shelters the corresponding invocation patterns. The procedure bodies themselves are contained within the INTERNAL STRUCTURE, while under the PROPERTIES descriptor the procedure environment is being captured: pre, post and sequencing conditions used to solve the priority conflicts raised by the pattern-directed invocation mechanism.

The knowledge base contains two categories of rules - backward and forward - supporting the goal-driven and respectively the event or situation-driven reasoning processes performed by the system. Backward rules have the following form:

```
(rule-name  (( conclusion )
             ( premise-1 ) ... ( premise-n )))
```

The semantic interpretation of backward rules is based on the two specific readings cumulated within logic programming:

- the declarative reading: the plausability of the conclusion is directly related to the plausability of the premises;
- the problem-reduction oriented reading: the conclusion represents a problem to be solved or a plan to accomplish, while the premises represent the corresponding subproblems, subgoals or plan decomposition respectively.

Forward rules have a form similar to the previous one:

```
(rule-name  (( situation )
             ( action-1 ) ... (action-n)))
```

The associated interpretation agrees with the generic reading applied on "situation-action" rules: whenever the specified situation is met within the current state of knowledge, the consecutive actions are to be performed by the system. The specified actions may involve:

- implicit modifications to be operated upon the current collection of knowledge pieces;
- system-driven dialogues aimed to obtain more support from the user;
- decisions concerning new goals to be treated, or other actions recommendable under the given circumstances.

When a new goal is chosen to be reached, all its solutions will, one by one, be propagated through the rest of the actions. The "conclusions", as well as the "situations", are represented by patterns that are to be matched by the problem statement or current knowledge state respectively. The unification mechanism is further responsible for the accurate propagation of bindings.

In the INTEXP system, backward and forward reasoning interleave. The later is completely subordinated to the former. The task of reaching a given goal is mainly relying on the backward reasoning process, that acts as a recursive goal reducer. Situation-driven inferences play the role of imprevisible but efficient information suppliers, enlarging the current knowledge horizon. Thus, the task of reaching the goal becomes easier since the subgoals generated on the basis of goal-driven inferences have a greater chance to be more directly fulfilled.

3. THE BASIC SOLVER

As it is known, the construction of an evaluation (search) scheme is essentially determined by the following elements:

a - the direction of evaluation within the problem space (backward, forward, bidirectional);
b - the conflict resolution strategy used to determine the selection priorities within the set of further alternatives available at each current stage;
c - the backtracking strategy used to determine a former stage to restart from and the selection priorities within the set of alternatives available at that stage.

According to the choices made concerning each one of the previous elements, the basic solver in INTEXP is actually a PROLOG-like backward reduction mechanism, providing automatic backtracking.

A resolutive process is started by a statement of the following form:

```
( REZOLVA  (( goal-1 ) ... ( goal-n )))
  (solve)
```

where (goal-i) is represented by some arbitrary pattern. The whole right-side goal conjunction corresponds to the problem to be solved. Goals are treated one at a time, from left to right, in a stack-like manner. The resolutive process contains two phases:

(i) retrieval: the system attempts to fulfill the goal requirement by direct or inheritance-based retrieval within the knowledge base;

(ii) inferential interpretation: in case of retrieval failure, the system "rewrites" the goal, expanding it into several subgoals according to the backward inference rules.

The second phase is based on a "recognize-rewrite" cycle applied on the set of backward rules, until there are no more rules applicable or the subgoals requirements are satisfied within the limits of phase (i). The resolutive process develops according to the following algorithm:

```
**  solve (GOAL, rules, varbind)
    // GOAL    - the conjunction of goals to be solved //
    // rules   - the subset of rules selected from the
                 knowledge base //
    // varbind - remembers the bindings of variables for
                 later use in answers and explanations //
          FAIL ←— false;
while     GOAL ≠ NIL & not FAIL  do
if        the first subgoal is directly retrieved
then      *  update (varbind);
          GOAL ←— *  var-update(rest(GOAL));
          ** solve(GOAL, rules, varbind);
or        the first subgoal is a solving procedure
then      *  execute the procedure;
          *  update (varbind);
          GOAL ←— *  var-update(rest(GOAL));
          ** solve(GOAL, rules, varbind);
else      // inferential interpretation is started //
          i ←— 1 & SOLVED ←— false;
```

```
while   i < the number of rules & not SOLVED  do
        var1 ◄── the first subgoal &
        var2 ◄── conclusion of rule (i);
if      * unify (var1 var2);
then    GOAL ◄── APPEND (* var-update(premises of rule (i)))
                        (* var-update(rest(GOAL)));
        * update (varbind);
        if  ** solve(GOAL, rules, varbind);
            then  SOLVED ◄── true;
            else  i ◄── i+1;
else    i ◄── i+1;
;
;
if      not SOLVED
then    FAIL ◄── true
;
answer  (FAIL);
```

4. REASONING FORWARD

By the explicit option of the user, the solver may act bidirectionally. Thus, it may insert forward inferences, each time a new subgoal is being achieved, in order to establish its direct or intermediate consequences. This type of reasoning is performed by the system for the determination of:

- the current knowledge status;
- the current course of processes already under development;
- new processes to be developed further on.

The final aim is to support backward reasoning, enhancing the knowledge accumulation and thus, making the subgoals not yet achieved easier to achieve. Forward reasoning is based on a recognize-act cycle applied within the set of forward rules until no more rules are applicable. The initial "situation" used to start the cycle is represented by the most recently achieved subgoal. Its consequences may lead to the occurence of new "situations" that reactivate the cycle. As a result of the recursive development of forward inferences, the knowledge base will be subject to "waves" of implicit modifications. A special case is represented by what we called "confirmations". Indeed, under certain circumstances (for instance, diagnosis situations) some fact needs to be precisely determined or confirmed. A confirmation may be completely implicit, depending totally on the system, which develops a resolutive process, whose goal is the given fact. As well, it may be half-explicit: that is, the confirmation is required by the system and supplied by the user. When some situation fits more than one forward rule, the whole set of applicable rules will be executed, since all the consequences involved by that situation are supposed to be useful for the later development of the reasoning process (see Figure 2).

5. THE EXPLAINER

The explanation mechanism in INTEXP offers the user the possibility to trace back on the reasoning line, checking the correctitude of the system's answer. A special feature of the explainer is given by its ability to show the causes of failures during the solving process. Unsolvable (sub)goals are mentioned, along with some suggestions concerning their possible solution. This makes the actions performed by the solver more reliable and also determines the user to play a more cooperative role in the solving process.

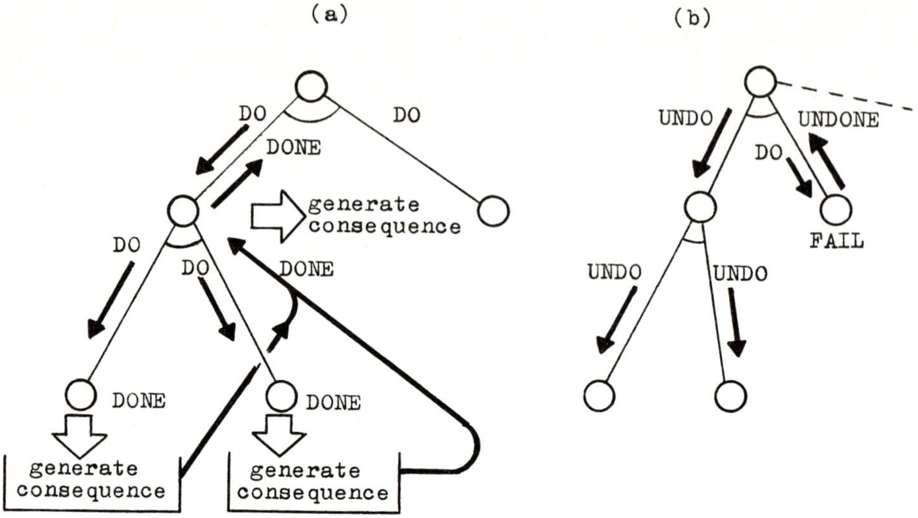

Figure 2
The interpretation tree for successful backward reduction and forward consequence generation (a), and the resetting of the previous context in case of failure (b)

The explanation facility may also serve to accomplish other tasks such as:

- education. since the user may ask questions and compare his own answers with those given by the system;
- knowledge-base adjustement, since erroneous or missing knowledge is reflected in the development trace of the reasoning process.

In order to fit the expectations of the user, the commands HOW, WHY and WHEN allow the explanations to be tailored according to some basic requirements:

- detailing degree deep enough to satisfy the interest shown by the user, who may choose by himself the depth in the inference tree where he wants the explanation to be stopped;
- concision degree high enough to make the explanation easy to understand; for instance, some details either too complex or too difficult to follow, such as procedure bodies or LISP forms may be replaced by their attached explanatory components;
- completeness: the system is able to justify easily any step of its behaviour, unless the developed processes have associated side-effects. In this case, the explainer keeps the traces af all the modifications operated upon the knowledge base.

6. FUTURE DEVELOPMENTS

At the present stage, the INTEXP system runs under its first complete version. We are going to develop new components to be integrated into INTEXP, concerning several further directions to follow:

- a special planning component, designed to improve the selectional strategy used to solve conflicts;

- a reviewing component, supporting an intelligent development of the backtrack analysis;
- acquisition and learning components, supplying efficiency gains in the solving process.

Along with the delivery of new INTEXP versions, we are also approaching new application domains - such as technical fault diagnosis - appropiate for automatic expertise.

REFERENCES

[1]. Charniak E., Riesbeck K.C., McDermott D.V., Artificial Intelligence Programming, Lawrence Erlbaum, 1980.

[2]. Cohen P.R., and Feigenbaum E.A. (eds.), The Handbook of Artificial Intelligence, vol.III, William Kaufmann, 1982.

[3]. Doyle J., de Kleer J., Rich C., Steele G.L., and Sussman G.J., AMORD, A Deductive Procedure System, MIT, Artificial Intelligence Laboratory, Memo 435, January 1978.

[4]. Georgescu I., Knowledge Representation with Hypernets,Central Institute for Management and Informatics, AI Research Group Report AI-FDo26, November 1982.

[5]. Georgescu I., Hotăran A., Predescu R., Vlasiu M., Petrescu F., Nicolăiţă D., and Nagy A., INTEXP - Manual de prezentare şi utilizare, Central Institute for Management and Informatics, AI Research Group, December 1983.

[6]. McDermott J., R1: A Rule-Based Configurer of Computer Systems, Artificial Intelligence, 19, (1982) 39-88.

[7]. Michie D., Expert Systems in the Micro-electronic Age, Edinburgh University Press, 1979.

[8]. Predescu R., Reasoning Lines, Central Institute for Management and Informatics, AI Research Group, Report AI-FDo39, September 1983.

[9]. Stefik M., Aikins J., Balzer R., Benoit J., Birnbaum L., Hayes-Roth F., Sacerdoti E., The Organization of Expert Systems, A Tutorial, Artificial Intelligence, Vol. 18, No. 2, March 1982.

[10]. Weiner J.L., BLAH, A System which Explains its Reasoning, Artificial Intelligence, 15 (1980) 19-48.

ARTIFICIAL INTELLIGENCE: Methodology, Systems, Applications
W. Bibel and B. Petkoff (Editors)
Elsevier Science Publishers B.V. (North-Holland)

DIGS: A DOMAIN-INDEPENDENT EXPERT SYSTEM FOR TECHNICAL DIAGNOSTICS

Vasil Sgurev, Danail Dochev, Christo Dichev,
Genadi Agre, Zdravko Markov

Institute of Industrial Cybernetics and Robotics,
1113 Sofia, Acad.G.Bonchev st., bl.2

In the present paper an attempt to formalize the technical diagnostics process has been made. A formal model of the technical diagnostics process (a diagnostic net), applicable to different classes of technical objects is suggested. The structure of problem-independent expert system for technical diagnostics is considered. An original mechanism of the inference machine, using versatile searching strategies, relevant to the diagnostic net for the given class of technical objects is described.

1. INTRODUCTION

An obvious method to improve the quality and the efficiency of the technical diagnostics is to automatize it. It is, however, hard to formalize the diagnostic work, as it depends on empirical and even intuitive knowledge, accumulated as a result of a long practice. Therefore it is advisable to enter this expert knowledge in the computer in order to be used by a wide range of low-qualified personnel. This idea has been recently realized in a number of existing expert systems (ES) |1, 2, 4, 5, 6 |.

The analysis of the up to date experience shows that the creation of an ES is a long and exclusively labour-consuming process, requiring a heterogenous group of highly qualified specialists. On the other hand there exists a strong tendency for renovation and improvement of the different classes of technical objects (TO). Therefore the building of an ES for diagnosis of a certain class TO might prove ineffective. A possible solution to this problem is the development of domain-independent ES, i.e. systems, permitting fast and easy adjustment for different TO classes by changing the expert knowledge and adaptation of the mechanisms.

The present paper describes a model of the technical diagnostics process and the developed domain-independent ES DIGS, based on this model.

2. TECHNICAL DIAGNOSTICS - BASIC CONCEPTS

The diagnostics of technical systems may be considered as a purposeful iterative process which consists of performance of tests in order to locate faults and/or to find the causes for the malfunctioning of the system. A <u>test</u> is a set of expert determined procedures, intended for obtaining quantitive or qualitive estimations of the state of the diagnosed system or its components. The test results are interpreted as <u>symptoms</u> of the diagnosed system. In this case the <u>faults</u>

are an expert defined subset of symptoms. A diagnostic session begins with a subset of symptoms, which will be called <u>initial symptoms</u>. Each symptom, not defined as a fault, specifies <u>an expert defined</u> subset of possible tests for execution.

3. A MODEL OF THE TECHNICAL DIAGNOSTICS

As a general model of the technical diagnostics (TD) process is considered a graph-like structure $S = \langle N, A, F \rangle$ (fig.1), where $N = \{N_i\}_{i=1}^{n}$ - a set of nodes corresponding to the symptoms and

$A = \{A_{ij}\}$, $i, j=1, \ldots, n; i \neq j$ is a set of arcs, which corresponds to the connection between the symptoms, i.e. the possible ways of branching of the process. A security factor P_{ij}, which is a complex measure, based on the probable existence of an expert defined set of symptoms, is assigned to each arc A_{ij}. An arc A_{ij} is passable, if both symptoms N_i and N_j exist. A set of switching functions $F = \{F_{ij}\}$, specifying the passability of the arcs, is defined on the set A. Each switching function is associated with a test specifying its value. The switching function mechanism enables finding of all possible passable paths in the structure S. The set of faults is the set NT N consisting of terminal nodes (nodes without successors). A set NF N consisting of nodes corresponding to the initial symptoms is also defined. The set NF is defined by the user in the beginning of the diagnostic session. This enables the beginning of the diagnostic session with a different level of localization which makes easier the initialization the system by users who differ in their qualification.

In terms of the described model the problem for finding a single fault comes to determination of a tree, consisting of passable arcs, with a terminal node (fault) as its root and the set of initial symptoms NF as its leaves. The solution of this problem is optimized by minimizing the number of switchings i.e. the number of tests performed by the user. Generally, the TD process consists of finding all simultaneously existing faults. The described structure S is called further a diagnostic net (DN).

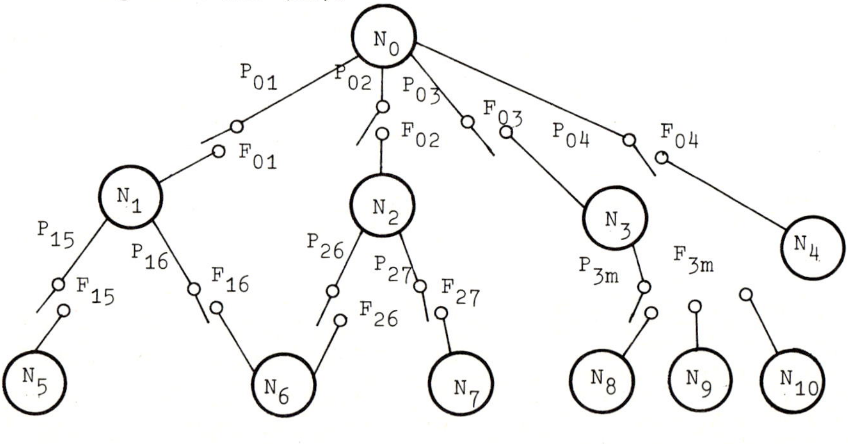

Fig.1

4. DESCRIPTION OF THE ES DIGS

Fig.2 presents the general structure of the system DIGS. The interface block (IB) and the block for explanation (BE) are not considered in the present paper.

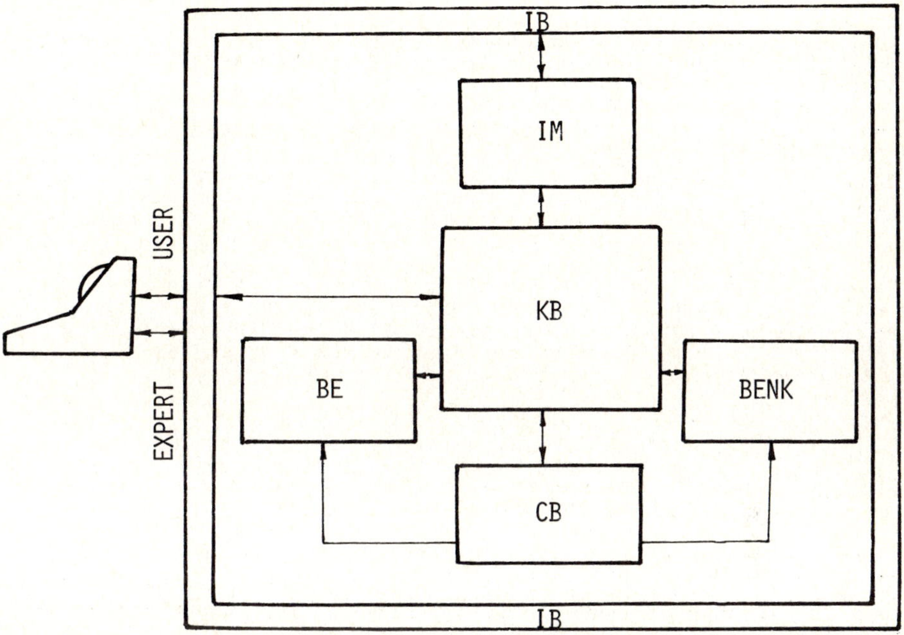

Fig.2

4.1. Knowledge base (KB)

The knowledge base as in all ES is the kernel of the system DIGS. KB is the skeleton of a DN, which the expert fills by means of the IB for each (concrete) TO class. The full KB contains the following structure elements:

- symptoms and connections between them;
- security factors, corresponding to the symptoms;
- tests (descriptions of the procedures to be performed by the user);
- switching functions, defining the correspondence between the result of the given test and the symptoms which cause the existence of the symptom initiating this test.

Two kinds of tests are considered in the system DIGS:

a) binary tests, i.e. tests checking the existence of a given symptom;

b) multi-valued tests, i.e. tests, determining one of several possible symptoms.

4.2. Block for the extraction of new knowledge (BENK)

BENK analyses the DN which has been built according to the expert knowledge and extracts additional properties and relations, facilitating the diagnostic process.

According to the TD model, a diagnostical session begins with entering the FN set (the set of initial symptoms), which may contain arbitrary nodes of the DN. Common nodes may exist in the paths, leading from the initial symptoms to the faults. Obviously such nodes play an important role in the diagnostics, since their existence may cause the appearance of a group of initial symptoms. In a DN common nodes are the nodes with more than one ancestor.

One of the functions of BENK is to find out all the common nodes, corresponding to a given set of initial symptoms. An important characteristic of the common nodes is their depth, i.e. the length of the longest path from the initial symptoms to such a node. This characteristic is evaluated for each common node and is used afterwards from the block for multiple input processing. A given set of symptoms may be classified as dependent or independent according to the existence or lack of common nodes. Such a decomposition of the symptoms permits the estimation of the minimal number of possible faults.

It is hard to get explicitly such type of knowledge from the expert especially for large and strongy connected DN. The new knowledge, obtained by BENK plays an important role in the diagnostic process. It permits to choose the most appropriate strategy for each case and in some cases may raise the abilities of the system above the expert level.

4.3. Inference machine (IM)

The IM operation will be described for DN, containing only binary tests since it illustrates best the IM mechanism.

The inference machine is a set of procedures, determining a terminal node N_t (fault) from a given initial node N_o (symptom). A set of nodes, for which there are paths, connecting each node with the node N_i, will be called hypotheses H_i. The depth of a hypothesis D (H_i) is the number of the arcs in the respective path. The security factor of a hypothesis $P(H_i)$ is a complex evaluation of the probability to pass the path from N_o to N_i and it is computed on the base of the security factors of the arcs, belonging to this path. A hypothesis is proved, if the result of the test T_i (i.e. the value of the corresponding switching function) shows the existence of the symptom N_i. A positive result of the test T_i is marked in the KB as $P_{i-1,j}= 1$. If N_i is a terminal node, it is a solution, i.e. N_i is the searched fault.

The test T_i is applied only if $P(H_i)\leq B$ where B is a threshold value.

The problem for detection of a single fault is solved step by step. At each step a hypothesis is built and is checked at the end of the step. In order to minimize the number of the applied tests it is necessary to minimize the number of the steps, i.e. to build hypotheses with maximal length. The length of the current hypothesis depends on the security factor P(H) and the threshold value B. The mechanism for hypothesis building ensures maximal $P(H_i)$. Let H_i be a current hypothesis, defined by the path $\{N_o,N_1,N_2,\ldots,N_i\}$. Each node N_j from thispath is chosen according to $P_{j-1} = \max \{P_{j-1,k}\}_{k=1}^{n_{j-1}}$ where n_{j-1} is the number of successors of the node N_{j-1}.

In the number of ES with a similar reference mechanism (APEX-3 |6| , PROSPECTOR |4|) a fixed threshold value is used. Such threshold does not depend on the concrete structure of the KB and therefore does not sufficiently reflect the characteristics of the particular diagnostic problem, i.e. this reduces the effectiveness of the TD process. In DIGS the threshold B is not fixed, but it is computed at each step. If $P_{oj} = \max\{ P_{ok} \}_{k=1}^{n_o}$ where n_o is the number of successors of the initial node N_f, then the initial threshold value is $B_o = \max\{ P_{ok} \}_{k=1,k\neq j}^{n_o}$. In this way the two most probable hypotheses are chosen from the set of all probable hypotheses. The maximal security factor determines the current hypothesis and the next to maximal security factor is used as a dynamic threshold value. At the end of the step after the application of the test T_i the threshold value is reevaluated. In case of a positive test result (proving the hypothesis) - the existence of the symptom N_i, N_i is considered as a new initial node and a new hypothesis is built with a threshold value chosen analogically. In case of a negative test result the threshold value B is not changed, as a new symptom is not detected. The lack of the symptom N_i is reflected in the KB by marking all arcs, leading to N_i, as not passable. A new hypothesis is built, which coincides with the previous one till the (i-1)-th node and the security factor is decreased proportionally to the security factor of the rejected (not passable) arc. If $P(H_{i-1}) \leq B$ the test T_{i-1} is executed and the above mentioned actions are repeated. Otherwise the current hypothesis includes the most probable successor of N_{i-1} node (excluding the rejected node N_i). This hypothesis is evaluated again according to the description above.

During the work of the IM the KB is updated and reflects the current state of the diagnosed object. Therefore the work of the IM is controlled by the expert knowledge and by the knowledge, obtained at the previous steps of the TD process.

The building of hypotheses may considered as a movement on the DN. Then the IM mechanism is a movement on a tree and realizes a "forward" strategy performed as a combination of moving in depth and in breadth, controlled by the actualized KB.

4.4. Control block (CB) and use of meta-knowledge

The IM, described in the previous chapter, finds a single fault by a single initial symptom. The real TD process is much more complicated - in general it is necessary to find several faults in the presence of a set of initial symptoms. The system DIGS uses the following classification of symptoms and faults:

1) Parallel faults, i.e. faults, the simultaneous existence of which causes appearance of given symptom;

2) Independent faults, i.e. each of them causes the appearance of a different symptom;

3) Dependent symptoms - at least one fault may cause their simultaneous appearance;

4) Independent symptoms - all symptoms, which are not dependent.

The control clock consists of 2 subblocks: a block for multiple input processing and a block for detection of parallel faults.

4.4.1. Block for multiple input processing (BMIP)

This block analyses the initial symptoms, entered by the user and by means of the block for extracting new knowledge (BENK) classifies them. Then the minimal possible number of the existing independent faults is estimated and as initial node for the beginning of the IM operation is specified. The determination of an initial node is an important point for the operation of the whole diagnostic system, as the choise of an appropriate node may reduce essentially the number of the applied tests, i.e. the time for fault searching. The common nodes in the DN, connected with the group of possibly dependent input symptoms, are candidates for initial nodes. The procedure for specification of an initial node checks the existence of the common node with maximal depth in the DN. In the correspondent symptom exists, it is transfered to the IM as initial node. Otherwise, the next deepest common node connected with the same group of possibly dependent input symptom is considered and the procedure is repeated.If such a node does not exist, the group of possibly dependent input symptoms is devided into subgroups and the same procedure is applied to each group.

The search for an initial node is completed when a symptom, corresponding to a common node, has been found, or the input symptoms are proved to be independent. In the last case the symptoms of the input group are used consequtively as initial nodes for the IM. The information, obtained during the process of searching for an initial node, is stored in the KB and it is used by the IM when hypotheses are built.

The whole process of searching for an initial node is controlled by metaknowledge - a set of heuristics, supplied by the knowledge engineer. Sometimes, when exhaustive deterministic algorithms are used, proving that the input symptoms are independent may take up considerable time and resources. In these cases the use of metaknowledge like estimations for the number of common nodes and input symptoms, their division in subgroups, the evolution of the diagnostic process, etc. is essential.

4.4.2. Block for detection of parallel faults (BDPF)

This block is activated when a fault has been detected by IM. After the removal of the faults the user specifies the existence of a parallel fault in a dialogue with DIGS. If the analysis confirms the existence of such faults, a new initial node for the IM operation is determined. Otherwise the control is transferred to BMIP for determination of an initial node for the next independent fault. The concept for searching of an initial node in BDPF is based on the fact that after the removal of the previous fault some of the proved symptoms remain to exist (in case of a parallel fault). The symptom best localizing the parallel fault (i.e., placed deepest into the DN) must be chosen as initial one. The searching strategy is controlled by metaknowledge, estimating the length of the path and the number of the steps for the previous fault detection.

5. MODES OF OPERATION OF THE SYSTEM DIGS

The expert works with DIGS in two modes of operation: filling the KB and testing the KB. In the first mode the knowledge entered by the expert, is transformed into an internal representation (DN) and is checked for correctness and completeness. These functions are performed by the interface blocks. The abovementioned checks are mainly syntactical and could not detect all possible errors and lapses of the expert in the primary entered KB.

In the test mode the adequatness of the obtained DN to the real TD process is checked by means of real data. The expert may localize and detect the existing errors and ommisions. T

The user of DIGS also works in two modes of operation - automatic and user mode. In the automatic mode the fault searching strategy is chosen by the system itself. In the user mode the fault searching strategy is chosen by the user. The user may build his own hypotheses and enter them in the system for checking, i.e. the system may respond to the question if it is possible for the symptom-hypothesis to cause the appearance of the initial symptoms. The system may reject or confirm the hypothesis and may point out the subset of symptoms, which are eventually caused by the symptom-hypothesis. The necessary test for proving the hypothesis is also described. In this mode DIGS realizes a pure backward strategy.

In order to permit users with different qualification to work with the system, it is possible to change the mode (automatic or user) after the execution of each test. Thus a mixed forward/backward strategy may be realized, which make the system more versatile and more effective.

6. REALIZATION OF THE SYSTEM DIGS

A great advantage of diagnostic system is the opportunity for its use directly on the user's working place. The personal computers are an appropriate hardware tool for realization of diagnostic systems due to their wide spreading, unpretentiousness and convenience for the mass user. For this reason DIGS is oriented towards personal computers (PC). The language PROLOG is a convenient tool for building expert systems |3| . An original version of PROLOG for PC (APPLE-II or IBM-PC) permitting the optimal use of the main and external memory has been developed for DIGS realization. The system DIGS is currently under development.

7. CONCLUSION

The experience of building up the system outlines the directions for its improvement and development. A direction for increasing the system effectivity is the perfection of the metaknowledge use in order to realize an automatic mixed forward/backward strategy and an automatic choice of an optimal system configuration, tailored to a given class of technical objects.

Another direction for the system development is the creation of mechanisms, permittimg the system to accumulate the experience of its own operation and to use it for perfection of the fault searching strategies, i. e. development of self-learning mechanisms.

REFERENCES

|1| Addis, T., Toward an "Expert" diagnostic system. ICL Technical journal, May, 1983, pp.79-105.

|2| Buchanan, B.G., Partial bibliography of work on Expert Systems. SIGART Newsletter, 84, (1983), pp.45-49.

|3| Clark, K.et F.McCabe, PROLOG for Expert Systems. Machine Intelligence, n10, Ellis Horwood, 1982.

|4| Duda, R., J.Gashing et P.Hart, Model design in the PROSPECTOR consultant systen for mineral exploration, in Expert Systems in the Microelectronic Age (ed.D.Mickie), Edinbourgh University Press, pp.153-167.

|5| Gini, G., M.Gini et R.Morpugo, A Knowledge-based consultation system for automatic maintenance and repair. Proc. of the PROLAMAT'82, North-Holland, 1983, pp.495-506.

|6| Merry, M., APEX-3: An expert system shell for fault diagnosis. The GEC Journal of Research, vol.1, 1983, pp.39-47.

ARTIFICIAL INTELLIGENCE: Methodology, Systems, Applications
W. Bibel and B. Petkoff (Editors)
Elsevier Science Publishers B.V. (North-Holland)

POSOH - THE INSTRUMENTAL EXPERT SYSTEM OF NL-MODULES DESIGN AND IMPLEMENTATION

Vladimir F. Khoroshevsky

Computer Centre Academy of Sciences
of the USSR, Moscow
U.S.S.R.

Nowadays, many NL-systems have been developped and utilized, but this systems' design is a very complex and labour-consuming job. That's why, the focus of researches in this field moves now to the creating of adequate environment for these goals. In the presented paper the questions of the problem oriented software of high level communication design are discussed.

INTRODUCTION

Nowadays, many NL-systems have been developped and used. This systems' design is a very complex and labour-consuming job. That's why, the focus of researches in this area moves now to the creating of adequate environment for these goals.

The first version of support development system named POSOH (Problem Oriented Software Of High level communication) was designed and implemented sometimes before at the Computer Centre Academy of Sciences of the USSR in Moscow. This system was described in (Khoroshevsky (1979)). The main goals of the instrumental complex POSOH were:
-using the modern programming technology in the field of the NL--systems design;
-special linguistic knowledge representation language based on the ATN-approach design and implementation.

But the first attempts of practical using of the POSOH, see, for example, (Selivanova, Khoroshevsky, Shubina (1981)), have shown, that the main profit can be received at the programming stage. But it is well known, that this stage represent approximately 17% of the labour-consumption of the system's design and implementation. The design stage is responsible also for the main bulk of buggs. This is the first reason of the POSOH-complex expansion. On the other hand, it is necessary to use domain experts' knowledge more widely.

These reasons made a demand to modify the first version of the POSOH-complex. Its development went by the following ways:
(a) design of different types of the ATNL-translators;
(b) extending of the instrumental knowledge representation languages;
(c) transforming the POSOH-complex into the instrumental expert system.
The last aspect is the core theme of the present paper.

PRELIMINARY REMARKS

During the last decade there has been a large progress in the field of the expert systems (ES) design (Buchanan (1981)). Nowadays, there exist several types of the ES's: consultation systems in the different problem areas, problem solvers, monitoring expert systems and "empty" expert systems. As for me, each kind of the ES has it own predecessors in the artificial intelligence and, more generally, in the computer science. For example, there are many similar features in the consultation ES and information retrieval systems. Then, execution modules of problem solvers are similar to applied packages of the programs. And instrumental expert systems spring from the "empty" expert systems, the technological support development systems, systems of the automatic programming and learning systems.

That's why, it seems to me, it's more convinient to name such kind of intelligent envieronment the instrumental expert systems, but not "empty" expert systems.

And at the finishing of this part of the paper I would like to name some predecessor ideas in this area. At first, this is the conseption of "empty" expert systems, such as EMYCIN (van Melle(1979)) AGE (Nii, Aiello (1979)), EXPERT (Weiss, Kulikowsky (1979)) etc., and instrumental tools conception, for example, TEIRESIAS (Davis, Lenat (1982)). Secondly, - the conception of automatic programming, supported by systems of PSI (Green (1977)) and PA (Rich, Shrobe (1978)) kind.

But, as to me, the advantages of POSOH new version lies in the unity of the
- -results in the field of programming technology;
- -syntax-directed translation and
- -empty expert systems.

POSOH-ARCHITECTURE

The general structure of POSOH new version is shown in fig.1, (the information links are duble, and the control links are single). It is convinient to distinguish four main blocks in this structure:
- -Block of control, which is comprised by the system's monitor and the communication with user module;
- -Explanation subsystem (it supports the domain experts, in this case - the designers of NL-modules or linguists, with the help of the received solutions and/or the results in the terms of the problem area);
- -Knowledge aquisition subsystem and
- -Executive block.

Now, a few words about these blocks.

Block of control. There are two ways for the system monitoring: executing of the domain expert requests and executing of another blocks' requests. As to system monitor functioning, the usual "data-driven" approach is used here. From the point of view of the goals of present paper the user communication module, which supports the "front-end" interface with the domain expert, is more interesting. In fact, this module is to implement the multilevel natural communication system. It will be descussed a little later.

Explanation subsystem. In general, the structure of this subsystem is usual. The specific of POSOH explanation subsystem is in its design and implementation, based on the using of the explanation subsystem generator, controlled by expert system's knowledge. The structure of such generator will be discussed at the next part of this paper.

Knowledge aquisition. It is supposed, that this block of POSOH will be organized as two-level structure. At the first level (it has been implemented nowadays) knowledge aquisition is done by the use of knowledge representation language family based at the ATN-approach. At the left end of the family stands the Augmented Transition Network Language ATNL-2.0 (Khoroshevsky,1983) and at the right end - the domain expert's languages, which may be developped on the base of the macrolanguage MATNL (Khoroshevsky (1984)). It is supposed that in future the pseudonatural knowledge representation languages will be designed. And they will consist of the high level of knowledge aqusition block.

Executive block. This is the problem solving block. That's why, the base of the executive block is the executive modules library. It comprises the job planning modules; knowledge representation languages translators and special editors, which support the knowledge aquisition processes; special linkage editors and also user help modules. By the way, the last are included into the executive block but not into the explanation subsystem, becaurse they consist of a special tutorial subsystem of instrumental expert system POSOH.

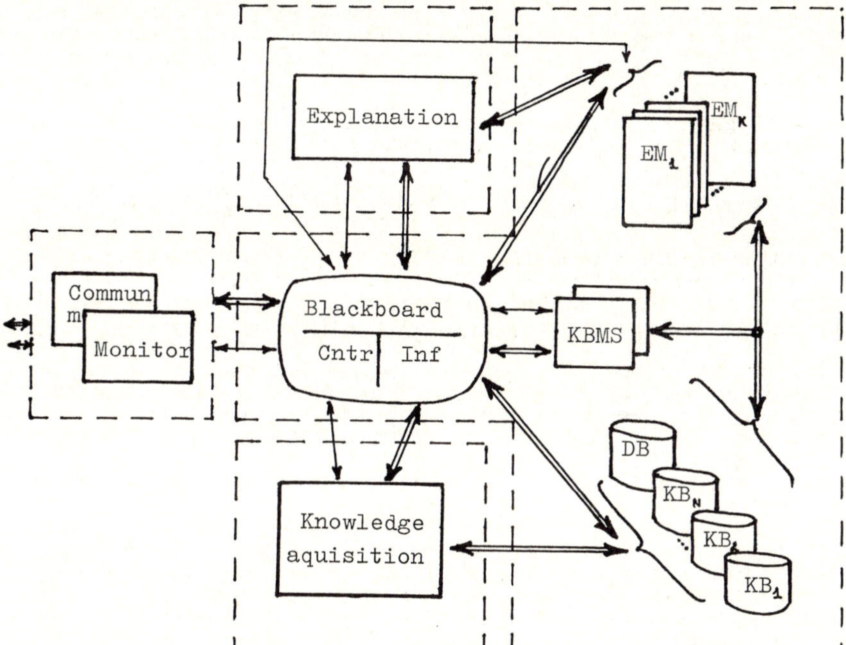

Figure 1
General structure of instrumental ES POSOH

SYNTAX-ORIENTED GENERATOR OF EXPLANATION SUBSYSTEMS

Now let's discuss the explanation generation concept. In our approach the explanation subsystems generators are similar to the syntax-directed translators, which are more complex, of course, than the analogous translators of the programming languages. Their complexity is determened by the complexity of the input language, more complicate knowledge base and by the dynamic character of its using.

Common structure of the syntax-directed explanation generator is shown in fig. 2.

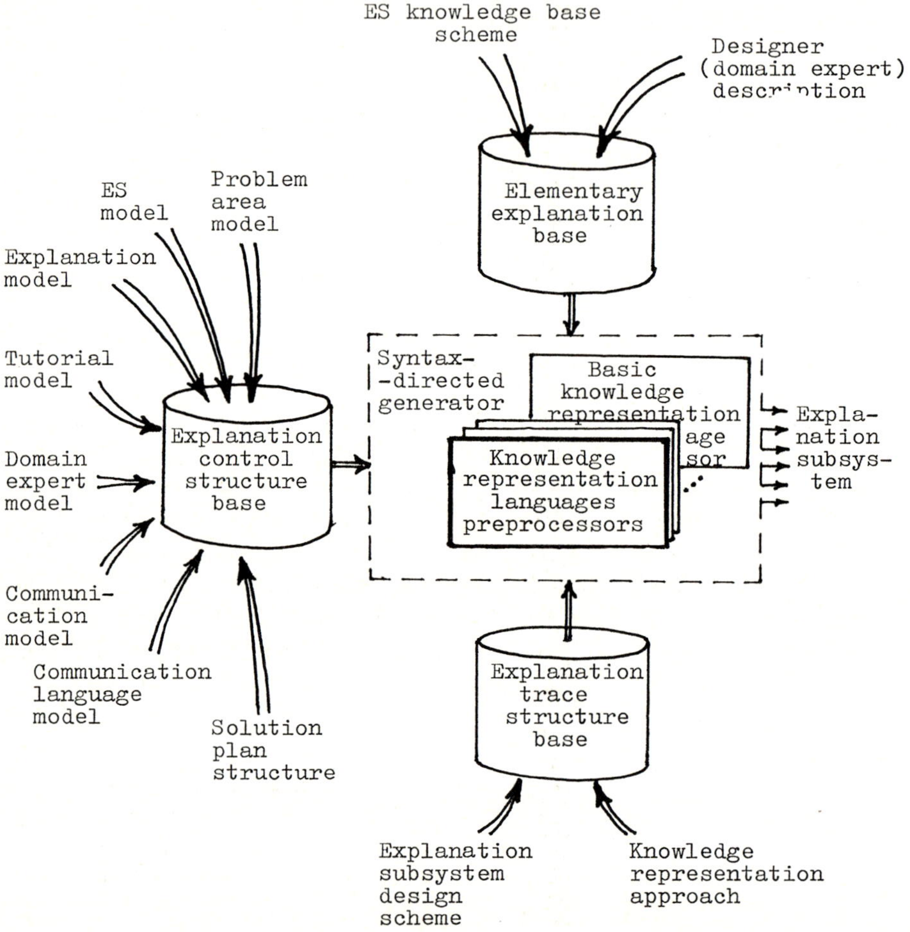

Figure 2
Common structure of the explanation subsystems generator

There are three main knowledge sourses in such generator. The first one is the elementary explanation base. It springs from the set of the elementary annotations. It must be generated from the ES knowledge base scheme and designers (in future, from the domain expert) descriptions.

The explanation control structure must be formed, on the one hand, on the base of the problem area model, explanation model, ES and domain experts' models, communication and tutorial models and on the base of the communication language model. On the other hand,the explanation control structure is formed on the base of the problem solving plan structure, constructed by the scheduler of ES executive programs.

The explanation trace structure is defined by the knowledge representation approach and used scheme of the explanation subsystem design. Blackboard-mechanizm supports the using of the explanation trace. In this case, the blackboard is the data base, and the scheme of this data base is the division of the knowledge base.

It is natural to use the knowledge representation languages family for the description of the above discussed knowledge sources. Then, the explanation subsystems generator may be presented as the set of the individual languages preprocessors and the basic knowledge representation language processor. Preprocessors' implementation in this case can be based on the macrogeneration technique. And basic language processor is implemented as an interpreter and/or a compiler (Khoroshevsky (1982)).

EXPLANATION SUBSYSTEMS GENERATION

Now let's discuss the main demands to the modern explanation subsystems and common principles of the syntax-directed explanation generator using. And, at the finishing, we'll give some remarks about such a systems design and implementation.

Nowadays, explanation subsystems must possess the following features:

- flexible using of the natural language in the explanation requests and in more precise requests, and/or in the case of incomprehension of the explanatory messages;
- adaptation to the communication language and/or qualification of the domain expert;
- using the developped help to the domain expert in the ES processing regime.

These features implementation intends the mutual using of the results, recieved in the experience of the explanation subsystems design, natural language processing and automatic tutors construction.

The general tasks of the explanation subsystems new generation design are concretized by the scheme in fig. 3. The scheme shows, that in such explanation subsystems, besides the problem area and communication language models, there are used the models of the ES, explanation, domain expert, tutorial and communication.

The coordinate functioning of different subsystems and its sub-subsystems is necessary in the new ES. It supposes the natural communication between different knowledge representation systems used in the whole communication processes description and implementation. It seems, that the unified formalizm of the different compo -

nents description is most useful in this case. The augmented transition network (ATN) formalism (Woods (1970)) is very convenient for this task. Naturally, some modifications and expansions should be made.

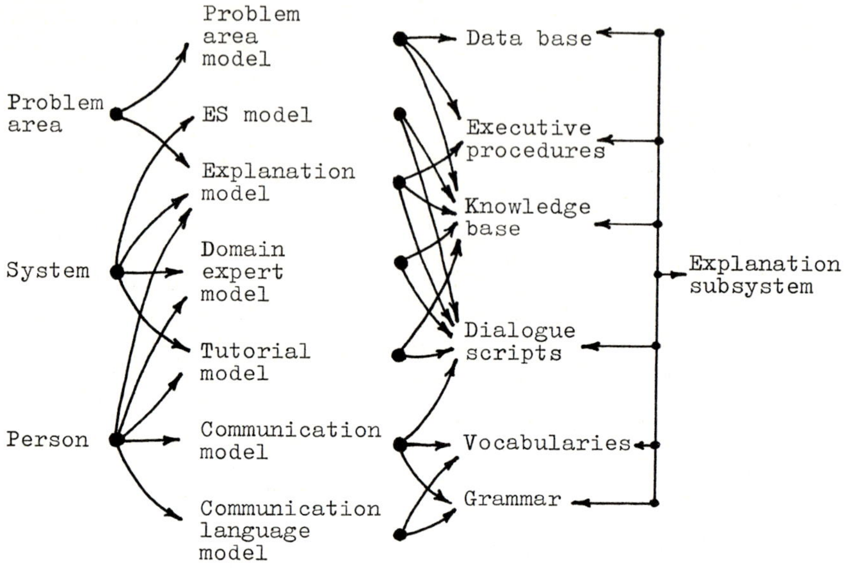

Figure 3
General scheme of the explanation subsystems design

When the ATN-approach is used, the problem area is described by the frames net, and the communication language - by the net grammars. The network approach is also very convenient with the dialogue scripts description. The multilevel transition networks are used in this case. The high levels of the networks represent the separate stages of the ES functioning, especially different dialogue types and communication goals. The intermediate levels of the networks describe the dialogue communication stereotypes. The knowledge about the ES itself, the models of the explanation, tutorial and communication, and the knowledge about different domain experts are represented here. Each model have its own control net and all of them use the common subnets. The domain experts models are defined dinamically by the reordering of the arcs in the explanation, tutorial and communication models' nets and subnets. Of course, they must be labelled at the beginning of the functioning of the expert system. At last, the lowest levels of the networks describe the analysis/synthesis subnets of the texts implementation of the communication between the domain expert and the explanation subsystem. Thus, we recieve the multilevel ATN-description of the explanation subsystem (see fig. 4).

The PUSH-arcs are used for the transition from one level to another in classic ATN (Woods (1970)) and in some of its developments (Khoroshevsky (1979); Khoroshevsky (1980)). All of them have the subroutine control manner. But the coroutines are more convenient in our case. Thus, the cascaded ATN idea (Woods (1980)), which is fixed in the knowledge representation language ATNL-2.0 (Khoroshevsky (1983)) is used to the ATN-based explanation subsystems implementation. The extralinguistic levels of knowledge are described in this case by the use of the ATN-oriented macrolanguages family (Khoroshevsky (1984)). They support the above discussed principles of the generation of the explanation subsystems on the base of the instrumental expert system.

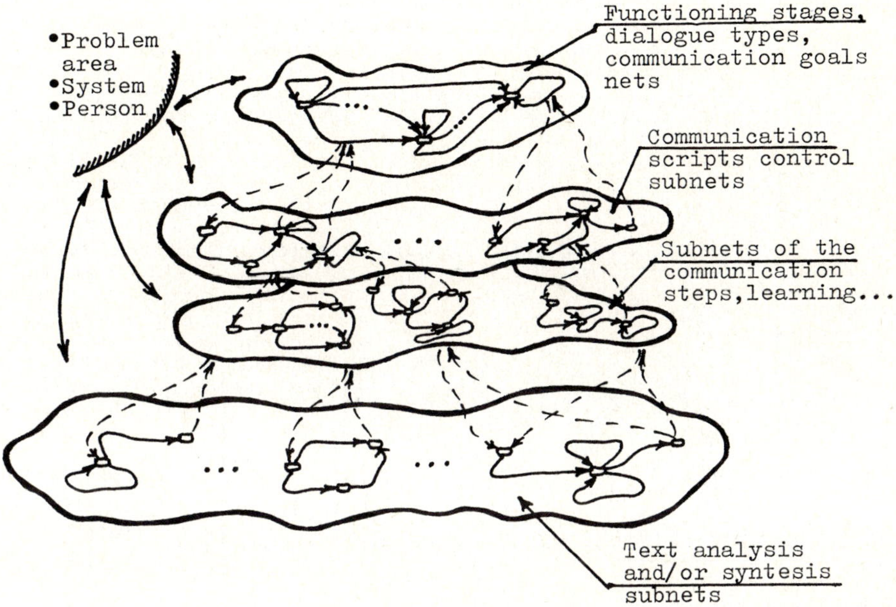

Figure 4
Multilevel ATN-description of the explanation subsystem

Thus, we discussed the main ideas of the explanation subsystems design and implementation in the framework of instrumental expert system POSOH.

CONCLUSION

The questions of the architecture, functioning and using of the instrumental expert system POSOH have been discussed in this paper. Now, the described version of POSOH is in progress. We use the metalanguage of recursive functions, which is the universal macrogenerator with the nonfixed input and output languages in the implementation of POSOH. And I. Nenova from Bulgaria implements now the ATNL-compiler by use the personal computer APPLE-II and Pascal.

REFERENCES:

1 Khoroshevsky,V.F., Mechanization of the Natural Language Processing for Dialogue Systems Design, Proc.Sov.-Fin.Symp."Dialogue Systems",vol.II, Tbilisy, Oct.,1979 (CC AS USSR, Moskwa,1979) (In Russian).
2 Selivanova,N.V.,Khoroshevsky,V.F.,Shubina,M.V., ATNL-based design of the linguistic processor for an intelligence information-control system, in: Nariniany,A.S.(ed.), Linguistic processors and knowledge representation (Novosibirsk,1981)(In Russian)
3 Buchanan,B., Research on Expert Systems, Report N° STAN-CS-81--837 (Stanford University, March, 1981).
4 van Melle,W., A Domain Independent Production-Rule System for Consultation Programs, Proc.IJCAI-79 (Tokyo, 1979).
5 Nii,H.P.,Aiello,N., AGE: A Knowledge-Based Program for Building Knowledge-Based Programs, Proc.IJCAI-79 (Tokyo, 1979).
6 Weiss,S.,Kulikowsky,C.A., EXPERT: A System for Developping Consultation Models, Proc.IJCAI-79 (Tokyo, 1979).
7 Davis,R.,Lenat,D., Knowledge-Based Systems in Artificial Intelligence (McGraw-Hill Inc., 1982).
8 Green,C., A Summary of PSI program synthesis system, Proc. IJCAI-77 (Stanford, 1977).
9 Rich,C.,Shrobe,H., Initial report on a LISP programmer's apprentice, IEEE Trans. on Software Eng., SE-4 (6),(1978) 456-467.
10 Khoroshevsky,V.F., ATNL-machine - Software & Hardware, Proc.of the IFAC Symp. on AI, Leningrad,USSR, 4-6 Oct.1983 (Pergamon Press Inc., 1984).
11 Khoroshevsky,V.F., The ATNL-based macroprocessor - software tool of the communication modules implementation, Proc.III Int. Conf. "Artificial Intelligence and Information-Control Systems of Robots", Smolenice, Czechoslovakia,June 11-15, 1984 (North--Holland, Amsterdam, 1984).
12 Khoroshevsky,V.F., Development of the NL-communicatiom systems on the base of the DBMS-software, Proc.II Int.Conf."Artificial Intelligence and Information-Control Systems of Robots", Smolenice, Czechoslovakia,18-22 Oct.1982 (Veda,Bratislava, 1982).
13 Woods,W., Transition network grammer for natural language analysis, CACM vol.13 N°10 (1970) 591-606.
14 Khoroshevsky,V.F., ATNL - linguistic knowledge representation language in NL-systems, in:Kuzin,L.T.(ed.), Questions of Cybernetics, vol.55 (Sov.Radio,Moskwa,1979) (In Russian).
15 Khoroshevsky,V.F., Adaptive analizers for dialogue systems, AS USSR (Moskwa, 1980) (In Russian).
16 Woods,W., Cascaded ATN grammars, American Jrnl. of Comp. Linguistics, vol.6 N° 1 (1980) 372-386.

ARTIFICIAL INTELLIGENCE: Methodology, Systems, Applications
W. Bibel and B. Petkoff (Editors)
Elsevier Science Publishers B.V. (North-Holland)

NEW EMPIRICAL RESULTS OF USER STUDIES WITH A DOMAIN INDEPENDENT NATURAL LANGUAGE QUERY SYSTEM

Matthias Jarke

Computer Applications and Information Systems
Graduate School of Business Administration
New York University
New York - U S A

Jürgen Krause

Linguistic Information Science
University of Regensburg
Regensburg - West Germany

The paper reports the results of several empirical studies which investigated the same domain-independent natural language query system (NLQS), using various applications in two different natural languages - English and German. The comparison of these NLQS experiments which involved over 12.000 queries has yielded methodological results and preliminary conclusions about this type of natural language interface, as well as gaps in the studies. The paper outlines some definitive results and plans to resolve several of the remaining issues.

0 INTRODUCTION

Natural language based question-answering systems are seen as one of the main research areas in artificial intelligence (AI) which are becoming important for commercial applications. The early skepticism of the industrial managers seems to have given way to last minute panic: there is hardly any major computer company which is not working on product development of natural language interfaces (NLI). One stimulus surely was the success of INTELLECT, the first commercially available NLI developed by the Artificial Intelligence Cooperation.
In connection with this development the impression is spreading that the theoretical background of NLI is safe enough. But that is neither true with respect to the techniques proposed, nor with respect to the transfer to application oriented software packages or evaluation methodology (see Krause 1982 and 1983).
It is still unclear in what sense NLI are preferable at all to formal query languages; concerning the overall architecture for implementing NLI, knowledge-based domain-specific NLI are contrasted with domain-independent so-called subset systems. The latter are rejected by the majority of the artificial intelligence community. Schwartz 1984 concludes:

> "Natural language systems lacking a knowledge base cannot understand anywhere near as wide a range of information retrieval requests as can knowledge-based systems." (p.247)

Nevertheless the subset type of NLI is the focus of our paper. One reason is that only subset systems have reached a degree of maturity where they can be subjected to rigorous empirical testing. Moreover even the knowledge-based systems implemented today use subsets when they are installed in practice. From a more elaborate point of view the problem appears to be only whether we build up the subset ad-hoc or whether we try to find regularities to define it.
We are postulating that defining a subset is one of the most important design decisions for all NLI. Nobody can implement all (or almost all) the possibilities which arise in man-man communication. Nevertheless theoretically based restriction rules are almost unresearched until now. One main point in this context is in which error situations users of NLI dispose of effective strategies to revise the initial formulation. Questions like this are of an empirical nature. Therefore this paper summarizes several field studies and laboratory experiments concerning the feasibility and practical desirability of a particular domain-independent NLI for database querying. Additionally we report preliminary results of a reanalysis of the experimental data in which we are investigating the stability of the user vocabulary and user strategies for rephrasing man-to-man requests and work tasks in man-machine dialog.

1 THE NATURAL LANGUAGE QUERY SYSTEM (NLQS) UNDER EVALUATION

The NLQS whose evaluation is reported here (see Lehmann 1978, Ott and Zoeppritz 1979, Krause and Lehmann 1980) consists of three main components:

a) a syntax analyser (see Zoeppritz 1984) which produces a surface oriented tree structure for natural language queries (English, German, Spanish)
b) interpretation routines which transform the tree structure into expressions of a formal query language with the help of a semantic analysis and
c) a relational database system.

The NLQS-design is especially influenced by the demand for portability. The intended users are non-EDP-professionals. They should be able to create and query their database without support by a linguist. As a result the potential number of users is greatly increased and the costs for the installation of an application reduced. However, this has two important consequences:

a) For each application one has to build up the vocabulary and the conceptualization.
b) No linguistic knowledge can be expected. Therefore NLQS dispenses with all information which only a linguist could give in the user specific part of the system. The consequence is that the NLQS generally works without semantic information in the user dependent vocabulary.

2 PREVIOUS EVALUATION STUDIES

The NLQS was investigated in several empirical studies using various applications in two different natural languages (English, German). Taken together, these experiments involved about 1oo subjects and over 12,ooo queries, constituting the bulk of empirical evaluations of NLI reported to date.

The evaluation studies can be seen as parts of an extended evaluation scheme. They started with real applications to be analyzed in field studies. The field studies were coupled with controlled laboratory experiments (paper and pencil tests) to answer special questions and to compare user performance in the NLQS against formal query languages.
Jarke/Krause/Vassiliou 1984 give an overview of all experiments with the NLQS (see also Zoeppritz 1983). In the first phase, the development team tested the system informally to uncover errors and gaps in coverage. The second set of experiments (the KFG study at Heidelberg and at the University of Regensburg since 1978) was still performed in part at the development site and with technical support by the development team but by an external researcher. The main field study of KFG was carried out by three teachers, supported by the system development team. For instance, the teachers wanted to know whether low grades in mathematics in earlier years have predictive power for grades of graduation. The database contained 41,250 grades for 430 students and further information about social background and class repetition. 7278 questions were asked in 46 sessions. At the heart of KFG was the long term observation (16 months) of a single user (6603 questions). Detailed qualitative analyses were performed, and the original field study was complemented by another field study and several minor laboratory experiments.

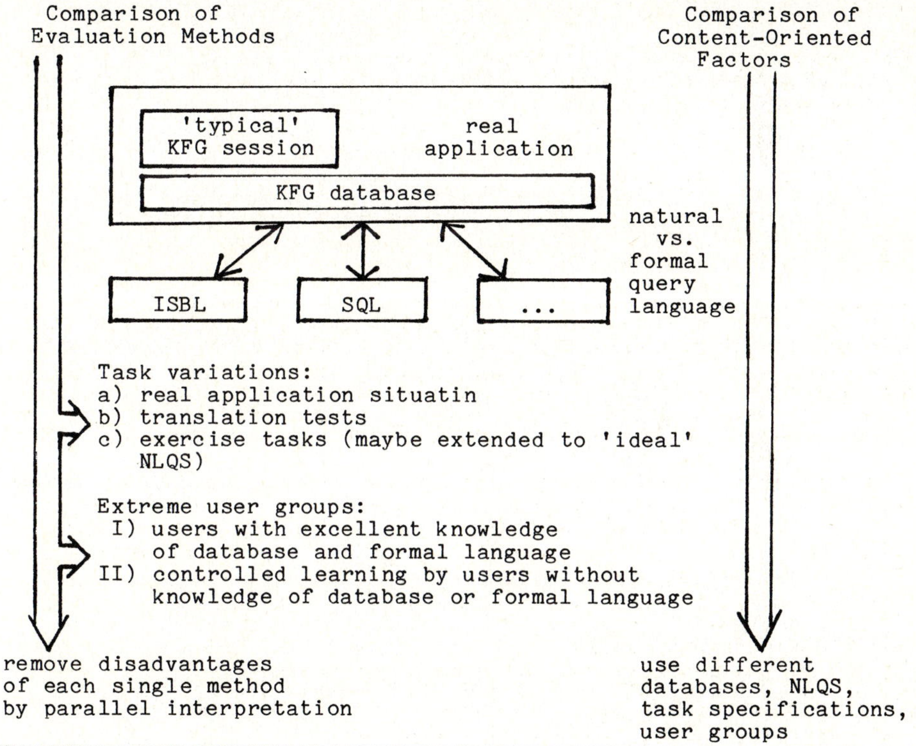

FIGURE 1: Overall Evaluation Plan - KFG Studies (partly realized)

For the third series of experiments (the Advanced Language Project (ALP) at New York University (from 1981-1983), the system was transferred to a different natural language (English), and to a site where little linguistic or technical support by the development team was available. A quantitatively oriented evaluation strategy was chosen for comparing the NLQS to the formal database query language SQL in a partially controlled field study and two controlled laboratory experiments.

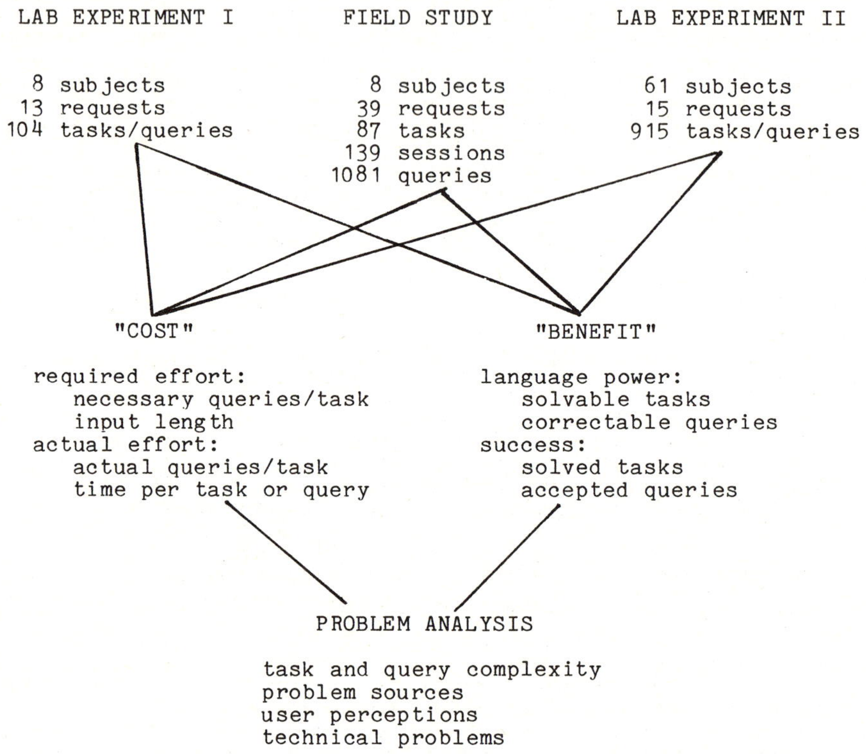

FIGURE 2: Evaluation Plan and Descriptive Statistics - ALP Studies

The application, a question-answering system about alumni of the Graduate School of Business Administration at New York University, maintains demographic data and donation histories of school alumni, foundations, other organizations, and individuals. The school has over 40.000 graduates as well as some 5.000 non-graduates who have given to the school over the past 20 years. The ALP database contained four base relations with approximately 100.000 tuples, substantially more than in previous applications. Data retrieved from this database usually serve as a basis for decision making in fund raising drives.

Based on the results of the KFG and ALP evaluation studies, the following five statements seem to have a fairly strong empirical backing.

a) Users do not communicate with a NLI in the way they do with a human. In particular, they are very careful in typing input, as evidenced by a low percentage of typographical errors. It is an open question how this would change with widespread availability of automatic spelling correction for NLI.

b) Small vocabulary subsets are sufficient for restricted application areas. This result may not extend to some of the knowledge-based systems which require the definition of all words used (including, in particular, values appearing in the database).

c) Natural language is more concise than formal query languages. In particular, SQL requires substantially longer input even for rather simple queries.

d) Formal query languages cannot be rejected on the grounds that a substantial effort is needed to learn them. In laboratory experiments, subjects achieved comparable success in formulating formal language queries as in formulating NLQS queries after the same short period of training.

e) Neither study confirmed the fear that natural language queries grow more and more complex over time.

3 RESEARCH IN PROGRESS

One of the methodological conclusions analyzing the ALP material was that the quantitative analyses must be complemented by qualitative interpretations. The latter are currently performed in a cooperation between the New York University and the University of Regensburg. Starting point is the material of ALP which concerns the NLQS, especially the protocols of the field study (8 subjects) and the natural language part of the second laboratory experiment (15 requests, 1o subjects without any knowledge of the NLQS, 34 subjects who were trained in the NLQS). At the moment our interest concentrates on user strategies of handling the task/request and the error situations, and on word usage and sentence patterns. The preliminary results can be summarized as follows.

3.1 DEFINITION OF THE VOCABULARY

Before working with the NLQS, the user has to define the application vocabulary, including the roles (arguments) attached to the verbs, nouns and adjectives. If different users need a different vocabulary (including the use of the roles) or if there are changes over time, NLQS will not work well. Therefore, it is important for the practical feasibility of NLQS whether there are major differences in vocabulary among users or over time.
The results of the evaluation studies are promising. The vocabulary and the roles used seem to be rather stable. They are rather stable with respect to different users, to different languages (German, English), to different training conditions, and to different methodological frameworks (laboratory or field experiment).

3.2 USER STRATEGIES

The subjects of the ALP field study wrote their work tasks down before working with the NLQS. We are now analyzing how this formulation changed when entering into real man-machine dialog. A simi-

lar shift appears between the given formulation of an exam question in the laboratory experiments and the NLQS solution proposed by a user. A third reformulation takes place when an error situation interrupts the man-machine dialogue and a question has to be reformulated by the user.
In studying these phenomena we hope to learn something about specific rules of 'computer talk' vs. written man-man-communication. There are first hints that such rules exist:

a) The questions in man-machine-dialogues are in all cases less complex than the initial formulation; in this respect there seems to be little difference between the field study and the laboratory experiments, and between the subjects with and without training in the NLQS.
b) In handling error situations the subjects of the KFG-study (German) have much in common with the ALP subjects. Using synonyms and the reduction of complexity by using formal extensions of the NLI (definition of variables) were the preferred strategies.

4 CONCLUSION

We are still at the beginning of the qualitative interpretation of the ALP material and its connection with that of the KFG study. The first preleminary results are promising. In the near future we hope to know more about how to define a subset for NLI (also for knowledge-based NLI) and about the question: what's that, computertalk?

LITERATURE

1. Jarke, M., Krause, J., Vassiliou, J., Studies in the evaluation of a domain-independent natural language query system, Working paper Series CRIS no. 72, New York University (April 1984).

2. Krause, J., Mensch-Maschine-Kommunikation in natürlicher Sprache (Niemeyer, Tübingen 1982).

3. Krause, J., Praxisorientierte natürlichsprachliche Frage-Antwort-Systeme: Zur Entwicklung vor allem in der Bundesrepublik Deutschland, Nachrichten für Dokumentation 34, 4/5 (1983), 188-194.

4. Krause, J., Lehmann, H., The User Specialty Language. A natural language based information system and its evaluation, in D. Krallmann (ed.): Dialogsysteme und Textverarbeitung (Essen 1980) 127-146.

5. Lehmann, H., Interpretation of natural language in an information system, IBM Journal of Research and Development 22, 5 (1978), 560-572.

6. Ott, N., Zoeppritz, M., USL - an experimental information system based on natural language, in L. Bolc (ed.): Natural Language Based Computer Systems (Macmillan, London 1979) 3-32.

7. Schwartz, S.P., Natural language processing in the commercial world, in W. Reitmann (ed.): Artificial Intelligence Applications for Business (Ablex, Norwood, NJ 1984) 235-248.

8. Zoeppritz, M., Human factors of a natural language enduser system, in A. Blaser and M. Zoeppritz (eds.): End User Systems and their Human Factors (Springer, New York et al. 1983), 62-93.

9. Zoeppritz, M., Syntax for German in the User Specialty Languages System (Niemeyer, Tübingen 1984).

ARTIFICIAL INTELLIGENCE: Methodology, Systems, Applications
W. Bibel and B. Petkoff (Editors)
Elsevier Science Publishers B.V. (North-Holland)

SYNTAX AND SEMANTICS FOR NATURAL LANGUAGE PROCESSING

G.Adorni*, A. Cappelli+, G. Ferrari%, L. Moretti+, I. Prodanof+

+ Istituto di Linguistica Computazionale - CNR - Pisa - Italy
* Dipartimento di Informatica, Sistemistica e Telematica
Universita' di Genova - Genoa - Italy
% Dipartimento di Linguistica - Universita' di Pisa - Pisa - Italy

This article deals with a computational model within which syntax and semantics are integrated in a single process. A general processor which handles several types of representations is discussed. A knowledge representation component and the ways by which it can be exploited by the processor are presented. Finally a system will be described by which experiments on semantic representation in different domains are being carried.

1. INTRODUCTION

This article discusses the following three basic issues which arised in the design of a computational model within which syntactic and semantic processing are integrated:

- how should the input string be processed in such a way as to i) cover a wide range of linguistic phenomena, ii) be able to handle symbolic representations of different nature, and iii) compete in efficiency with current parsers;
- how does the output representation look like and which are the conceptual operations involved in the construction of such a representation;
- to what extent does the application domain affect semantic representation and whether it is possible to create a mechanism that automatically switches from a domain to the other.

2. AN EXPERIMENTAL GENERALIZED PROCESSOR

A processor intended to map natural language strings directly onto a knowledge structure is required to recognize a wide variety of surface structures including those in which pronouns, gaps or ellipses occur. Consequently, in addition to normal structuring and storing actions it has to perform structure manipulating operations such as antecedent-pronoun binding or gap filling.

Furthermore, the structure resulting from the analysis of the string need not be a mere parse tree nor need it be directly dependent upon the parsing algorithm and the recognition grammar. On the contrary, it is expected to manipulate syntactic information together with knowledge structures by means of a rich set of memory accessing functions triggered and controled by the surface distribution. Such a triggering may not unambiguosly coincide with the beginning of a constituent: for example the linguistic phenomenon known as pied-piping shows how the nature of a constituent (relative clause) can be recognized many words after its beginning.

2.1. The EXAM-LC Model

Having these requirements in mind, EXAM-LC-ATN (Extended Access and Manipulation of the Left Context, see 15) has been developed at the Istituto di Linguistica Computazionale - Pisa. The sentence recognition process is based upon the traditional ATN parsing algorithm. The basic features of ATN parsers, i.e. the network formalism and the non-deterministic top-down recognition algorithm, are kept, while the data structure and the whole set of actions and forms have been modified such that the resulting parsing model is closer to a context-free parser. Instead of the traditional register table, the data structure consists in an unstructured space of memory into which information is stored and accessed by explicit structure specifying functions. The data structure is a list which is mainly accessed with a typical LIFO stack policy. It represents a unique memory space non splitted into registers. The state saving mechanism necessary for the treatment of non-determinism is provided by ND-LISP, the dialect of LISP (see 1, 13) in which the system is written. At any point in which non-determinism is called, the previous context, in particular the data, is saved and only the new values are set in the current context. Therefore, there is no difference between the use of the traditional register table and this special list since both of them are handled in the same way. This (LIFO) list contains at any point of the process the entire left context literally represented. The augmentations, i.e. forms and actions, have been modified in order to provide a collection of specialized techniques for the parsing of a large set of linguistic phenomena. They consist in a set of operations of access and manipulation of the left context literally represented. Also the use of the push-down mechanism has been modified to some extent.

An experimental version has been implemented which runs a functional grammar a la M. Kay (12). Its basic representational unit is the attribute-value pair (functional description) where an attribute is a symbol (label) and a value is a symbol or another functional description. Thus the left context is represented in terms of attribute-value pairs and the implemented actions manipulate them. The list of the funtions in Backus notation is:

```
1.Actions
  a. <storing actions>::=
       ADD pair location
       ASSIGN label path
      <location>::= NIL | <form >
      <label> ::= any label
      <pair> ::= label value
      <value> ::= * | <form>
  b. <list manipulation>::=
       PUSH |
       POP |
       INSERT data item
      <data> ::= any data
      <item>::= <form>
2.Forms
       FIND path test level dtype |
       FINDVAL path test level dtype |
       LOCATE path test level dtype
      <path>::= <label+>
      <test >::= T | any test
      <level> ::= T | CL
      <dtype>::= T | ND | L
```

They represent the following set of accessing actions:

- starting (PUSH) and ending (POP) the storing (ADD) of the information related to a phrase/clause in a current subspace subsequently merged with the global space;
- retrieving (FIND/FINDVAL) information according to several types of

restrictions, including morphological features, syntactic idiosyncrasies, semantic features or cognitive descriptions, syntactic determination of the scope of the search, etc.;
- modifying already built structures (INSERT);
- relabelling already processed constituents (ASSIGN).

2.2. Efficiency

A relevant claim is that the data structure and the set of actions of EXAM-LC-ATN improve the computational efficiency of an ATN parser. This depends upon two peculiarities of the parser, the reduction in register setting and storage accesses and the limitation of backtrack.

In ATN, register setting is done by searching through a register table; if the called register is already present it is set to the new declared value, while if it is not, it is initialized and filled. In EXAM-LC-ATN ordinary register setting (SETR) is substituted by an operation which stores information in an already initialized memory subspace. Thus, for an equivalent grammar, the number of storage accesses in EXAM-LC-ATN is exactly the same of a traditional ATN, but no searching or initialization is performed. There is a similarity between a register initialization operation and the opening of a new memory subspace (PUSH). However, this is done only for the higher level constituents, such as S, NP, PP, etc., while in an ATN new registers are activated even for the storage of terminals or features.

Extra register setting, commonly used in an ATN to laterally pass parameters to different levels of computation from the current one (SENDR, LIFTR), is unnecessary in EXAM-LC-ATN. In fact, the required parameters are retrieved if and when they are needed from the level where they are needed. This guarantees efficiency in two ways. On one hand, the SENDR/LIFTR - GETR pairs are substituted by a single search through the left context. Within a memory subspace the search proceeds linearly as for pattern-matching. On the other hand, the overhead due to the sending or lifting of parameters which turn out to be useless at the next upper or lower level is eliminated. In conclusion, the average of storage spaces activation operations and storage accesses is in favour of EXAM-LC-ATN.

Backtrack is the typical mechanism by which non-deterministic depth first parsers like ATN manage the choice of alternatives. It consists in going back to the nearest choice point and trying the following alternative. It involves also a restoring of the input pointer to the element in the input string where it was before the current alternative was chosen, and reprocessing of the input from that point in the new alternative. Generally this mechanism is activated when some incoming piece of information signals that the chosen alternative is the wrong one. In some cases, the information give meaningfull indications about the correct alternative analysis to be chosen. In these cases backtrack can be substituted by special techniques for modifying the output of the analysis without reprocessing the involved segment of the input string. INSERT is a case of such a modification action and avoids backtrack. The full access to the left context allows for the introduction of other ways of limiting backtrack.

3. KNOWLEDGE COMPONENT

If the process of understanding is seen as a direct mapping on to a knowledge base, attention needs to be focused on those cognitive operations which store and manipulate knowledge. In particular it is necessary to individuate:

i) the formalism to represent knowledge objects in a knowledge structure which

simulates a sort of long-term memory (LTM);
ii) the actions, which manipulate objects and are triggered by linguistic facts.

3.1 A formalism for representing knowledge

The representation formalism that has been adopted for this experimental step is the one offered by SI-Nets. This formalism is realized by a Knowledge Language, KL-Magma which is a version of KL-ONE implemented in MAGMA-Lisp (1). It is similar to the one described in 2, 3, and it also takes into account the versions given in 16 and 7. As in KL-ONE, KL-Magma formal objects are Concepts, Roles and Structural Descriptions.

KL-Magma is a language isomorphic to SI-Nets formal objects, since it contains functions for creating and manipulating single objects within the network. The problem which then arises is to establish a correspondence between the objects and the operations of an SI-Net and those used by natural language.

For this purpose, a new language, KL-Conc, has been designed which manipulates the LTM (see 6, 7). The functions of this language try to simulate the conceptual operations underlying the communicative use of natural language realizing, in this sense, the interpretative aspect of many linguistic elements such as articles, adjectives, PPs, relative clauses etc. In other words, we have reduced the conceptual aspect of many linguistic units to a set of functions of a KL, which can be manipulated by the processor. Thus there are in the processor a set of functions directly affecting the knowledge stored in the LTM.
This is the list of the functions so far designed:

GEN : creates a new generic concept
NEWIND : creates a new individual concept
JUSTONE : returns the unique instance of its argument concept
ANYONE : returns anyone instance of its argument concept
SOME : returns some instances of its argument concept
ALL : returns all the instances of its argument concept
LAST : returns the last instance of its argument concept
ADD_CONFIGURATION_OF_PROPERTIES : adds a configuration of roles
TEST_CONFIGURATION_OF_PROPERTIES : tests the presence of a configuration of roles

In this way, within the processor it is possible to handle, at the same time, different classes of symbolic systems.

3.2. Hypothesis of integration

We have already stated that KL-Conc functions try to simulate conceptual operations underlying the communicative use of natural language. KL-Conc functions enable the user to individuate or to create objects, to test properties of objects etc. represented in a data base of knowledge (LTM). These conceptual operations are assumed to be analogous to those used by human beings to communicate facts. In a model of comprehension they act as the basic cognitive operations by which a message in natural language is understood.

These functions are integrated into a processor of the type described above as cognitive generalized actions for storing and manipulating fragments of structured knowledge. In this way the processing is also charged with part of the interpretation and manipulation of the representation of the world, in terms of the storing and retrieving of the information which is necessary for the completion of the analysis.

The actions of knowledge manipulation are distributed along the analysis path and are triggered as soon as cognitively relevant linguistic units occur, without waiting for syntactic structures to be completed. Thus, for instance, the string

i capelli rossi (the red hair)

is recognized by the diagram shown in Fig. 1, where the appropriate KL-Conc functions appear on the corresponding arcs and are bound to their arguments.

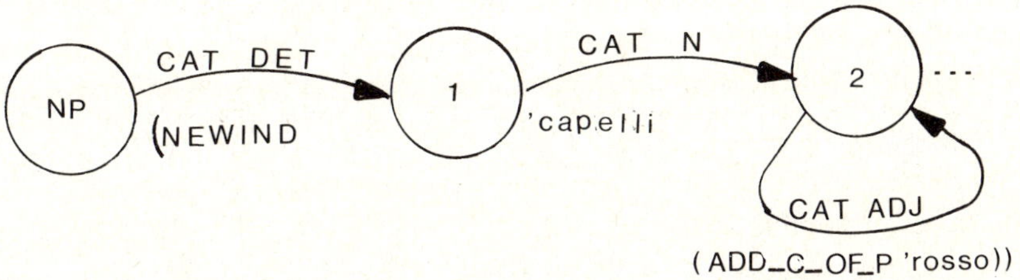

Figure 1

The processor acts as a control structure which establishes the sequence of cognitive operations in accordance with the surface distribution of linguistic units and of purely syntactic facts such as the opening, closing, and embedding of constituents. More complex clauses require more complex configurations of functions.

This model is assumed to be intuitively analogous to the human process of understanding (see 4).

4. DOMAIN-DEPENDENT SEMANTICS

On a purely theoretical ground it is desirable to account for the meaning of words and sentences as a unique abstract entity. However, in concrete communication the understanding of a sentence yields different behaviours according to the domain into which the utterance is to be situated (see 9, 10).

In order to investigate the mechanisms that induce these differences and the possibility of developing a "grammar of the semantic switching", a system has been developed at the Department of Communication, Computer, and Systems Science - Genoa. As the focus is on semantic switching, the syntactic analyser and the semantic representation have been simplified, while a conversational facility has been added to rapidly modify the semantic description of words. The system has been experimented in two practical application domains, a command language for robots and a data base query for a relational data base implemented in INGRES.

4.1. The Analyzer

The analysis of the input sentence is performed by a lexical scanner, which associates a lexical description to each word, and a variable context length LL(k) parser with a maximum k=3. It runs an attribute grammar and sentences are represented in terms of networks. They have two types of nodes, simple concept nodes, which represent words or phrases playing a definite role in the linguistic structure, and a compound nodes which are used to connect two or more concept nodes among which some (logical) coordination relation holds. Both nodes are assigned, by special arcs, a set of attributes which include lexical features of the corresponding concept; the attributes of a compound node may be 'raised' from the connected concepts or computed in connecting them. Oriented arcs connect concepts one to the other; the direction specifies the domination relation, while a label on the arc identifies the functional relation.

The grammar recognizes two basic networks (structures), the proposition and the noun group. In the proposition network the dominating position is assigned to the main verb of the sentence, i.e. the predicate which indicates the action to be performed, and the arcs connect it to its linguistic arguments such as subject, object, agent, etc. A relatively superficial case frame with some resemblances with traditional functional grammar (8) has been adopted, the effective predicate- arguments binding being performed at the semantic level. Noun groups are completely symmetric to propositions and a restricted case frame is also represented.

4.2. Semantic Interpretation

Starting from the syntactic representation sketched above, the semantic interpretation is performed by matching it towards a semantic net and activating the corresponding routines. Semantic representation is based upon the semantic networks technique, in which key-word nodes are connected by labelled arcs. By key-word a common noun is meant, which indicates some object characteristic of the application domain. Thus, in a data base query 'data base', 'relation' and 'domain' will be key-words. Also the main action verb is a key-word. Each key-word has a semantic routine associated to it; once a semantic net has been built or activated, the corresponding routines are run and they perform the required task in the defined application domain. The nodes are connected by labelled arcs which specify the type of relationship holding between key-word nodes.

The sentence

Erase the relation "subscribers" form the database "customers".

is matched against the prototypical situation 'to erase a given relation from a given data base'. The interpretation is represented in Fig. 2

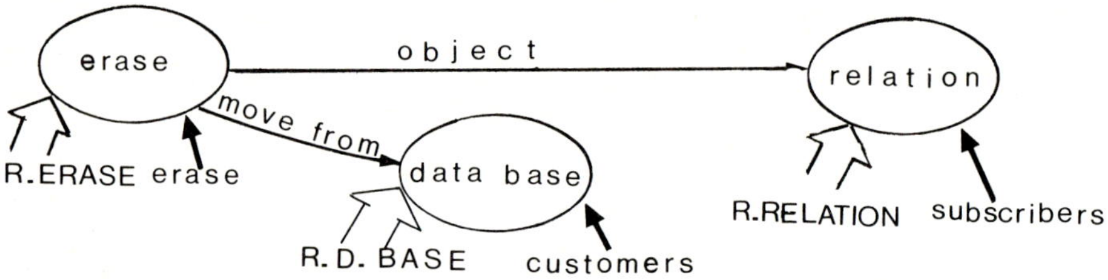

Figure 2

where the network represents the prototypical situation and the semantic routines (in capital letters), implemented in a programming language and stored elsewhere, are attached to key-words by their names. Once the sentence has been related to the corresponding prototype, the declared values are bound to the corresponding key-words and the instance-routine is finally executed.

4.3. Acquisition of semantic information

The acquisition of a network of prototypical situations (queries or commands) is done at run time during the analysis of the input sentences by a rich interaction with the system. In fact, an input sentence either fall into an already known situation or contains new unknown words. In this latter case a dialogue is started by the system in order to identify which of them are key-words and which are not. Information about lexical and syntactic features of each word are also asked. On the basis of this knowledge, as well as the syntactic functions, a new branch of the semantic network is built. The user interface has also facilities to modify part of the lexical information and to erase or insert lexical entries.

Suppose that the typical situation of Fig. 2 is already stored and, in addition, that the words 'nome' (first name) and 'cognome' (family name) have already been described as specifying the key-word 'dominio'.

The sentence

(3) cancella il nome 'Luigi' e il cognome 'Bianchi' dalla
    erase the firstname Luigi and the name Bianchi from the
    relazione abbonnati
    relation subscribers

will cause the following interaction

vuoi associare una routine semantica alla parola chiave dominio? si
dimmi quale R.DOMAIN
vuoi associare una routine semantica alla parola chiave relazione? si
dimmi quale R.RELATION
vuoi associare una routine semantica al verbo inserire? si
quale? R.ERASE

which will cause the integration to Fig.2 shown in Fig.3

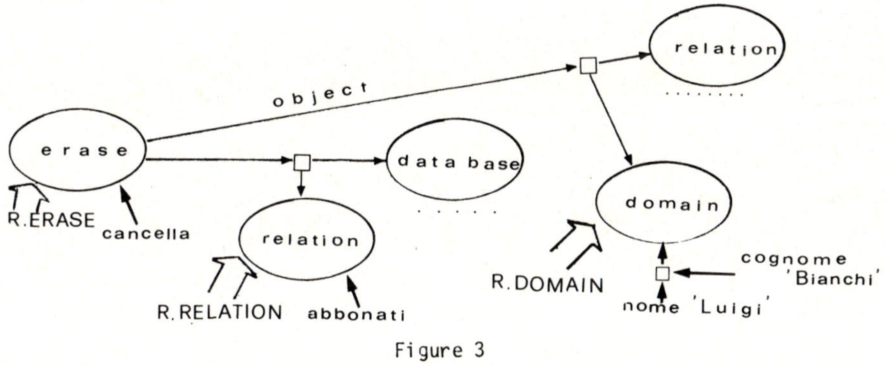

Figure 3

and the appropriate update of the database.

4.3. Perspectives

Despite strong similarities between this system and semantic grammar a' la LIFER (11), the fact that syntactic and semantic representations of a sentence are neatly separated allows for a better domain independence of the analyser and a mechanism of domain specification easier to be handled. Moreover, this system offers the concrete possibility for creating a mechanism of switching to different coexisting semantic systems, thus realizing an intuitively natural model of human comprehension.

However two major improvements to the system turned out to be useful in order to carry effective experiments. The difficulty of comparing and managing interpretations represented in code suggests their description in a high level knowledge language. Tha factoring of common parts of the semantic procedures would help in identifying the specific parts in situated utterances.

REFERENCES

[1] Asirelli, P., Lami, C., Montangero, C., Pacini, G., Simi, M., & Turini, F., MAGMA-Lisp Reference Manual (N.T. C75-13). Pisa: IEI-CNR, 1975.
[2] Brachman, R.J., Ciccarelli, E., Greenfeld, N., & Yonke, M., KLONE Reference Manual. (BBN Report 3848). Cambridge, Mass.: Bolt, Beranek and Newmann Inc., 1978.
[3] Brachman, R.J., On the Epistemological Status of Semantic Networks. In N. Findler, (Ed.), Associative Networks: Representation and Use of Knowledge by Computers. New York: Academic Press, 1979.
[4] Cappelli, A., Ferrari, G., Moretti, L., Prodanof, I., A Framework for Integrating Syntax and Semantics, in B.G. Bara & G. Guida (Eds.), Natural Language Processing, Amsterdam: North Holland, to appear.
[5] Cappelli, A., & Moretti, L., An Approach to Natural Language in the SI-Nets Paradigm. In Proceedings of the First Conference of The European Chapter of the Association for Computational Linguistics, Menlo Park, Ca., 1983.
[6] Cappelli, A., Moretti, L., Aspetti della Rappresentazione della Conoscenza in Linguistica Computazionale. Pisa: Pacini, 1983.
[7] Cappelli, A., Moretti, L., Vinchesi, C., KL-CONC: A Language for Interacting with SI-Nets. In Proceedings of the Eighth International Joint Conference on Artificial Intelligence. Los Altos, Ca.: Kaufmann, 1983.
[8] Dik S.C., Functional Grammar, Amsterdam, 1978.
[9] Ferrari G., Analisi automatica del significato, in Delmonte (ed.), Linguistica Computazionale, Padova, 1983.
[10] Ferrari G., Un confronto fra linguistica teorica e computazionale: il lessico nell'interpetazione semantica, in Omaggio a R.Ambrosini, Pisa, to appear.
[11] Hendrix G., Sacerdoti E.D., Sagalowicz D., Slocum J., Developing a Natural Language Interface to Complex Data, in ACL Transactions on Data Base Systems, vol. 3,2, pp.105-147.
[12] Kay M., Functional Grammar, in Proceedings of the 5th Meeting of the Berkeley Linguistic Society, Berkeley, 1979, pp. 142-158.
[13] Montangero C., Pacini G., Turini F., ND-LISP Reference Manual, NT C76 - 3, IEI CNR, Pisa, 1976.
[14] Porta, O., & Vinchesi, C., Un Sistema per la Rappresentazione della Conoscenza: Aspetti Concettuali e di Implementazione. Unpublished thesis, Pisa: Istituto di Scienze dell'Informazione, 1981.
[15] Prodanof, I. , Ferrari, G., Extended Access to the Left Context in an ATN Parser. In Proceedings of the First Conference of the European Chapter of the Association for Computational Linguistics, Menlo Park, Ca., 1983.

This article presents and discusses the results of three different projects which, through discussions between the authors, turned out to share several points of view on Natural Language Processing. It is, in fact, the merging of three papers presented at AIMSA84.

ARTIFICIAL INTELLIGENCE: Methodology, Systems, Applications
W. Bibel and B. Petkoff (Editors)
Elsevier Science Publishers B.V. (North-Holland)

ON EXPERIMENTAL LINGUISTIC PROCESSORS FOR MAN - COMPUTER DIALOGUE IN BULGARIAN

Radoslav Pavlov, Galia Angelova, Elena Paskaleva

Laboratory of Mathematical Linguistics
Institute of Mathematics with Computing Centre
Bulgarian Academy of Sciences
1090 Sofia, BULGARIA

The investigations are described on the creation of formal models of Bulgarian. As an instrumental tool, an automated software environment is used for programming of algorithms on the basis of the ATN formalism. As an application of the well-known approach for realization of applied dialogue systems, the currently developed experimental version of a linguistical processor for access of users - nonprogrammers to a relational data base in a language, close to the natural,is described.

In recent years, a number of investigations and program systems appeared in connection with developments in artificial intelligence which are oriented towards the realization of man - computer dialogue in a natural language. The goal of these investigations is to maximally draw the computer nearer to its end users.

In this article, the state of the art of investigations, currently being carried out by the Laboratory of Mathematical Linguistics at the Institute of Mathematics with Computing Centre, BAS, concerning the creation of systems for man-computer communication in Bulgarian language, is discussed. The investigations are described on the creation of formal models of Bulgarian oriented towards the whole of the language as it is represented in normative grammars. As an instrumental tool, an automated software environment is used for programming of algorithms on the basis of the ATN formalism. As an application of the well-known approach for realization of applied dialogue systems, the currently developed experimental version of linguistic processor for access of users - nonprogrammers to a relational data base in a language, close to the natural, is described. As a problem area of this version, the extracurricular work in Bulgaria is chosen, as it is conducted by the Union of Mathematicians in Bulgaria.

By a language, close to the natural, we shall understand a professionally oriented subset of the language of the end user, which admits without constraints:

a) morphological structures inherent of natural language;

b) syntactical structures inherent of the common stylistic layer to which belongs the language of the end user (e.g. formal, scientific and technical, economical, etc.);

c) semantical structures inherent only of the problem area and of those elements from the common vocabulary of natural language, used in it.

This definition, as well as the fact that Bulgarian has quite a developed morphology, enforce the necessity for a complete morphological analysis of the query text, which will supply information necessary in essense for building the structure of the text.

The development of the linguistic processors' morphological component is accomplished in two main directions:

a) development of procedures for a complete morphological analysis (by means of dictionaries of vocabulary and morphological elements). These procedures substantially decrease the bulk of the dictionaries of applied dialogue systems.

b) development of morphological analysis algorithms not using a vocabulary dictionary (since the latter is very much dependent on the particular problem area and in many cases will not cover newly input texts). Such algorithms automatically determine the bounds of morphological elements and are particularly useful as a supplement to the common morphological analysis procedure. This is so since they give us means for initial processing of new words, not recorded in the processor dictionary part.

Within the framework of the automatic "Text - Morphological Level" transition, and vice versa, a formal procedure for generating Bulgarian word-forms is worked out (Paskaleva (1982)) which is a necessary component of each dialogue system, since it ensures a final shaping in the generation of the system's answers. The procedure, in a detailed way, represents the data and the mechanism of Bulgarian declension and conjugation in terms of a finite automaton.

The morphological analysis results, as well as the detailed characteristics of Bulgarian lexemic and morphological elements used in the morphological synthesis, allow us to uniquely determine the content and character of this information, attached to each Bulgarian word-form, which constitutes the input characteristics to the syntactical component, necessary for the automatic building of the syntactical structure.

Besides these, a basic prerequisite for accomplishing the "morphological representation - syntactical structure" automatic transition is the choice of syntactical representation for the Bulgarian phrase.

The fact that Bulgarian is on the one hand analytical (like English) and, on the other hand, it has a relatively free word order and formally expressed links of syntactical subordination (like Russian) does not allow us to choose as dominating one of the two basic syntactical formalisms, the constituency or the dependency system. The type of syntactical structure adopted by us, even though it reflects the basic groupings into constituents, necessarily presupposes labeling of the types of links between constituents (at all levels of grouping). This labeling is done in accordance with two parameters:

a) the content of the link, i.e. its syntactico-semantic nature;
b) the direction of the link, i.e. marking a master and a slave word.

Investigation along this line is being carried out of the basic kernel structures of Bulgarian. In Bulgarian linguistics a similar investigation, directed towards computer modeling, has not been realized (excepting certain isolated studies at the Institute for Bulgarian Language of the Bulgarian Academy of Sciences).

This makes it necessary that the work on the processor syntactic component be realized in two parallel directions:
a) investigations of the Bulgarian syntax in terms of the model chosen;
b) creation of instrumental tools for processing of the derived syntactical dependences.

Recently, in the Laboratory of Mathematical Linguistics investigations are carried out in connection with the utilization of the ATN formalism for description of algorithms for analysis and synthesis of Bulgarian phrases. The aim of these investigations is on the one hand to study the applicability of the formalism for Bulgarian constructions and its eventual modification and, on the other hand, to evaluate the computing resources needed in the analysis process.

For instrumental maintainance of investigations in this field, an automated software environment is developed for programming of analysis and synthesis algorithms on the basis of the ATN formalism, including means for entry, editing, debugging and execution of programs. As a basis for this realization, a concrete version of the formalism, viz. the language for representation of linguistic knowledge, ATNL, developed at the Computing Centre of the Soviet Academy of Sciences, is chosen. The input language of the realized translator, MicroATNL, is a subset of ATNL, including its basic means for analysis and synthesis of natural language phrases (Nenova (1984)).

This realizations has two major goals:
a) the convenience of the transportability of the program system, as well as the results from translation;
b) using in the operational process of a reasonable number of computing resources.

Reaching these goals would allow on the one hand to use the implemented system on widespread personal computers for experimental investigations of language and, on the other hand, to realize on its basis linguistic processors enabling an access in a language close to the natural, to the program products with various purposes being developed at the Laboratory of Mathematical Linguistics (as learning systems, linguistic data automated retrieval systems, information-retrieval systems, etc.).

In parellel to this approach for building program tools for ATN representation of linguistic knowledge, in the Laboratory of Mathematical Linguistics investigations are carried out concerning knowledge representation in artificial intelligence. The feasibility of various knowledge representation models is studied. As a basic model for knowledge representation in a specific problem area semantic networks are chosen. Since by a problem area in artificial intelligence it is natural to understand such a part of world knowledge which is semantically connected, it might be supposed that the description in terms of a semantic network is always a connected graph. A conception of the problem area as a semantically connected part of the world is in agreement also with our intuitive notions about the way in which the reality is being segmented in order to be studied and described. On this conception, an experimental procedure for semantical analysis of user request is developed which is made use of in the developed version of a linguistic processor for access of users - nonprogrammers to a relational data base in a language close to Bulgarian (Pavlov, Angelova (1982), Pavlov, Angelova (1983)). As an input to the algorithm is treated the user request in a language close to Bulgarian, the request being to some extent pre-analysed lexically and syntactically - the syntactical dependencies in the sentence are determined (the question of structural ambiguities however is not solved). As an output, a query to the relational information retrieval system is obtained, expressed in its query language. The algorithm uses descriptions of the problem area in terms of a semantic network. It is supposed that the user puts a query, semantically "correct" with respect to the problem area, and this query is treated as a semantically connected phrase of Bulgarian; thus the internal representation of the user query is a connected subnetwork of the semantic network describing this problem area. The connectibility of the internal representation of the user request is treated as a condition on its correct internal interpretation and as a criterion on the correctness of the question being put. The algorithm for analysis and generation of queries to a relational data base performs the following basic steps:

- isolates in the internal representation of a user query all objects which are relations and attributes in the logical scheme of the superstructured generation of the data base;

- checks the correctness of the links between them and, in the case of incorrect internal representation, executes a dialogue with the user;

- makes the so called target list of the query to the data base and all conditions from the qualification of the query which are of the form:
<name_of_relation> . <name_of_attribure_of_the_relation> $\left\{\begin{matrix}<\\=\\>\end{matrix}\right\}$
<literal_value> ;

- makes these conditions from the qualification of the query which are of the form:
<name_of_relation> . <name_of_attribute_of_the_relation> $\left\{\begin{matrix}<\\=\\>\end{matrix}\right\}$
<name_of_relation> . <name_of_attribute_of_the_relation> ;

- checks the "connectedness" (in the sense of the decomposition, used in the INGRES system) of the internal representation obtained; in case of connected internal representation, a query is generated to the relational data base in accordance with the query language syntax. In case of non-connected internal structure and in accordance with the keys in the data model an attempt is made to "connect" the query in terms of the problem area description, a particular query being generated afterwards. The connection of the different parts of the query is accomplished by means of adding to the qualification of the query of conditions of the following type:
<name_of_relation> . <name_of_attribute_of_the_relation> $\left\{\begin{matrix}<\\=\\>\end{matrix}\right\}$
<name_of_relation> . <name_of_attribute_of_the_relation> .

The system ML-1, developed at the Laboratory of Mathematical Linguistics, is considered as a basic product to be experimentally superstructured with different versions of linguistic processors. ML - 1 is an information retrieval system of a relational type, being capable of carrying on correspondence. The system can be generated over different data bases. The user data are structured in an arbitrary number of relations with an arbitrary number of attributes. The physical relations are represented as index or sequential files. Since the more complex user queries are being answered by decomposing the request into simpler requests, the index organization of the data base files, having more keys, substantially reduces the time needed to answer some of the users' questions. ML - 1 disposes of a flexible language of requests from a relational type which is oriented towards users-nonprogrammers in the sense that it is enriched by elements from Bulgarian, Besides the standard operators for keeping up the data base like ADD, REPLACE, ERASE and the operator FIND for outputing references in the language of the system, ML - 1 uses the PRINT LETTER operator which allows outputing official correspondence and documents by a standard part of the text given in advance. Each particular letter is automatically edited in accordance with Bulgarian orthography by an editor developed at the Laboratory of Mathematical Linguistics. The editor formats the text in accordance with the desired length of the line, there being a possibility, if needed, to carry a word over on to the next line.

The ML - 1 system is developed for the SM-4 computer controlled by the DOS RV-B operating system (compatible with PDP 11/40 and the RSX operating system, respectively). Despite the fact that ML - 1 can be used and distributed as an autonomous product, for us it is predominantly an instrumental environment for building up of dialogue systems. Both the means for ATN representation of linguistic knowledge, and the algorithms for analysis in terms of a given semantic network, are oriented towards the creation of applied dialogue systems for conversing with computers in a language, which is close to Bulgarian. Investigations of a similar type completely unify the efforts in the Laboratory of Mathematical Linguistics spent on the diverse problems to be met in dialogue systems.

Because of the richness of expression of the relational model of data base description, as well as its flexible query language, which is easily superstructured (or changed by those working with the system), and its specific internal architecture, designed ad hoc, the ML - 1 system can be looked upon also as a basis for building of different applied systems in the field of artificial intelligence, in which it is necessary to keep up and accomplish references over a data base.A first step in this direction is the project for "intellectualization" of ML - 1 realizing an intelligent main body of an information retrieval system with built-in capabilities for autonomous reactions. The rules for description of reactions constitute a production system. The aim is to automate, in view of the user non-programmer, the activities concerned with keeping the data base integrity and with sending of special signal messages on occurence of preassigned conditions on the data in the data base.

The above-mentioned software product realizations are basically directed towards personal and mini-computers, including those manifactured in the Soviet Union and in Bulgaria.

REFERENCES:

[1]. Nenova , I., On the implementation of the ATNL-language , in: W. Bibel and B. Petkoff (eds.), Proc. of the International Conference "Artificial Intelligence Methodalogy Systems Application - AIMSA'84, Varna, Bulgaria, 17-20 September 1984 (North-Holland, Amsterdam, 1984).

[2]. Pavlov, R. and Angelova, G., On one approach for designing linguistic processors, Proc. of the Second World Conf. "Mathematics at the Service of Men", Spain, July 1982.

[3]. Pavlov, R. and Angelova, G., Linguistic processors, in: J. Denev and B. Uhrin (eds.), Proc. of the Joint Bulgarian-Hungarian Workshop on Mathematical Cybernetics and Data Processing, MTA SZTAKI Tanulmanyok 147/1983, Budapest.

[4]. Paskaleva, E., A formal procedure for Bulgarian word form generation, Proc. of COLING'82, Prague, Czechoslovakia, July 1982.

APPLICATIONS

ARTIFICIAL INTELLIGENCE: Methodology, Systems, Applications
W. Bibel and B. Petkoff (Editors)
Elsevier Science Publishers B.V. (North-Holland)

IURES: A HUMAN ENGINEERING APPROACH TO NATURAL LANGUAGE QUESTION-ANSWERING SYSTEMS

Dan Tufiş
Central Institute for
Management and Informatics
B-dul Miciurin no.8-lo
Bucharest 1
ROMANIA

Dan Cristea
Al.I.Cuza University
Str. Berthelot no.16
Iaşi
ROMANIA

The paper presents an operational natural language question-answering system. IURES is intended not only as a question-answering system, but rather as a general and flexible framework for building natural language interfaces.

INTRODUCTION

Human engineering, as a well settled research area, can be defined in terms of its objective: overcoming the comunication gaps between a human user (not a programmer specialist) and a computer. Natural language is a central research topic in artificial intelligence (AI) as well as in human engineering (HE), but although the two research areas use many theories, technics and instruments in common, one may say that they differ mainly with respect to their ultimate objective. While in the framework of AI the focus of natural language research is the understanding and modelling the fundamental aspects of human communication as well as discovering linguistic and psychologic models (implementable on a computer) able to testify the language understanding theories, the HE community approaches the topic more pragmatically, in order to develop operational natural language systems (NLS) using current technology.

A certain class of NLS was given a special attention in the HE research: the question-answering systems (QAS). The current natural language QAS that are operational and available for commercial use are, most of them, typical implementations of the pragmatic point of view of HE /1/, /2/. The priviledged status of the natural language QAS is not arbitrary. Some of the most important reasons are the following:

- the informative processes are easily modeled by a question-answering dialogue;

- the question-answering situations are the most frequently met in the interaction of naive users with computers;

- the results of linguistics are (from the computer science point of view) much better developed for interrogatives than for other types of utterances;

- the semantic interpretations of a question are drastically limited by the knowledge the answerer has about a certain domain.

In our research, we have taken into account some facts and hypotheses amoung which the most significant are given bellow:

- in a limited universe of discourse, the structures of a fair questioner utterances are, in general, predictable; we call this assumption "the non-hostile questioner" hypothesis;

- some experiments /3/ have shown that human subjects of a computer question-answering session make use of a limited vocabulary and a limited set of semantic structures; we consider this stereotipy (probably determined by the information the questioner knows or presumes he might obtain from the system) a key implementation premise in QAS design;

- in a limited universe of discourse a classical syntactic analysis is "an unaffordable luxury... The syntactic parse would take time and not yield much information about the meaning of the sentence "/4/. The semantic grammars /2/, /5/, /6/ are more appropriate in such cases.

On this background we developed a knowledge-based system for building QAS, called IURES (an acronym for I Understand and Respond by Eliminating the Syntax) entirely written in DM-LISP /8/ for the romanian minicomputers (PDP11/34 compatible). In our project we had to meet a number of requirements from which some are given bellow:

- the query language must not be (in a limited universe of discourse) too much restricted, that is an unexperienced user may ask for information in natural language without being apriori told how to ask it;

- in case a question is not syntactically perfect, but its meaning is clear, the system has to correctly process it;

- the pronominal references and ellipses (as well as other usual anaphorae) must be permitted and correctly processed;

- the answers of the system have to be (when it is the case) cooperative;

- the system has to be code independent on the universe of discourse as well as on the natural language.

SYSTEM OVERVIEW

The IURES system consists of two independent parts with clearly defined functions: the knowledge base design assistant (KBDA) and the question-answering system (QAS).

The knowledge of the system is represented in a semantic network /9/ logically divided into a conceptual (intensional) network and a referential (extensional) network.

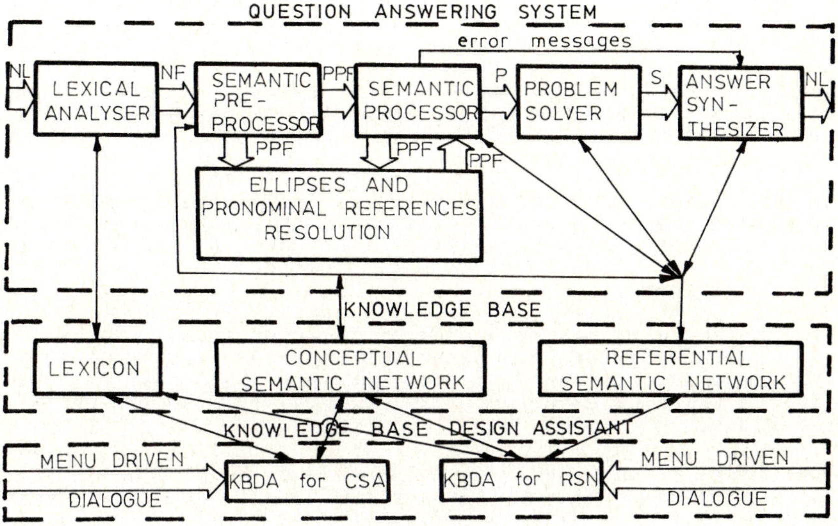

Figure 1
The architecture of IURES

The conceptual semantic network (CSN) contains information about the concepts of the domain, the properties that they may have, as well as the linguistic information needed for parsing and generation of natural language sentences.

The referential semantic network (RSN) contains knowledge about the particular objects of the domain, the properties that they really have, as well as the linguistic information needed, for instance, to recognize that a syntagm (a sequence of words) refers to a certain object, or to generate a natural language referent for a given node of the network.

Besides the domain-dependent relations, the knowledge representation model includes also the taxonomic relations (largely described and analysed in /lo/). These relations connect the RSN to CSN and make possible for network manipulator to assure the property inheritance regime when it is the case.

Because of the way we designed our representation network, the RSN consists of many partial and particular copies of the structures in the CSN.

THE KNOWLEDGE BASE DESIGN ASSISTANT

The KBDA is responsible for knowledge acquisition and manages the creation, augmentation of a knowledge base for a certain application. It also provides the user with automatic creation and augmentation of the lexicon. The knowledge acquisition is done in two distinct phases.

The first one refers to the conceptual knowledge acquisition, that is the CSN construction. Because of the absence of a metaknowledge level, the conceptual definition of a new universe of discourse is entirely under the designer responsability. As a consequence, this phase is critical with respect to the accuracy of the acquired knowledge. However, in order to restrict error possibility, the designer is allowed to define concepts only in a step-wise refinement manner. In this way it is impossible, for instance, to define an unreachable node of the network.

When defines a concept, the designer specifies its name (automatically entered (root-form) in the lexicon), its synonims or the associated syntagmae, as well as the classes in which its instances will take the values for their properties. The names of the synonims and the words appearing in a syntagm are automatically entered in the lexicon (root-form).

Besides the encoding the knowledge of the conceptual objects of a certain domain, the CSN represents the semantic grammar of the system. The relations between concepts, the way the concepts are linked reflect the semantic structures of the questions the system is able to understand.

In this phase, every concept is associated with one or more segments of text as well as with some special procedures which, in the question-answering sessions, will serve for answers generation.

The second phase of knowledge acquisition is the RSN construction. This process is entirely system controlled. In fact, the referential knowledge acquisition is an instantiation process of the conceptual structures previously defined in CSN. In this step, the designer of the application has the possibility to define synonims or syntagmae for individuals. As in the first phase, the corresponding words (root-form) are automatically entered in the lexicon.

An interesting feature of our KBDA (largely described in /11/ and /12/) is its ability to acquire procedural knowledge. This is a consequence of the augmentation of the classical semantic network model (a declarative representation scheme) with what we call the procedural nodes of the network. These special nodes are sensitive to the network navigation, that is when the network manipulator reaches such a node,the associated procedure becomes active. The result of an attached procedure activation is (or must be) always a network node. Yet the interesting aspect of such an activation is its side-effects. One may think, for instance, of changing the state of the network manipulator, or altering some global parameters, or changing the answer search strategy and so on. However, when the procedures associated to the procedural nodes are written by the designer, (as opposed to those provided by the system) we have to note that the responsability for semantic correctnes of procedures effects is entirely in charge of the designer.

There are 6 types of network functions available to the designer of an application. They allow the network designer to:

- define a node and its structure;
- update a node structure;
- delete a network node a relation between two nodes;
- list the instantiated structure of a referential node;

- define the synonims or syntagmae of an object as well as the text segments required by the answer synthesizer;
- print the semantic network.

THE QUESTION-ANSWERING SYSTEM

The QAS manages the natural language question-answering dialogue, the understanding and answering question being entirely based and dependent on the knowledge base created previously with KBDA. The natural language processing (both the analysis and the generation) is made according to the semantic grammars model. Our linguistic processor makes no use of syntactic categories such as <nominal-group> or <verb-group> or <prepositional-group>, but instead heavily relies on semantic cotegories such as <implementation-language> or <program> or <computer> etc.

The linguistic processor (see Figure 1) transforms an understood question into a labeled tree structure, processable by the problem solver. The solution offered by the problem solver as well as the error or clarification messages are converted into natural language sentences by the answer synthesizer. The main steps in a question processing are briefly given bellow.

The lexical analyser has the task to normalise the input, that is to replace the inflected words with their root forms and to drop up the unnecessary words (the words that have no network associated information). This normal form (NF in Figure 1) is further processed by the semantic preprocessor.

The semantic preprocessor firstly searches for syntagmae and in case some are found, everyone is replaced by a single network symbol. Afterwards, for each symbol in the NF, this module generates (by inspecting the semantic network) an association pair: (CONCEPT_i VALUE_i). In case the current symbol was located in CSN (hence being a concept) its corresponding pair has the form (CONCEPT_i ?) where CONCEPT_i represents the concept denoted by the symbol. In case the current symbol was located in RSN (hence being an instance of a certain concept) its corresponding pair has the form (CONCEPT_k INSTANCE_k) where INSTANCE_k represents the instance denoted by the symbol and CONCEPT_k represents the prototype of the instance. If several pairs of the same type (that is with the same concept as CARs) are neighbours, they are clashed into a single pair. A clashed pair has the following structure: (CONCEPT_k (clash-operator INSTANCE_k1 INSTANCE_k2. . . INSTANCE_kn)) where clash-operator is one of '&' (and), '!' (or), '-' (not), depending on the instances appearence in the initial question. In Figure 2 we present the equivalent pairs for some natural language strings.

```
   COBOL, ASSIRIS, FORTRAN =(LANGUAGE(& COBOL ASSIRIS FORTRAN))
 COBOL, ASSIRIS OR FORTRAN =(LANGUAGE(! COBOL ASSIRIS FORTRAN))
 NEITHER COBOL NOR FORTRAN =(LANGUAGE(- COBOL FORTRAN))
```

Figure 2
Clashed pairs

In case the question contains some pronominal references or typical linguistic constructions that generally, signal an elliptic utterance, the list of the aforementioned pairs is directed to the ellipses and pronominal references resolution module.

The anaphorae resolution is made, roughly speaking, by a selective matching of the current question structure against the structure of previous question. This module provides the QAS with the ability to correctly process a large number of anaphoric questions, as the examples in the following paragraph will show.

The next processing step is achieved by the semantic processor. This is the most important as well as time consuming processing phase of a question. The task of this module is to assign a meaning to the sequence of pairs built up by the previous processor. If the input of the semantic processor (PPF) contains contextual ambiguities (that is pairs whose concepts have more than a single meaning) this module tries to solve the indeterminations on the basis of the surrounding pairs and the list of the possible meanings of the corresponding ambiguous concepts. If it fails, a clarification dialogue is initiated, the user being asked to choose one of the system proposed interpretations. The meaning of a question (we called it a "problem" P) is a tree-like structure containing the search criteria, that will be inferentially matched by the problem solver against the RSN in order to find the answer.

In Figure 3 is given the meaning of a typical question:

"WHAT PROGRAMS FOR STATISTICS DO YOU KNOW WHICH ARE WRITTEN IN FORTRAN AND REQUIRE LESS THAN 5o KBYTES OF CORE MEMORY ?"

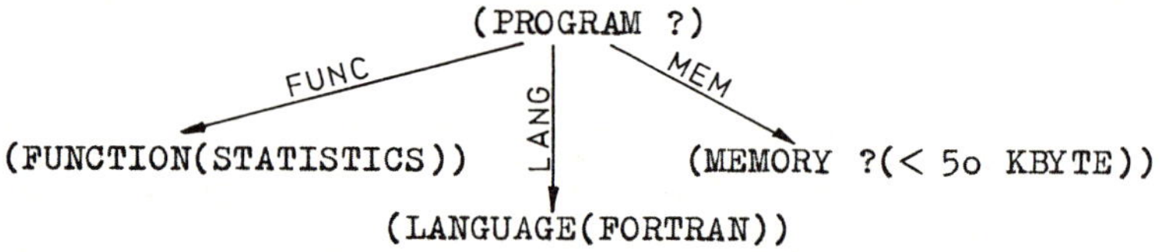

Figure 3
A typical problem

The problem solver is a deductive pattern matcher which makes intensive use of the inheritance structures of the semantic network. In searching for a solution, it is able to adopt either a forward or a backward strategy, depending on the structure of the problem. The result of the problem solver processing is a forest of tree structures, obtained from the problem structure by instantiation. The search criteria are pruned from these structures. In Figure 4 is given the solution of the previous example problem.

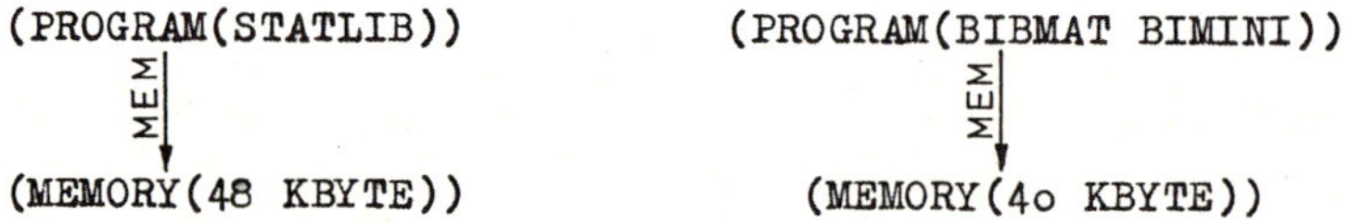

Figure 4
The solution of the problem in Figure 3

The solution of a problem is finally processed by the answer synthesizer. As we have previously shown, every concept in CSN has associated with it some segments of text. These text segments represent rude natural language strings that after processing will be assembled in natural language answers. Depending on the concepts present in the solution, the answer synthesizer will select the appropriate segments, will work out the necessary number agreements and then will join them as a natural language answer. For instance in case of the solution in Figure 4, the answer synthesizer will choose from the concept PROGRAM of the first tree the text "THE PROGRAM", leave it in the singular, from the concept MEMORY the text "REQUIRE" which is transformed in "REQUIRES", add the value 48 and the plural for **kbyte** "KBYTES" and finish verbalisation of the first part of the solution. Similarly will be processed the next tree, such as finally the answer will be the following:

"THE PROGRAM STATLIB REQUIRES 48 KBYTES AND THE PROGRAMS BIBMAT AND BIMINI REQUIRE 4o KBYTES"

EXAMPLES

In this section we provide a few examples fron one of IURES implementations. These examples represent an almost mot-á-mot translation of the original questions, which were entered the computer in romanian language.

Q: IN WHAT LANGUAGE IS IMPLEMENTED BIBMAT ?
A: THE PROGRAM BIBMAT IS WRITTEN IN FORTRAN

Q: WHERE WAS IT MADE ?
A: THE PROGRAM BIBMAT WAS IMPLEMENTED AT CENTRAL INSTITUTE FOR MANAGEMENT AND INFORMATICS

Q: WHAT IS ITS ADDRESS ?
A: CENTRAL INSTITUTE FOR MANAGEMENT AND INFORMATICS HAS THE FOLLOWING ADDRESS: B-DUL MICIURIN NO:8-1o TOWN BUCHAREST

Q: I SHOULD LIKE TO KNOW THE CATALOGUE NUMBER, THE LANGUAGE AND THE AUTHOR FOR STATLIB !
A: THE PROGRAM STATLIB WAS IMPLEMENTED BY CENTRAL INSTITUTE FOR MANAGEMENT AND INFORMATICS , IS WRITTEN IN FORTRAN AND HAS THE CODE A-o1-1-76F

CONCLUSIONS

IURES was used to implement 3 experimental natural language question-answering systems in 3 different universes of discourse:
- an information retrieval system for National Program Library;
- a computer instruction aid for geography education;
- a tutorial system for prognosis elaboration.

Another application, a decision support system, which is now in progress, faced us with some limitations of IURES system. These limitations reffer mainly to the QAS module. More precisely, the difficulties appear in the problem solving phase. We are confronted with requirements for hypothetical inferences ("what would be the productivity ratio of the plant if the personnel would be enlarged with 15%"), planning capabilities ("how could I achieve a minimum supplying cost for building materials"), uncertain knowledge manipulation and so on. In this context, a new linguistic competence feature was claimed for, namely processing ability for fuzzy natural language expressions. Although, at present, IURES does not cope with these problems, they being current research topics, the three aforementioned systems, implemented with IURES were successfully experienced. The results can be summarized as follows:

- the unfamiliar users of IURES were able to interact with computer in natural language, without an apriori training;
- the building of a new dedicated QAS appears to be a quite non-technical activity, and when we say this, we rely on the fact that two non-LISP programmers, with a little assistance from us, succeded in implementing an interesting application (the 3-rd one);
- although only romanian language was used in our experiments, we do not see any reason why IURES would not work with any other language;
- the cooperativeness of the system is satisfactory.

REFERENCES

/1/ Gevarter, W.B., An Overview of Computer-Based Natural Language Processing, NBSIR 83-2687, U.S. Department of Commerce (april 1983).

/2/ Barr, A. and Feigenbaum, E.(eds.), The Handbook of Artificial Intelligence 2, (HeurisTech Press-W.Kaufmann, inc., 1982).

/3/ Thompson, B.H., Linguistic Analysis of Natural Language Communication with Computers, Proceedings of the 8-th International Conference on Computational Linguistics, COLING (198o).

/4/ Brown, J.S., and Burton, R.R., Multiple Representation of Knowledge for Tutorial Reasoning, in: Bobrow, D.G. and Collings A. (eds.), Representation and Understanding (Academic-Press, New-York, 1975).

/5/ Bonnet, A., Les grammaires sémantiques, outil puissant pour interroger les bases de donnée en langage naturel, RAIRO Jrnl. 2 (198o).

/6/ Hendrix, G.G., The LIFER manual. A Guide to Building Practical Natural Language Interfaces, Technical Note 138, Artificial Intelligence Center (february 1977).

/7/ Barr, A. and Feigenbaum, E. (eds.), The Handbook of Artificial Intelligence 1, (HeurisTech Press-W.Kaufmann, inc., 1982).

/8/ Sotirescu, D. and Stefănescu, M., Report on the Interactive Programming System DM-LISP, Polytechnic Institute from Bucharest (july 198o).

/9/ Findler, N.(ed.), Associative Networks. Representation and Use of Knowledge by Computers (Academic-Press, New-York, 1979).

/1o/ Tufiş, D. and Cristea, D., The IURES system. Conceptual Knowledge: representation and acquisition. User manual, CIMI, (august 1984).

/11/ Tufiş, D. and Cristea, D., The IURES system. Referential Knowledge: representation and acquisition. User manual, CIMI, (may 1984).

/12/ Tufiş, D., Knowledge representation in the SDLR system, Research Report, Research Division (august 1982).

/13/ Tufiş, D. and Cristea, D., How to Solve it with IURES, CIMI, (october 1984).

ARTIFICIAL INTELLIGENCE: Methodology, Systems, Applications
W. Bibel and B. Petkoff (Editors)
Elsevier Science Publishers B.V. (North-Holland)

ON AN IMPLEMENTATION OF THE ATNL-LANGUAGE

Irina Nenova

Laboratory of Mathematical Linguistics
Institute of Mathematics
Bulgarian Academy of Sciences
Sofia, Bulgaria

This paper describes the implementation of MicroATNL, a language programming tool for algorithms developed on the basis of the ATN-formalism. The implementation represents a basic component of a portable ATN programming environment including program input, editing, debugging and execution facilities.

INTRODUCTION

The Augmented Transition Network formalism (ATN-grammars) was developed by William Woods at the beginning of the 70's as a comfortable tool for describing natural language phrase analysis (1). In the last decade it has actively been used as a formalism for linguistic knowledge representation for natural language communication with computers. Most of the natural language systems of the American firm BBN (LUNAR is the best known) are based on the ATN-formalism and its modifications. It has also been used for the development of systems like PLANES (2), HAM-RPM, DIALOG, DILOS, etc. A number of different versions, the so called ATN-dialects, are developed using the basic formalism and are usually implemented in the LISP language.

Recently, at the Laboratory of Mathematical Linguistics, research is focused on the use of the ATN-formalism for describing algorithms for the analysis of Bulgarian natural language phrases. It has two basic purposes - to clear the applicability of the formalism to Bulgarian natural language constructions, and to provide an estimation of computational resources used in the process of analysis. An automated programming environment for ATN based algorithms supporting research in this area is being developed. It includes program input, editing, debugging and execution facilities. A concrete version of the formalism, the linguistic knowledge representation language ATNL (3), has been chosen for the implementation.

Two basic aims are pursued by the implementation:
a) portability of the programming system and the translation results
b) use of reasonable amount of computational resources in the operation mode.
Accomplishing the above stated aims would allow to run the implementation on personal computers, available in Bulgaria, for experimental research in the natural language field. On the other hand, it would provide a possibility on the basis of the implementation for developing natural language man-computer communication systems (4).

This paper describes the main component of the programming environment which ensures the translation and execution of MicroATNL-programs. The input language of the developed translator - MicroATNL - comprises a subset of ATNL including its basic tools for analysis of natural language phrases.

MICROATNL-PROGRAM

Any MicroATNL program comprises three components - a program identification division, a vocabulary description division and a network description division. The first two divisions are optional while the last is mandatory. The program identification division has a commentary status and serves for fixing information about the developed program. The vocabulary description division includes descriptions of vocabulary of the processed natural language phrases. The algorithms for analysis of the input and synthesis of the output phrases are described in the network description division. The descriptions in the last two divisions follow the classical traditions of the ATN-formalism. The vocabularies comprise a set of vocabulary entries which include a key for searching in the vocabulary and a list of feature-value pairs. The network is described as a set of "bushes" every one of which corresponds to a particular state of the network and comprises the arcs which come out of it. Four types of arcs - TST, CAT, PUSH and POP - are used in ATNL and MicroATNL. A condition allowing transition through the arc in case of validity and a set of actions which are carried out while passing through the corresponding arc are associated with every arc. The transition along the TST and CAT arcs is associated only with the validity of the condition and the current token of the input string. The PUSH-arc serves as a recursive call to a subgraph of the network while the POP-arc serves for returning from this subgraph in the call point. The state which a given arc leads to is registered with the help of a final action. The intermediate results in the process of analysis/synthesis are obtained with the help of the so called forms and stored in system and user registers. The filling up of the registers is done by the actions while their values are used for the computation of forms and conditions. This short description of the pecularities of the ATN-formalism and the MicroATNL-programs allows us to discuss some basic decisions which were made for the MicroATNL implementation.

IMPLEMENTATION PRINCIPLES

Three approaches are used generally for the implementation of programming languages: translation of the source program into a machine code program, direct interpretation of the source program and translation into an intermediate representation with a following interpretation. The data structures used in the MicroATNL-programs and their processing algorithms do not correspond to the traditional computer architectures which makes the translation into machine code difficult and uncomfortable. Such an implementation would, in addition, be totally unportable. An implementation basd on a full interpretation could be portable if the tolls for its realization are chosen accordingly, but it would require a considerable amount of computational resources which would make its use on personal computers currently popular in Bulgaria impossible. If a suitable intermediate representation and tools for the implementation are chosen the approach based on translation of the program into an intermediate representation with a following interpretation of this representation ensures portability of the implementation and use of reasonable amount of computational resources for making it operational. Following the above stated aims, we have chosen such an implementation scheme and used the high level language Pascal which is available in compatible versions for a large class of computers (fig.1).

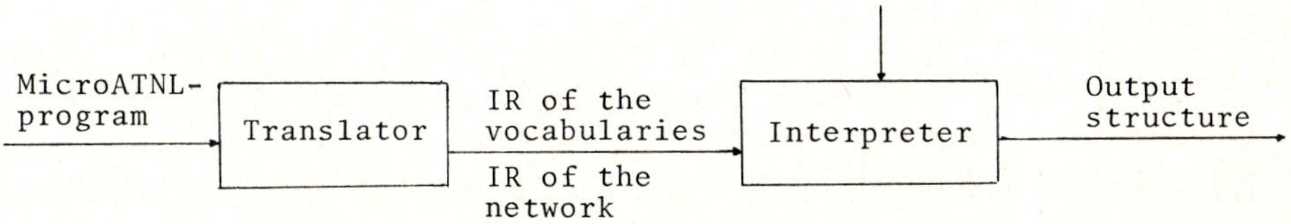

Figure 1

INTERNAL REPRESENTATION

The choice of the internal representation of the program is a basic factor determining the portability and the amount of computational resources for those systems which are based on translation followed by interpretation. The MicroATNL-program representation that was selected allows its effective interpretation. It is not bound to a particular computer architecture or a given data representation on external data carriers. During the design process a possibility for augmentation of the language without changing the already implemented constructions has been pursued. In addition, the internal representation is close enough to the source program which enables a relatively easy implementation of a system for a dynamic program debugging in terms of the source language.

In the computer storage the MicroATNL-program is represented as a set of several types of interconnected data structures. The vocabulary representation (fig.2) has a different particular realization in accordance with their size.

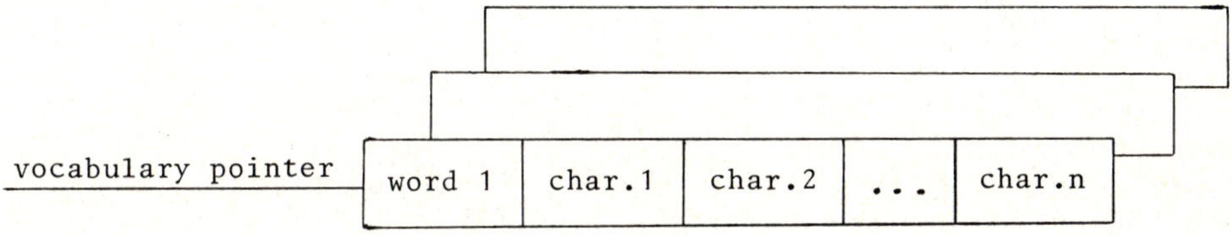

Figure 2

The network representation we use (fig.3) ensures direct access to any particular state.

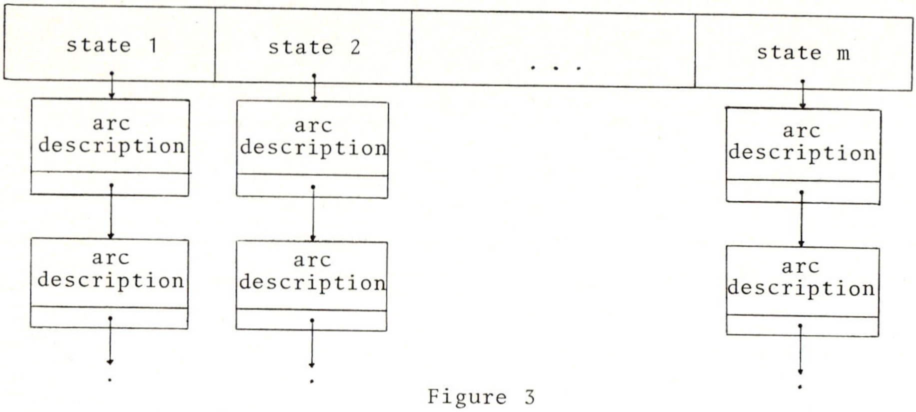

Figure 3

The arc description has different structure depending on the arc type (fig.4 - a,b,c,d). The fields describing conditions and actions are pointers to the representation of forms and conditions as tree-like structures.

a)

TST	condition	actions	next state

b)

CAT	vocabulary set of words	condition	actions	next state

c)

PUSH	initial state of the subgraph	condition	actions	next state

d)

POP	condition	form

Figure 4

TRANSLATION

The internal representation of the MicroATNL-program is in fact representation of the source program in a form that allows effective interpretation. The process of translation into internal representation is reduced to building a table of symbols of the source program followed by encoding the identifiers in accordance with the functions they execute and subsequent representation of the program in the form of the above described data structures. The formation of an interpretable representation is carried out simultaneously with the syntactic and semantic analysis of the program. The syntax of MicroATNL is described by a LL(1)-grammar. It is a one-pass syntactic analysis that is carried out by the recursive descent method. The internal representation obtained in this way could be directly interpreted or stored linearly on an external data carrier and used for subsequent interpretation. A possibility for output of the symbol table in the appropriate form is also given, thus enabling a dynamic control of the program in terms of the source language, by feeding the symbol table together with the internal representation into interpreter.

INTERPRETATION

In the process of interpretation of the program represented in this way, it is necessary to develop special environment for supporting the realization of the specific recursive calls in the language and the realization of the register operations that constitute a specific form of stack storage. The registers are considered as partitioned in layers any of which corresponds to one level of recursive calls and is represented as a list-like stack containing register-value pairs. A stack of pointers to the beginning of every layer is supported. This implementation scheme allows the transmission of information between the different recursive levels and operation with variables of stack character which are not common of the classical programming languages. At the same time the necessity for fixing an upper bound of the register number is eliminated and the copying of their contents is made easy in the process of backtracking.

The interpretation of the MicroATNL-program is carried out by a program interpreter and in the cases when it is not immediately after the translation it begins with the input of the internal representation into the main memory and its reverse transformation from linear into standard form. The separate arcs, conditions, actions and forms are interpreted by corresponding procedures in correspondence with their semantics. The execution of some basic actions like selection of the next arc, organization of the interpretation of the next bush, preparation of the registers for a call to a subgraph and memorizing the information necessary for coming back from it etc. is provided by special procedures.

REFERENCES

(1) Woods, W.A., Transition Network Grammars for Natural Language Analysis, Communications of the ACM, 13 (1970) 591-606.

(2) Finin, T.W., The Planes Interpreter and Compiler for Augmented Transition Network Grammars, in: Bolc, L. (ed.), The Design of Interpreters, Compilers, and Editors for Augmented Transition Networks (Springer-Verlag, 1983).

(3) Khoroshevsky, V.F., ATNL-Machine - Software and Hardware, Proc. of First Symp. IFAC and IFIP on AI, Leningrad, USSR, 4-6 oct. (1983).

(4) Pavlov, R., Angelova, G. and Paskaleva, E., On experimental linguistic processors for man-computer dialogue in Bulgarian language, in: Bibel, W. and Petkoff, B. (eds.), Artificial Intelligence Methodology Systems Applications (North-Holland, Amsterdam, 1984).

ARTIFICIAL INTELLIGENCE: Methodology, Systems, Applications
W. Bibel and B. Petkoff (Editors)
Elsevier Science Publishers B.V. (North-Holland)

EXPERIMENTAL SYSTEM FOR RECOGNITION AND CLASSIFICATION OF ARCHAEOLOGICAL CERAMICS

Valentin Tomov, Stephen Sahno

Institute of Mathematics with Computer Center
Bulgarian Academy of Sciences
Sofia, Bulgaria

The system is intended for partial automation (by means of a computer) of archaeological finds data processing. The basic problem consists in recognition of the type of a concrete ceramic article and classification of this article to already studied ceramic culture. This problem is solved by means of a production system. The user's language, the rule description language, the rule interpreter (written in LISP), and a set of production rules, representing a description of a concrete domain, are considered.

GENERAL FORMULATION OF THE PROBLEM AND THE APPROACH TO ITS SOLVING

The experimental system for recognition and classification of archaeological ceramics (ESAC) represents a simple rule-based system. The problem this system solves is making an inference about the belonging (or not belonging) of a concrete ceramic article to a definite ceramic culture. This problem is solved by a production system on the basis of the description of the ceramic culture and the data of the concrete ceramic article. The main components of the production system (Fig. 1) are the following: a rule description language, a rule interpreter, and a set of production rules.

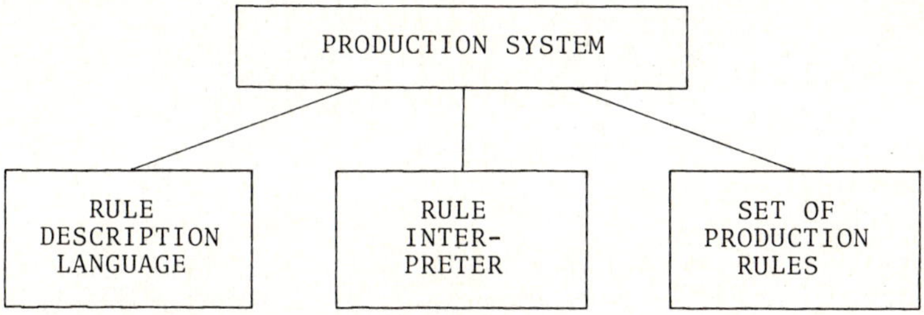

Figure 1
The main components of the production system

The rule interpreter carries out the problem-solving process. The rules are given according to the syntax of the rule description language and represent in essence a base of archaeological knowledge about the ceramic culture..

An advantage of the adopted approach is the clear separation of general knowledge about the domain (the production rules) from the information about the current problem (the input data) and the procedures that apply the general knowledge to the problem (the rule interpreter). This partitioning makes possible the gradual refinement and extension of the knowledge about the concerned domain through improving old rules and adding new ones. It is possible to use the rule interpreter for problem solving in another domain, where knowledge can be represented in a similar way. The same knowledge can be used for different purposes, such as teaching the user. In conformity with the set new purpose this can be achieved by additionally extension of the interpreter's capabilities and adding new specific rules.

A dialogue regime for working with the experimental system is adopted. The communication with the system is performed by means of a terminal, from where the user enters the information about the current problem. He participates in the dialogue mainly through answers to questions asked by the computer. This way of working extricates the user from the necessity of keeping in mind all properties of the ceramic article, which possibly will be of significance during the problem solving.

The data representation in the system is simplified. The main construction being used for description of the ceramic articles (both within the data base and within production rules) is the following: (<ELEMENT> <PROPERTY> <VALUE>)
The contents of the concepts "element", "property", and "value" is concretized depending on the application domain. In the instance of the archaeological ceramics ELEMENT means mainly a part of a ceramic article, for example: body, neck, handle, etc. PROPERTY stands for the various properties of the elements, for example: shape, opening, orientation, etc. The values corresponding to these properties are designated by VALUE, for example: globular, wide, horisontal, etc. The description of a concrete ceramic article represents a list of descriptors of the above type, for example VESSEL1:
(body shape biconic) (neck length tall)...(bottom profile concave).

PRODUCTION RULES

They represent archaeological knowledge about a concrete ceramic culture and some common archaeological knowledge. Rules, describing the ceramic culture, are formed on the basis of the ceramic articles classifier elaborated by archaeologists. The classifier represents a description of the basic types of ceramic articles through combinations of values of the articles' properties (shape, proportions, decoration, composition of the pottery clay, etc.).

A simple language for rule description was developed. Its syntax is shown in Fig. 2.

```
<rule>::=<name>: IF <condition> THEN <consequence>
<name>::=<identifier>
<condition>::=<conjunction>|<disjunction>|<subcondition>
<conjunction>::=<operand>AND<operand>|<conjunction>AND<operand>
<disjunction>::=<operand>OR<operand>|<disjunction>OR<operand>
<subcondition>::=<descriptor>|<identifier>
<consequence>::=<subcondition>|(<consequence><subcondition>)
<operand>::=<subcondition>|(<condition>)
<descriptor>::= (<element><property><value>)
```

Figure 2
The syntax of the rule description language

The condition-part of a rule can be a logical expression of descriptors combined by the connectives AND and OR, for example

```
R9: IF (neck length low) AND (neck shape bent) THEN B5
R10: IF (neck length tall) AND ((neck shape funnel-wide) OR
                                ((neck shape cylindric) AND
                                 (rim deflection broad) )) THEN BT
```

The condition of a rule can contain also a subcondition defined by another rule, for example:

```
R11: IF (neck opening normal) AND B5 THEN B6
```

The archaeological knowledge thus represented is entered into the knowledge base of the system. Then the rules are compiled and a set of production rules directly usable by the rule interpreter is generated. These rules are used mainly during the inference process, when a conclusion is drawn about the type of the ceramic article and its belonging to the ceramic culture.

The set of rules forms a tree-like structure (search tree) of the type AND/OR. The tip nodes usualy represent descriptors (see Fig.2), i.e. they specify values of properties of the ceramic articles and their elements. The nodes of upper levels are defined by means of the rules.
A set of rules, describing Moravian archaeological ceramic articles and serving as an experimental example, was formed on the basis of the classifier ellaborated by archaeologists. This set of rules represents a description of the various types and variations of pots and beakers according to the classifier given in {6}.

Archaeological knowledge about the prehistoric ceramic culture described in {5} is being formalized with the help of experts-archaeologists.

GENERAL FUNCTIONAL STRUCTURE OF THE EXPERIMENTAL SYSTEM

The specific functions being performed by separate parts of ESAC differentiate four subsystems in it: subsystem for knowledge base maintenance, subsystem for data base maintenance, rule interpreter, and subsystem for user's language processing (Fig. 3).

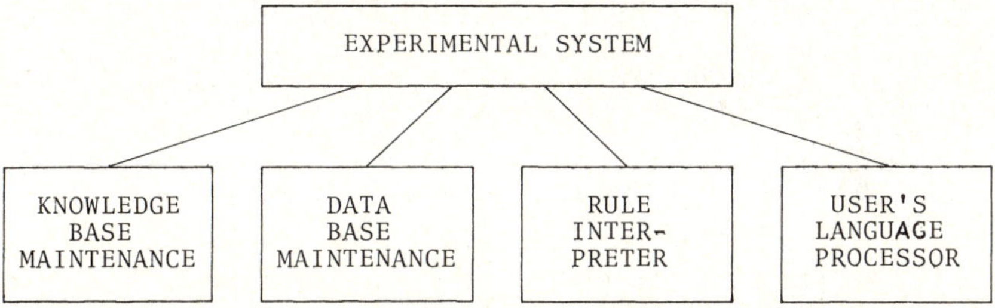

Figure 3
General functional scheme of the system

The subsystem for knowledge base maintenance performs operations connected with the entering of the set of rules and its extension and modification. Syntax analysis and control are done during the initial entering of the rules. Then they are compiled into an internal representation which is more convenient for processing.

The search tree relevant to the set of rules is created at this stage also.

The subsystem for data base maintenance performs operations connected mainly with the data entering and the modification of the data base. A simplified logical structure of the data base was fixed on. The sections within the base contain successions of objects' descriptions.

The inference process is the basic activity of the rule interpreter. At this stage of the problem solving the set of rules is used with the purpose of generalizing the evidence about the concrete ceramic article and, if it is possible, classifying this article to the ceramic culture concerned. The generalization is carried out by means of a forward chaining (data-driven reasoning) through the search tree. Each node of a higher level is considered as a hypothesis, whose verification is done by means of a backward chaining (goal-driven reasoning). This verification is accomplished in order to be found a combination of characteristic features of the ceramic article, which confirms the hypothesis.

The control strategy implemented in the rule interpreter is of mixed type. Due to the procedural character of the control problem, this strategy is described semiformally in a dialect of PASCAL (Fig. 4).

```
Procedure CONTROL;
Repeat Data input;
       Call DOWNTOP to make conclusions;
       Call NEW-HYP to generate a hypothesis H;
       Call TOPDOWN(H) to try to confirm H
until  the problem is solved
```

Figure 4
The control strategy implemented in the rule interpreter

The rule interpreter carries out inductive and deductive analyses. The procedures for data-driven (DOWNTOP) and goal-driven (TOPDOWN) reasoning are used alternatively (Fig. 5).

```
Procedure DOWNTOP;
Select a set A of applicable rules;
While A is nonempty and the problem is unsolved
do begin
   Choose a rule R from A;
   Apply R; Update the data;
   Select a set A of applicable rules
   end

Procedure TOPDOWN(H);
Select a set D of rules that determine H;
If D is empty then ask the user about H else
   while H is not confirmed and D is not empty
   do begin
      Choose a rule R from D;
      If the condition C of R is not examined
         then call TOPDOWN(C);
      If C is satisfied then apply R
      end
```

Figure 5

The procedures for data-driven
and goal-driven reasoning

The rule interpreter's algorithm includes in essence recursive processing of list structures. That is why LISP was chosen as an implementation language. The inference procedure (and all subsystems of ESAC) represents a set of LISP functions.

The available in LISP means of property lists (P-lists) processing were used in the rule interpreter's implementation. The constructing and the use of the working list structures maintained by the interpreter are fulfilled by means of P-lists. These structures contain the internal representations of the data about the current problem, the search tree, the intermediate hypotheses and conclusions, etc.

During the analysis a P-list is constructed for each element of the object. The properties of the elements serve as indicators. The corresponding values of the properties are associated with these indicators.

A P-list is constructed for each node of the search tree also. In this case lists containing information about the parent nodes and the successor nodes are associated with the indicators.

Further information, obtained during the inference process or by means of the user's answers, is collected in P-lists also. Thus the second examination of a hypothesis and asking the user one and the same question are avoided.

The communication means are in conformity with the dialogue style of working with the system. A convenient user's language was developed. It includes: operators with a simple structure, which are used for data entering by the user; questions asked by the system, related to definite properties of the ceramic article concerned or the choice of a definite regime of working; user's commands, which specify the operations the system has to perform.

The commands in the user's language can be divided according to their functional destination into several groups: operations with the knowledge base (rule entering and modification); operations with the data base (data entering and updating); data processing; etc. The destination of some of the main commands is briefly described below.
By means of the command ENTER-PROPERTIES the specialist-archaeologist can enter into the knowledge base a set of properties, which are basic for a definite ceramic culture. Questions about the values to be associated with these properties are asked by the system during the examination of a ceramic article or to facilitate the entering of an object's description by the user.

The command READ-RULES is used when a set of rules has to be read from the knowledge base.

The description of an object, that will be examined, is entered by the user with the help of the command ENTER-OBJECT. Through answers to questions asked by the system the user enters the values of the basic properties first. This directs the rule interpreter (in the beginning of the tree searching) to the rules, related to the concrete object concerned, and thus hastens the analysis. After that another characteristic features of the object may be entered. During the execution of this command each question is asked about a value to be associated with a property of an element. Thus new descriptor is created and added to the description of the ceramic article.

The user may enter a hypothesis and test its truth by means of the command HYPOTHESIS. In this case the rule interpreter carries out top-down analysis. The goal-driven control strategy is used only

(Fig. 5, Procedure TOPDOWN). This command enable the skilled and well-experienced user to formulate at will appropriate hypotheses, whose confirmation directs the course of the further analysis. Thus he may conduce to a possible shortening of the analysis.

On typing the command CLASSIFY an attempt is made to be classified the entered object to one of the archaeological cultures known to the system. The mixed control strategy (Fig. 4) is used during the analysis.

The following example illustrates the manner, in which the dialogue is usually carried on, and the use of some of the basic commands of the user's language. Each line typed by the user is marked by the symbol "→".

```
→(START)

 the system is started
 if you wish to survey the commands enter (H)
 enclose each command in round brackets
 next command ?

→(READ-RULES)

 for which ceramic culture ?

→MORAVIAN

 Moravian ceramics set of rules is read
 next command ?

→(ENTER-OBJECT)

 data entering
 values of the basic properties:

 body shape ?
 (globular/1 oval/2 biconic/3)
→1

 neck length ?
 (low/1 tall/2)
→2
 ...
 other descriptors ?
 enter a triple (element property value)
 or E to end

→(NECK SHAPE BENT)
 ...
 next command ?

→(HYPOTHESIS)

 attempt to be confirmed the hypothesis:

→BEAKER-TYPE2
 ...
 the hypothesis is not confirmed
 next command ?

→(CLASSIFY)
 ...
 ? is this true:
 (neck opening wide)
 (yes/Y no/N unknown/X)
→Y
 ...
```

the concerned object is classified to:

culture Moravian ceramics
class Beaker
type Beaker-type1

next command ?
...

Further development of the user's language and enlargement of the rule interpreter's capabilities are envisaged.

Means of explanation are being developed also. The system will give explanations about the problem-solving process. These means will enable the user to follow up the steps of the problem solving. Thus the user will be able to estimate the trustworthiness of the analysis. These means will supply references to the archaeological literature also.

IMPLEMENTATION AND EXPERIMENTS

The experimental system for recognition and classification of archaeological ceramics is developed in the Institute of Mathematics with Computer Center at the Bulgarian Academy of Sciences.

The archaeological part of the research is done by a group of archaeologists led by professor doctor of historical sciences Henrieta Todorova of the Archaeological Institute with Museum at the Bulgarian Academy of Sciences.

The system is programmed in STANDARD LISP {7}.
The system SINTER {3,4} for interactive work on EC1040 computer in the Computer Center of the Institute of Mathematics with Computer Center at the Bulgarian Academy of Sciences is used. The present version of the experimental system uses 120 K bytes of the main storage.

More complex real examples from Moravian archaeological ceramics {6} were examined with the help of the experimental system. The obtained results witness the system's capabilities for correct classification.

In conclusion, we should like to note that the adopted approach to automated solving of the archaeological problem concerned proved perspective. The results, obtained from the experiments with the system, in our opinion are hopeful. This stimulates us to continue its developing further. We hope that the experimental system, completely developed, could be used as an assistant of the archaeologists in their research work.

The authors wish to acknowledge the competent consultations on the archaeological problems and the help, they received from professor doctor of historical sciences Henrieta Todorova of the Archaeological Institute with Museum at the Bulgarian Academy of Sciences.

We are grateful for the support, given by the Institute of Mathematics with Computer Center at the Bulgarian Academy of Sciences and the Archaeological Institute with Museum at the Bulgarian Academy of Sciences during the realization of this interdisciplinary research work.

REFERENCES

{1} Winston, P.H., Artificial Intelligence (Addison-Wesley Publishing Company, Inc., 1977).

{2} Winston, P.H., Horn, B.K.P., LISP (Addison-Wesley Publishing Company, Inc., 1981).

{3} SINTER - General Manual (Interprogramma, Sofia, 1979).

{4} SINTER - User's Guide (Interprogramma, Sofia, 1979).

{5} Todorova, H., Vasilev, V., Ianushevich, Z., Kovacheva, M., Valev, P., Fouilles et recherches VIII - Ovcharovo (Institut d'archeologie et musee, Sofia, 1983).

{6} Podborsky, V., Kazdova, E., Kosturik, P., Weber, Z., Numericky Kod Moravske Malovane Keramiky - Problemy Deskripce v Archeologii (Universita J.E. Purkyne, Brno, 1977).

{7} Fitch, J., Manual for STANDARD LISP on IBM System 360 and 370 (University of Utah, Symbolic Computation Group, Technical Report No. TR-6, August 1978).

{8} Duda, R.O., Gaschnig, J.G., Knowledge-Based Expert Systems Come of Age, Byte Publication, September 1981.

{9} Stefik, M., Aikins, J., Balzer, R., Benoit, J., Birnbaum, L., Hayes-Roth, F., Sacerdoti, E., The Organization of Expert Systems - a Tutorial, Artificial Intelligence, vol.18, No.2, 135-173, March 1982.

{10} Nilsson, N.J., Principles of Artificial Intelligence (Springer-Verlag, 1982).

{11} Buchanan, B.G., Duda, R.O., Principles of Rule-Based Expert Systems, in: Yovits, M.C.(ed.), Advances in Computers - Vol.22 (Academic Press, 1983).

{12} Hayes-Roth, F., Waterman, D.A., Lenat, D.B. (eds.), Building Expert Systems (Addison-Wesley Publishing Company, Inc., 1983).

ARTIFICIAL INTELLIGENCE: Methodology, Systems, Applications
W. Bibel and B. Petkoff (Editors)
Elsevier Science Publishers B.V. (North-Holland)

AN EXPERT SYSTEM IN RELIABILITY - STRUCTURE AND KNOWLEDGE REPRESENTATION

Ivan Popchev, Neli Zlatareva
Institute of Industrial Cybernetics & Robotics
Bulgarian Academy of Sciences
Acad.G.Bonchev Str. Bl.2, 1113 Sofia, Bulgaria

INTRODUCTION

Various interpretings and definitions of the term "Expert System" (ES) exist and they reflect to a great extent the meaning which the different authors asume in it. For this reason quite differing in respect of function, structure and abilities systems are termed "expert".Because of the forementioned we would like to formulate in prior the main principles of the base on which ES in reliability is elaborated, namely:

- ES is a system based on knowledge;
- ES implements human experience and skill;
- ES has the ability to explain in "human" way the decision made;
- ES is a personal adaptive device, totally subordinated to the idea of user's convenience.

The principle for "personality" determines to the utmost extent the technical base on which ES in reliability is implemented, and namely personal computer, which in this respect supposes a number of peculiarities in the very organization of the system.

ES in reliability (ESYRE) is designed for the broadest specter of users (scientists, engineers, constructors, specialists in the field of standartization of reliability, students, etc.). The main group of problems defining it problem domain at the present stage are as follows:

(i) general problems of reliability;

(ii) choice of criteria and standartizing the level of reliability of products;

(iii) computation, evaluation, optimisation, forecasting and modelling of reliability.

A large number of these questions concern the unformal problems of reliability. For example, the choice of index for reliability is connected with a very serious and difficult question - what should one expect from the computation of this index and advantage as well.

The standartizing of the index is natural extansion of the question and is still a pure intuitive process, and the real-time possibility to be controlled is training of the reliability intuition.
Besides the specialists' experience and intuition of long years duration, the solving of the forementioned problems requires knowledge on Theory of Probabilities, mathematical statistics and standard base. All this makes the problems mentioned extremely difficult which in this respect leads to their neglecting and conscious sliding over by the persons concerned.
These problems and difficutlties demanded the creation of ES in reliability which is designed to solve the conflict which has occurred - "necessity-possibility".

SYSTEM ARCHITECTURE

The particular requirements demanded from the ESYRE impose certain chainges in the traditional ES structure. They are connected with some additional functions, implemented in the following subsystems:
(i) "Help" - supplies the user with teaching information on reliability, probability and mathematical statistics;
(ii) "Data base (DB) interconnecting and supporting subsystem" - executes fast and competent answer of questions connected with the necessary information searched (standards, methodologies, etc.);
(iii) "Computation subsystem" - supporting the computing moduls library for different reliability calculations;
(iv) "Disketts' library control subsystem" - allows a practically unlimited system extension.
The structural scheme of ESYRE is given on fig. 1. It is designed for an 8-bytes personal computer and this defines the peculiarities of its software implementation, connected first of all with the main memory restrictions. The main principles of this implementation are:
1. Hierarchical problem solution;
2. Modularity and extendability;
3. Transparency.

KNOWLEDGE REPRESENTATION

It is evident from fig. 1 that the knowledge base (KB) and DB support different system functions. Besides them, a scenario library and a computing moduls library exist. These so different in contents system information level elements could be described by frames. Two kinds of frames - describing and computing - exist in the system. The first one supposes the searching procedures activation in the DB or a new information input, while the second one is connected with the application programs or computation moduls running.

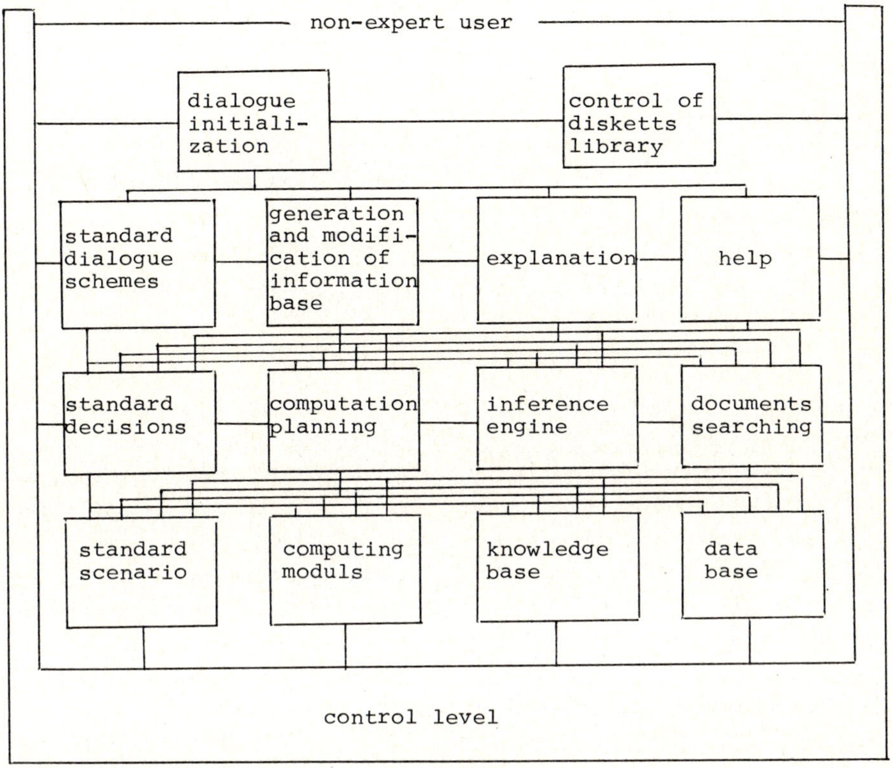

Fig. 1

The procedure knowledge in the system, defining to a great extent the inference engine, are represented by production rules of the following type:

IF: (antecedent 1)

...

(antecedent n)

THEN: (consequence 1) with certainty factor CF_1

...

(consequence m) with certainty factor CF_1

The production rule is an "antecedent-consequent" or a "situation - decision" pair, in the left hand side of which a list of antecedents or conditions is contained. The set of antecedents is termed a situation, i.e. $\sum_{i=1}^{n}$ antecedents$_i$=situation$_j$. When a particular situation is considered, it is necessary to take in account inaccuracies in its description because of the different subjective factors, acting on its formulation from an expert's or user's side. A certainty factor (CF), receiving values in the closed interval (0, 1), which evaluates the expert's or user's certainty in the existance of a given fact could be used for this purpose.

So, the system procedure knowledge could be described by a table (table 1) and a production rule illustrating its content is given on table 2.

Table 1

antecedent 1	CF_{11}	CF_{12}	...	CF_{1i}
antecedent 2	CF_{21}	CF_{22}	...	CF_{2i}
...				
antecedent n	CF_{n1}	CF_{n2}	...	CF_{ni}
consequent 1	B_{11}	B_{12}	...	B_{1i}
consequent 2	B_{21}	B_{22}	...	B_{2i}
...				
consequent m	B_{m1}	B_{m2}	...	B_{mi}

Table 2

1.The device is serially produced	1	1	0	1
2.A continuous observation is performed in exploitation	1	1	0.5	0.9
3.The stochastic variable distribution law is a normal-logarithmic one	1	1	0.5	1
4.An observation (N,U,N) plan is used	1	1	1	0
5.No failure has occurred during a fixed period of time t	1	0	1	0
1.The observation results for a fixed period of time t are satisfactory	1	0	0.2	0.3
2.The probability requirements for a reliable work are not confirmed and it is necessary to perform additional observation	0	1	0.2	0.3
3.It is necessary to perform additional investigation			0.6	0.4

The upper left part of the table contains a set of antecedents, which is called basic. The antecedents are simple (describing facts contained in KB), which are not subjected to changes in the solution process, or complicated (they themselves could be a solution of a subproblem). Complicated antecedents also represent production rules containing in their left side a corresponding set of premises whose check has been performed and has been given a positive result before the corresponding solution in the higher level production rule (in forward chaining), or the opposite - to evaluate the certainty of a given antecedent, it is necessary to evaluate the corresponding conditions of a lower level production (in backward chaining). The hierarchy, thus obtained, leads to some main advantages:

(i) it is possible to classify by importance the problems solved by ES a priori;

(ii) complex problems' solution could be represented as a sum of its subproblems' solutions;

(iii) it is presumed that when one makes a decision he has not more than six to eight problem's domain components in mind.

The hierarchy introduced allows the system to take into account human abilities in the process of description. When the system can not solve the problem set with the knowledge available, it asks the user one or several questions, in order to add to the KB the missing facts necessary to make a decision. A part of the system's decisions are connected with an additional dialogue initialization.

It is possible to generate decisions, which demand further concretization. For this purpose there exist the so called "help tables", which have a structure analogic to that of the basic table, but the search space is restricted in the frame-work of the decision already made.

The hierarchy of tables describing the system procedure knowledge and interaction among them are given on fig. 2.

It is evident that the pure knowledge declarative elements are not present in the system. This leads to a greater homogeneity of the information contained in the KB and DB and makes the searching much more easier.

INTERACTION WITH THE SYSTEM

The interaction with the system is performed by means of the developed network of subsystems and moduls menu. It is based on the idea of adaptive dialogue and includes tools such as "initiative variation", "special user's reactions", "portion information input and output", "predeveloped scenarioes" and provides the user with developing of scenarioes by himself.

CONCLUSION

ESYRE is designed for a personal computer which makes it accesible, convenient and cheap. Other advantages are:

(i) extendability - this is an open system which can include other tools and reliability knowledge;

(ii) computation abilities make much more easier the work of users in the field of computing and evaluating the reliability, collecting and reliability information processing;

(iii) the information searching abilities provide the user with necessary documents or references from DB;

(iv) system teaching abilities;

(v) ability for preliminary analysis of the effectiveness by introducing a new device;

(vi) the optimisation abilities allow optimisation of the reliability requirements towards the device, which are defined in the initial stage of the design.

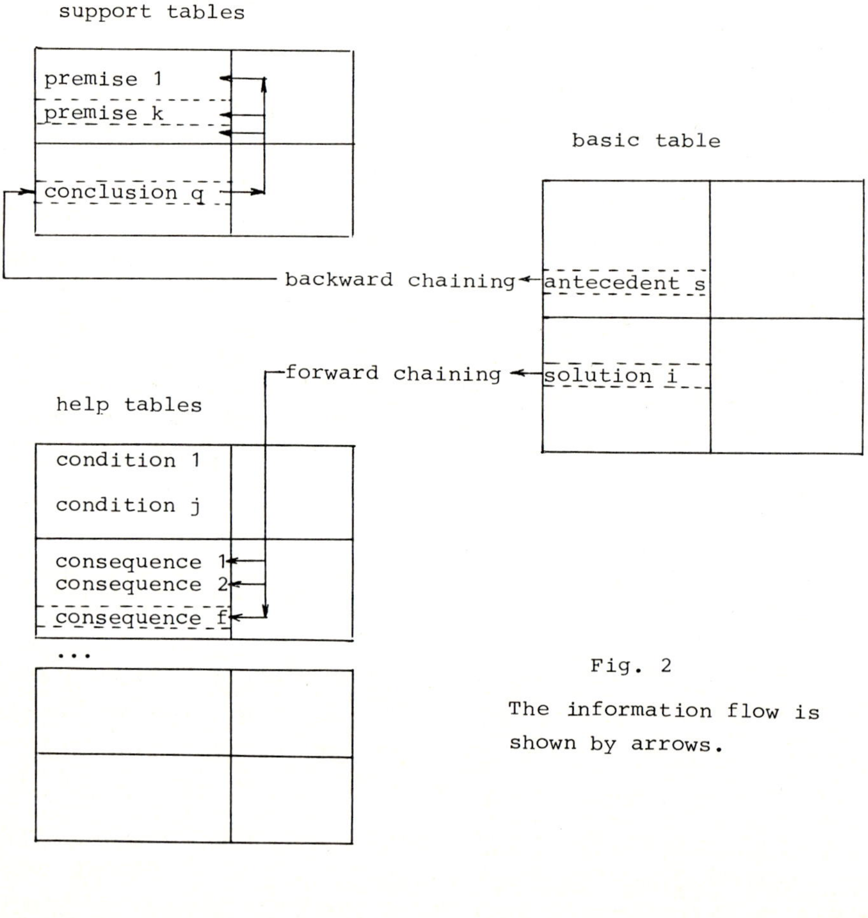

Fig. 2

The information flow is shown by arrows.

REFERENCES

/1/ F.Hayes-Roth, Waterman, D.Lenat, Building expert systems, vol. 1 (Addison-Wesley Publishing Comp., 1983).

/2/ B.Buchanan, R.Duda, Principles of Rule-Based Expert Systems, Advances in Computers, vol.22, 1983.

/3/ V.M.Briabrin, Adaptive dialogue base of personal calculation system, Linguistic processors and knowledge representation, Novosibirsk, USSR, 1981 (in Russian).

ARTIFICIAL INTELLIGENCE: Methodology, Systems, Applications
W. Bibel and B. Petkoff (Editors)
Elsevier Science Publishers B.V. (North-Holland)

SPACE REPRESENTATION AND OBJECT POSITIONING IN NATURAL LANGUAGE DRIVEN IMAGE GENERATION

Mauro Di Manzo, Fausto Giunchiglia and Ernesto Pino

Department of Communication, Computer and System Sciences
University of Genoa
Viale Opera Pia 11A, 16145 Genoa, Italy

In this paper we are faced with the problem of positioning obiects in an inferred environment described by means of natural sentences. More specifically, after a brief discussion of the overall system (NALIG: Natural Language driven Image Generator) we will focus on the coding of the meaning of some spatial prepositions in a "suitable" space representation.

INTRODUCTION

The development of an artificial system, able to draw a scene on a screen described by means of natural language sentences, is a challenging matter which requires a lot of sophisticated knowledge. Such a system must be coped with all the problems deriving from the seemingly infinite complexity of the real world and the intrinsic ambiguity of any natural language sentence. On the other hand this is an interesting domain because of all the potential applications which can be, for instance, the interaction with a "domestic" robot (that is a robot able to work in a not specially organized environment) or the implementation of "non-standard" user-friendly CAD systems.

The aim of this paper is to describe some aspects of a system, currently under development in our department, called NALIG (NALIG is an achronym which stands for NAtural Language driven Image Generator) [6]. More specifically, after a brief discussion of the overall system the paper is focused on the coding of the meaning of some prepositions in a "suitable" space representation approaching the problems related to the actual placement of objects in the "imagined" scene.

SYSTEM OVERVIEW

A basic feature of NALIG conceptual processing is the extensive use of qualitative reasoning even if the final positioning step must handle numerical values. This approach, which is becoming popular in AI research [7,8,4], allows us to reach meaningful conclusions even with ill-defined problems for which very few information is available and which are therefore hard to formalize using quantitative models. Qualitative reasoning in NALIG is faced with problems such as preposition disambiguation, environment setting, instantiation of unmentioned objects, naive positioning strategies and stableness analysis and so on [3,2,1,6], solving also the "frame of reference problem" [3], discussed in the literature [10]. In some sense the qualitative modules of NALIG are a model of human common sense reasoning about objects and space; however the basic semantics of all symbolic relations relies on a deeper quantitative model of space in which geometrical and physical properties of objects are taken into account. For example, hearing the sentence "Put the water on the table", it is possible to infer, on the basis of a qualitative taxonomy of objects, that "on" means, in this case, that the table gives support to the water by means of physical contact on a nearly horizontal surface [3] (we call this relation H_CONTACT(a,b)); moreover, it is possible to infer that the water is contained by some suitable container, as a bottle [1], and this container is likely to stay in a upright position on the table [2]. However, there is no way, through a purely syntactic approach, to know if there is enough available free space on the table top to allocate the bottle of water. More generally, a mere syntactic problem solving technique has been discarded both because is too far from human reasoning and because (when it is possible to adopt this solution) there are problems of consistency and execution time in the definition (and eventually modification) of such a formal system [11]. Quantitative checks may cause the rejections of some solution inferred by qualitative rules and the activation of a new reasoning cycle; they are the main tool to ensure the global consistency of the "imagined" scene, solving problems which are typically related to the coordination of several pieces of knowledge (deriving, for instance, from several sentences), as the problem of unique object identification, approached in the next section.

The modules handling the two kinds of reasoning, qualitative and quantitative, are interfaced in NALIG through a semantic network, which is built by qualitative modules by translating the input sentences into a set of unambiguous syntactic relations. This network is the starting point for all the conceptual activities involved in the evaluation of the actual object positions.

COMMON SENSE REASONING AND SPACE REPRESENTATION

The actual position of an object in the space is defined by the coordinates of its barycentre and by the orientation of its own coordinate axes with respect to the current reference system. Unfortunately, this information is rarely available in the semantic network. In fact even if it is unambiguous, it carries no more information than the input sentences do, and it is rather uncommon to hear that "the chair is on the floor, the coordinates of its barycentre are (x*,y*,z*), it is upright and turned 25 degrees with respect to the window". A strong specification like the previous one is (rarely) used, only when a precise position is needed, in order to achieve a very specific goal. Even if NALIG is able to represent and manipulate it, this is only a particular case, in a sense out of the scope of the work (NALIG has been developed to deal with common sense reasoning, that is with everyday descriptions of space).

Therefore, the assignment of positions to objects is the result of an inferential activity which looks for the most "reasonable" coordinate values taking into account several sources of knowledge, as the semantics of the stated relationships, the geometrical and physical properties of the involved objects, naive representations of the most common physical processes, likely organizations in a given environment, object functionality, overall scene consistency and so on. Let's consider, for instance, the conceptualization H_CONTACT(chair, table). The semantics of the relation H_CONTACT allows to consider only the table top surface. On this surface the shape of the supported object (i.e. the chair) may put constraints on the set of allowable positions. First of all, the analysis of equilibrium positions (it is made in NALIG by means of proper qualitative rules [2]) usually selects only a subset of stable orientations: a chair on a table may be upright, lying or reverse, as shown in fig.1. Each equilibrium position limits the rotational degrees of freedom and may put constraints also on the allowable values of the barycentre coordinates. For example, in the upright position the chair may be everywhere on the table top, but, in the reverse position, movements of the barycentre are limited within a relatively narrow strip along the table border. Since in most cases object shapes and dimensions are not explicitly stated, they are extracted from a knowledge base which contains an object dictionary where object structures are modeled by means of generalized cylinders [9]. The result of this step is the codification of the meaning of a single conceptualization as the set of all the possible positions of the barycentre (the Variation Volume VV) and the related object orientations (the Orientation Set OS) for each equilibrium position and assumed shape and dimension

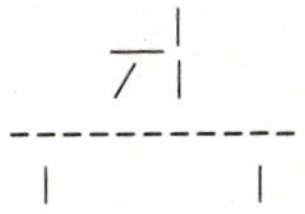

fig.1a: upright position

fig.1b: reverse position

fig.1c: lying positions

of the object. In some cases functional considerations or other sources of knowledge may give preference to some specific positions within the set of those allowed by the equilibrium analysis. For instance, thinking of "a cigarette on the ashtray" we probably imagine it lying on the ashtray border in a nearly axial orientation. Therefore, a kind of likelihood may be introduced in the definition of VV and OS (they are actually modeled as fuzzy functions [12]).

At this step, the system knowledge about the scene, deriving from the relation H_CONTACT(chair, table) is represented by the graph in fig.2 where one (or more) VV and related OS are associated to the labeled arc.

```
                H_CONTACT
 ----------                ----------
 | table1 |<------------| chair2 |
 ----------                ----------
```

fig.2: reference graph

Suppose now to add a new piece of knowledge, consisting of the relation H_CONTACT(ashtray, table); the resulting reference graph is shown in fig.3.

```
        H_CONTACT                          H_CONTACT
 --------          --------      --------          ----------
 |table1|<---------|chair2|      |table3|<--------|ashtray4|
 --------          --------      --------          ----------
```

fig.3: multiple reference graph

The question is: can nodes "table1" and "table3" be merged in a single one? In other words, how many objects of the same type must be supported to exist, due to the multiple references in the semantic network? Sometimes the semantic network itself gives evidence for separate instantiations. For example, the relations H_CONTACT(book, table) and H_CONTACT(book, shelf) strongly suggest the existence of two distinct books, since the two reference objects, a table and a shelf, cannot be merged. If it were analyzed in terms of VV's and OS's (but in this case it is not necessary), the hypothesis of a single book could be rejected considering that the table and the shelf cannot share the same space for not embedding reasons, and therefore the two books have not overlapping VV's (of course, we should not exclude the very special case of a book supported partially by a table and partially by a shelf, but we can tolerate that NALIG gets confused of such a situation, taking in account that, maybe, the same would be for a human listener). However, conclusions at a symbolic level must be drawn in a very conservative way, because the criterion of "different objects if linked to different references" does not always work. If we say, for instance, "the book on the table" and "the book near the window", the second relation S_NEAR(book, window) gives not enough information to reject the hypothesis of the same book in both phrases. Only a particular class of relationships (we call them "strong relationships" [5]), which are directly related to a supporting action involving physical contact, can give this kind of evidence. The VV's and OS's associated to strong relationships have a distinguished role in the final object positioning, so we call them "ground" functions; we will discuss later the role of "weak" relationships.

If the attempt to reason at the symbolic level fails, a deeper analysis of VV's and OS's functions must be performed. First of all, NALIG completes (if not completed) the reference graph in fig.3 making some standard inferences based on the criterion that all not-flying objects must be supported by other objects. Therefore, a chain of strong relations is created using default knowledge about the most typical positions of objects in a given environment. Assuming that the current environment is a dining-room the most likely inference is "table on the floor", so the graph in fig.4 is obtained. This inferential mechanism can be recursively activated until an already existing object is referred to or an object is instantiated, which delimits the current environment (for a deeper discussion of the use of this mechanism and the environment setting, which is out of the scope of this paper, see [5,3]. Now table1 and table3 have a common reference, so their ground VV's and OS's can be compared in order to find reasons to accept or reject expectations. Expectations are raised, in this case, by default knowledge about the typical organization of dining-rooms, where is unlikely to find a large number of tables (a restaurant environment will raise different expectations); hence the expected number of tables is one. The VV's of table1 and table3 fully overlap; infact, since there are no explicit constraints in the semantic network, the previous discussed quantitative inferential mechanism assumes that they can be placed everywhere on the floor. Therefore there is no evidence against the expectation of a single table and two nodes, table1 and table3, can be merged in the final graph of fig.5. Let's turn now to weak relationships. If the information "the ashtray is near the centre of the table" is added to the graph in fig.5, the weak relation H_NEAR(ashtray, centre(table)) simply results in modifying the profile of the ground VV function which describes the position of the ashtray relatively to the table referred to by the strong relation H_CONTACT. On the other hand, if we say that "the ashtray is near

```
           H_CONTACT --------  H_CONTACT   --------
 --------   ---------|table1|<-------------|chair2|
 |floor5|<-|         --------              --------
 --------   |        --------             ----------
            ---------|table3|<------------|ashtray4|
           H_CONTACT -------- H_CONTACT   ----------
```

fig.4: final graph

```
          H_CONTACT          H_CONTACT   --------
--------           --------   ---------|chair2|
|floor5|<----------|table1|<---|        --------
--------           --------    |        ----------
                               ---------|ashtray4|
                     H_CONTACT   ----------
```

fig.5: final graph

the chair", we establish a new weak connection between the chair and the ashtray (see fig.6) which does not modify their ground VV's (the chair and the ashtray may be still everywhere on the table). Of course all this discussion is valid if the two ashtrays can be merged in one, how this is made with weak relationships is beyond the aims of this paper and it is not discussed. However, when a specific position will be chosen for the chair, then the ground VV's of the ashtray will be influenced by this weak link. This fact may be described associating to the link H_NEAR an influence VV and the related OS which represent a codification of the relative positions of the chair and the ashtray. Influence VV's and OS's describe only explicitly stated (or inferred) influences. Implicit influences may rise from the interference among the ground VV's of several objects linked to the same reference object through strong relations.

The solution of influences into ground functions is the last step of the process of object positioning. Unfortunately this evaluation can be made in a rather simple way only simulating a specific placement. The resulting representation must be kept distinct from the reference graph, which describes the actual knowledge of the system, otherwise the inference activities were easily misleaded. During the positioning step, each object corresponding to a node of the reference graph with one or more entering are associated to strong relationships represent a local context for the linked objects. Since positioning is a simulation of a specific placement, general repositioning activities in a local context may be stated by events which are not necessarily connected to deep modification of the reference graph. A first, obvious source of repositioning requests is the lack of place while attempting to add a new object

```
          H_CONTACT          H_CONTACT   --------
--------           --------   ---------|chair2|<----
|floor5|<----------|table1|<---|        --------    |
--------           --------    |        ----------  | H_NEAR
                               ---------|ashtray4|---
                     H_CONTACT   ----------
```

fig.6: final merged graph

in a local context. This situation, however, is quite easy to detect, but there are other, more subtle situations. Consider, for instance, the scene in fig.1b: if we add the information that the table is near the wall, in contact with it may be there is no longer place to put the chair in that position. These events are quite common with objects which define an open contact as tables, shelves and so on. When these objects are used as local context, the available space may depend on their relationships with other surrounding objects; weak relationships are the most relevant, in this case. Object allocation is performed by NALIG in a rather naive way. Each object is described in the knowledge base at several levels of details. The first level consists of the Occupancy Volume (OV), which represents the minimal parallelepiped in which the object itself can be embedded. Using OV's to check not embedding conditions, NALIG tries to allocate objects according to the maximum values of their VV's and OS's functions; preference in picking objects is given to objects with selective ground VV's, large OV's and high number of links in the reference graph. If the available space is not enough, before starting a replacement procedure an attempt is made to use "holes" in OV's, looking at more detailed object descriptions. Object transparency with respect to specific relationships is also taken in account in some simple cases [3]. Space occupancy is described by means of oct-trees which allow an easy verification of not embedding conditions through a comparison of the state of discrete pieces of space.

CONCLUSIONS

Presently NALIG is at a rather advanced state of development. All the theory concerning the symbolic model has been developed while some problems of how to use efficiently (from a conceptual point of view) fuzzy logic exist.

The first implementation was totally written in FRANZ LISP while the current second version is in C_PROLOG and C (the first language has been used to implement the reasoning parts, the second to implement the computational ones). All the system has been developed under UNIX Operating System on a DEC VAX 11/750.

REFERENCES

1. Adorni, G., DiManzo, M., and Giunchiglia, F., "Some Basic Mechanisms for Common Sense Reasoning about Stories Environments", Proc. 8th. IJCAI (Karlsruhe, West Germany, August 1983).

2. Adorni, G., DiManzo, M., and Giunchiglia, F., "Natural Language Driven Image Generator", Proc. 10th. COLING (Stanford, California, July 1984).

3. Bona,R. and Giunchiglia,F., "The semantics of some spatial prepositions: the Italian case as an example", DIST, Technical Report, Genoa, Italy (January 1983).

4. DeKleer, J., "Qualitative and Quantitative Reasoning in classical Mechanics", in: Winston, P.H. and Brown, R.H. (eds.), Artificial Intelligence: an MIT Perspective, Volume I (The MIT Press, Cambridge, 1979).

5. DiManzo, M. and Giunchiglia, F., "Reasoning about scene descriptions in natural language", Tech. Rep. DIST; University of Genoa, Genoa, Italy. (1984).

6. DiManzo, M. and Giunchiglia, F., "A Primer of NALIG", DIST, Technical Report, University of Genoa, Genoa, Italy (in progress).

7. Forbus,K., "Qualitative Reasoning about Space and Motion", in: Gentner, D. and Stevens, A. (eds.), Mental Models (LEA 1983).

8. Hayes,P.J., "The Naive Physics Manifesto", in: Mitchie, D. (ed.), Expert Systems in the Micro Electronic Age (Edimburgh University Press, Edimburgh, 1979).

9. Marr, D. and Nishihara, H.K., "Representation and recognition of the spatial organisation of 3-D shapes", Proc. R. Soc. London D. (1978).

10. Sondheimer,N.K., "Spatial Reference and Natural Language Machine Control", Int. Jrnl. Man-Machine Studies 8 (1976). 329-336

11. Waltz,.D.L. and Boggess, L., "Visual Analog Representations for Natural language Understanding", Proc. 6th. IJCAI (Tokyo, Japan, August 1979).

12. Zadeh, L.A., "The concept of a Linguistic Variable and its Application to Approximate Reasoning I-II-III.", Information Sciences 8-9-10 (1975). 199-249, 301-357, 43-80

ARTIFICIAL INTELLIGENCE: Methodology, Systems, Applications
W. Bibel and B. Petkoff (Editors)
Elsevier Science Publishers B.V. (North-Holland)

3-D OBJECT RECOGNITION - PREPROCESSING OF STRUCTURALLY ILLUMINATED SCENES AND INTERPRETATION WITH LOCATION CONSTRAINTS

G.Stanke and P.Florath

Dept. of Artificial Intelligence
Central Institute of Cybernetics and Information Processes
Academy of Sciene of the GDR, DDR - 1086 Berlin, Kurstr.33

An approach to 3-D object recognition in scenes illuminated by structured light, especially by light grids is described. Special problems arising by preprocessing of grid like patterns are discussed and algorithms are proposed to overcome these problems. The procedure of object identification and determination of location bases on 3-D object models and models of object location constraints. A decision tree classifier and a generalized Hough-transform are used. Algorithmic components of latter method regarded here in some detail are 3-D orientation estimation and restriction verification using local features.

INTRODUCTION

In various technical and scientific fields vision systems can be successful used for inspection and supervision tasks. Especially the fast progress of industrial automation and the wide spreaded usage of robots demand the application of vision systems. 2-D vision systems have reached a stage of industrial application /1/. Their drawback is they are able to process 2-D information only. Some tasks in industry (e.g. assembly) demand 3-D information about the scene. 3-D recognition systems include algorithms to determine identity and location (i.e. position and orientation) of objects in space. The basic problem is only projections of 3-D objects are available. In order to overcome this difficulty many approaches extract so called 2-1/2-D information from the scene (e.g. distances, orientation of surface points). Using this information as well as a priori information they try to describe the 3-D reality /2,3,4,5,6,7/. Common features are: to apply techniques allowing to excerp 2-1/2-D information in a more simple way (e.g. structured light) and to use a-priori information as much as possible (e.g. location constraints, object models). Already existing techniques for processing images of 2-D scenes (e.g. filtering, window operators) and existing special hardware solutions are commonly used.

Our approach partly outlined in this paper is characterised by the following features (cf./8/):

- the scene is illuminated by grid like patterns
- the object models are known
- there is a priori knowledge about the location constraints
- the method of interpretation is independent of actual preprocessing and segmentation
- data driven and modell driven procedures are combined.

The following paragraph contents a remark to data acquisition. Further details and a systematisation can be found in /9/. Then the basic problems for preprocessing of grid illuminated scenes are formulated, algorithms to tackle these problems are described in detail and illustrated by examples. The last paragraph outlines steps of interpretation.

3-D DATA ACQUISITION

For 3-D vision systems the data acquisition is the best investigated field. A broad spectrum of physical principles can be used. Basic problems are:

- to limit the acquisition time to a resonable range of one second
- to determine the correspondence between image and scene.

Two approaches seem to be most prosperious. Both use triangulation for range measuring. The first one /10/ reaches a high scanning rate using a position sensitive photodetector which is synchronized with a laser light point projector. The second one uses the projection of special light patterns onto the scene. Thus the image must be taken only once and a coded grid can make more simply the recovery of corresponding points into the scene and the image /9/. For both approaches well known processing techiques for binary and grey level images are applicable (a distance picture produced by a laser range finder can be handled as a grey level picture). Of course, special algorithmic steps have to be added. These two approaches will probably lead to the first successful solutions for 3-D vision systems.

For certain classes of recognition tasks approaches on the base of numerically controlled shutters in the light beam /11/ or on the base of Moire-techniques can lead to solutions economically usable.

PREPROCESSING OF GRID LIKE PATTERNS

The reconstructed grid pattern contains the information about the region boundaries and surface properties. In our approach the first step of preprocessing of images resulting by acquisition of grid illuminated scenes is to reconstruct the ideal distorted grid pattern. The detection of shadows is also treated on the level of preprocessing. Grid reconstruction and shadow detection will be described in detail for binary pictures. For effective and simple hardware solutions we use as much as possible 3x3 window operators. All basic steps can be extended for grey level pictures.

In general, preprocessing, especialy thinning by 3x3 window operators is well investigated /12,13/. Usually large sets of crossings (as in grid like patterns) does not apear as basic elements in images. Exceptions are e.g. chinese characters and so called polygon maps. For chinese characters in /14/ a well working procedure is proposed. Larger windows then 3x3 have been used. For polygon maps an interesting approach can be found in /15/. In each pass of a quasi parallel thinning procedure pixels are relabelled in the range from 0 to 3 where the figures have a special meaning. The information is coded in a non-binary picture.

We divide the process of skeletonizing into four steps. First a restoration procedure filles in gaps of one pixel breadth in the contour. Second smoothing removes single pixels and one pixel from end of tails (of one pixel breadth). Next a contour of one pixel breadth is removed in alternating stripping from left/top and from bottom/right. The result is a line structure of one pixel thickness. It is not the skeleton for pixels in the surrounding of crossings. A last step gives the real skeleton.

The basic problem in skeletonizing grid like patterns is that crossings in the original picture are split into two branchings in the skeleton (see fig.1).

```
xxxx       xxxx        -x--        --x-
 xxxxx   xxxxx          -xx--    --xx-
  xxxxxxxxxx             --x----x--     - eliminated pixel
    xxxxxx                 -BxxB-
  xxxxxxxxxx             --x----x--     B - branching point
 xxxxx   xxxxx          -xx--    --xx-
xxxx       xxxx        -x--        --x-
```

Figure 1 Original image Sleletonized image

This splitting by thinning cannot be avoided on the level of window masks of resonable size. Therefore we have to carry out a special procedure for estimation of the location of the crossing points.

For estimation of crossing points (by merging of branching points) distances between adjoining branching points as well as angles between branches must be taken into account. To use distances between branchings for estimation of the crossing points is not sufficient. The distance from a branching to its actual neighbour (e.g. d(C1,C2) in fig.2) can be larger then the distance to a "foreign" branching (e.g. d(C1,C1a) or d(C1,C1b) in fig.2).

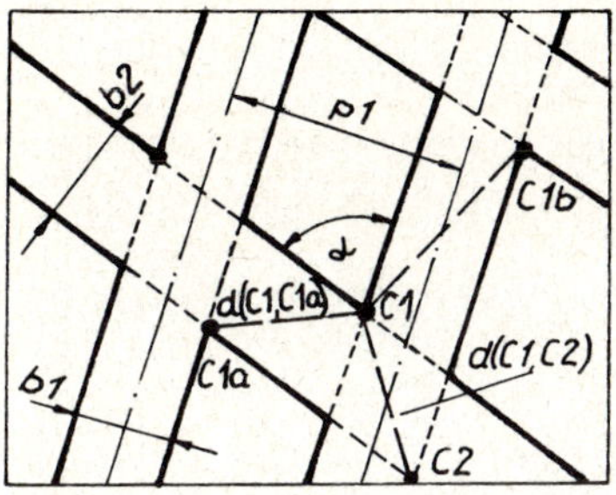

d(Ci,Cj) - maximal distance between associated branching points

α - angle of grid distortion

b1,b2 - line breadths

p1,p2 - distances between grid lines

If $b=b1=b2$, $p=p1=p2$ and $n=p/b$ then
$\alpha(d(C1,C2)=d(C1,C1a))=\arccos(n/2-1)$

Figure 2 Example for geometrical relations in a distorted grid

However for n>4 and for equal line breadth the distance criterion allows a quite sure discrimination between associated and "foreign" branchings. This derivation holds only for ideal grid lines. If there are some "thickinings" due to nonideal illumination and imaging the situation can be worther.

At object edges irregularities of crossing shapes can arise. Fig. 3 gives an example. Even in such cases it is not possible to infer a crossing only from the (little) distance between two branchings. Merging must not be done here.

```
-x-     -x-     -x-
 -x-    -x-    -x-
  -x-   -x-   -x-
   -x--x-   -x-
    -xB-- -x-                B - branching point
     -x---x-
      -x-x-
       -B-
       -x-
       -x-                   Figure 3
```

In a corresponding manner it can be shown that a comparison of angles of branches of the branching points (cf. fig.4) is not sufficient for merging two branching points. Therefore, let T, TR, $T(\alpha)$ be suitable specified thresholds , let dr(Ci,Cj) be the real distance between two branching points then the decision procedure for merging two branching points is as follows (see fig.4):

1. If
$$\alpha 1 < T(\alpha)$$
$$\alpha 2 < T(\alpha)$$
$$|\beta 1 - \gamma 1| < T$$
$$|\beta 2 - \gamma 2| < T$$
then C1 and C2 are candidates for mergin.

2. Evaluate r(Ci,Cj) = dr(Ci,Cj)/d(Ci,Cj). If $r > 1$ then Ci is no more a candidate (i=1,2; j=1a,1b,2a,2b).

3. If r(C1,Ci)/r(C1,C2) > TR, i=1a,1b, and r(C2,Ci)/r(C1,C2) > TR, i=2a,2b, then merge candidates C1 and C2.

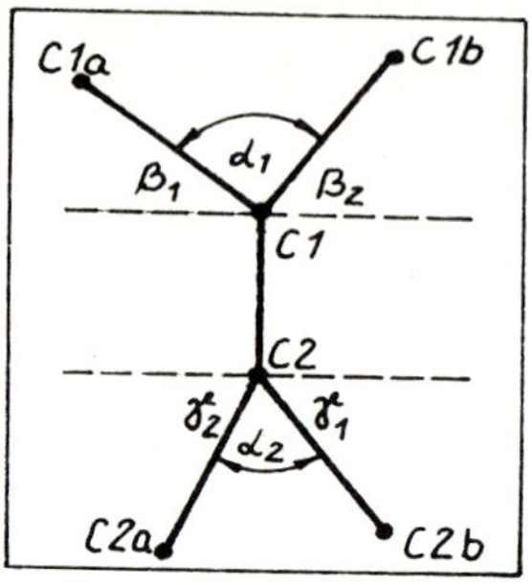

Figure 4

This procedure seems to need a great effort fortunately the amount of data is already drastically reduced (e.g. from 488x390 pixels to less than 800 branchings and crossings). Figure 5 gives an example for grid reconstruction for a region of a polyhedron.

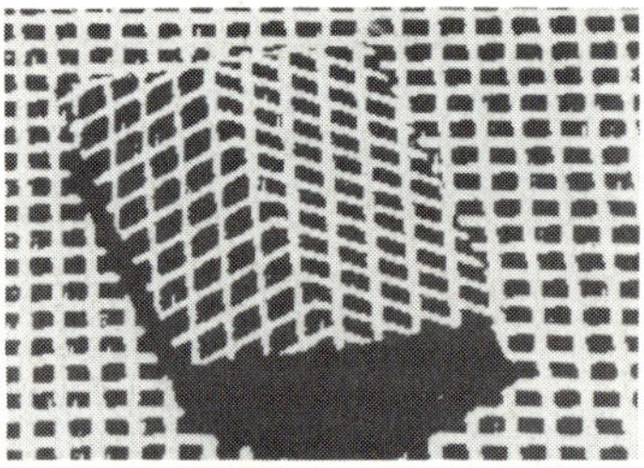

a)

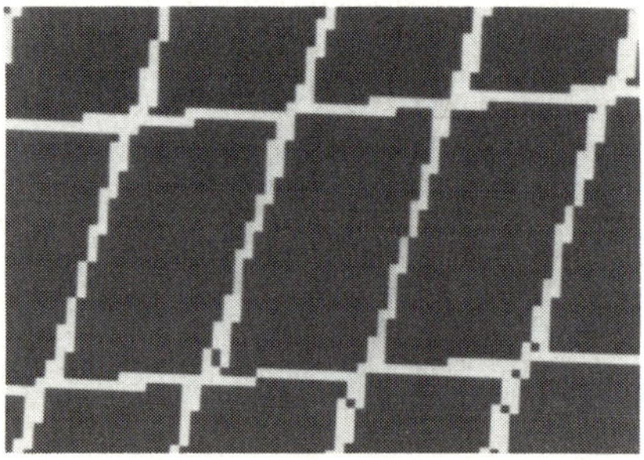

b)

c)

a) Original image

b) Skeletonized grid overlayed by reconstructed grid

c) Reconstructed grid

Figure 5

The result of grid reconstruction is a list of ends, bends, branchings and crossings with their geometrical properties and topological relations. The segmentation at the feature level bases on this list. Homogenuous grid regions are labeld by a comparision of neighbour crossings. The determination of edges of such regions is done by help of a sequence of a Hough-transform, a clustering and a clique search algorithm. These latter steps are not described here.

At the level of preprocessing the shadow detection for grid like patterns can be done in a quite simple manner. This is useful for the processing of grey level images when for diffuse light the grey level of shadows can increase the grey level of some object region and an adaptive threshold procedure gives a clear binary grid pattern. Then several thinning passes over the dark regions not preserving topology are applied. The problem is when to stop thinning. Consecutive stripped contours of a region (without tails of 3 pixel breadth or less) differ by 4-8 pixels. This fact will be used to determinate when stopping. Of course parts of shadows with a diameter in the magnitude of grid patches will be also removed. The example image contains one shadow region and many grid patches (fig. 5a). The sequence of numbers of removed pixels in each step is
10304/ 6693/ 2960/ 550/ 396/ 327/ 308/ 283/ 274/ 261/ 250/ 240.
Here is a clear breakpoint after 3 passes. The patches are nearly eliminated. (see fig.6a). The theoretical magnitude of 4-8 pixels between two consecutive stripped contours is reached after 6 thinning passes (see fig.6c) but the top right part of the shadow is also eliminated. In order to approximate the original shadow a thicking with an equal number of passes follows (see fig.6b and 6d). Smoothing of the shadow contour is not done. A comparision with the original image gives a good fitting.

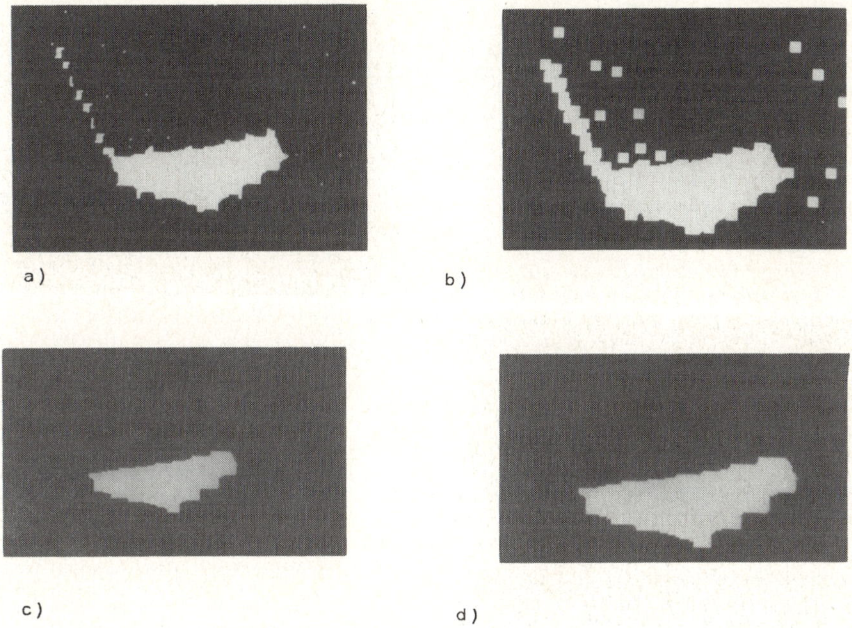

Figure 6 Detected shadow (a,c) Shadow after thicking (b,c)

INTERPRETATION

3-D interpretation or recognition means here interpreting the image data in terms of known 3-D models of objects, i.e. determining the identities and locations of the objects seen in the image.

In the contrast to 2-D recognition for 3-D recognition the object models cannot be described by a small set of so called image models, i.e. object location is not so strongly restricted that only a few projections different with respect to shape can occur. Therefore 3-D interpretation must be based on local image and model features (geometric elements) and can be understood as inexact matching of geometric structures.

There are several approaches to inexact matching of geometric structures as particular cases of relational structures /16,17,18/. Our approach follows the idea of geometrical Hough-transform /19/. It assumes that the set of 2-D and/or 2-1/2-D geometric elements are detected (respectively can be detected) from the image and that the object models are also described by geometric elements and their spatial relations.

After initialization of a suitable accumulator array the algorithm iteratively performs the following main steps /8/:

1. Choosing an appropriate pair of image element and model element.
2. Calculating possible object location ranges where the regarded image element would be approximately caused by the object model element taking into account the scene model and the imaging geometry at hand.
3. Updating the accumulator array.

We will roughly present some ideas and results concerning step 2, a more detailed description will be contained in /20/.

The calculation of possible object location ranges for a given pair of image and model elements can be regarded as a process of inexact constrain satisfaction where the constraints result from the image as well as from a priori knowledge. Our approach to this task has the following main components:
- Formulation of the a priori known location constraints as transformation matrices containing free variables
- Computing transformation matrices describing the constrain location range of the regarded model element with respect to to camera coordinate system using parameter values of image and model elements (location estimation)
- Combining the location estimation result and a priori constraints by analyzing some matrix operations describing the relationship between the relevant coordinate systems (location verification).

Assuming perspective projection the problem of location estimation can be difficult or even analytically unsolvable. It is much more simple if orthographic projection holds. Location estimation with perspective projection can be reduced to that with orthographic one if the so called perspective normal projection /21/ is approximately valid, i.e. if regarded geometric elements are very small compared to the object element distance to the camera.

Location estimation in this case is then performed by first location estimation assuming orthographic projection with respect to a virtual camera showing directly to the regarded object element using adequately changed image element parameter values and second a correction of this result by the coordinate transformation between the real camera and the virtual one.

We have investigated location estimation and verification for simple geometric model elements of two groups:

- so called point-like elements, e.g.
  - . an ray (point plus one line direction)
  - . an angle (point plus two line directions)
  - . a planar junction of three rays
  - . a spatial 3-corner (point plus three arbitrary line directions)
- extended elements, e.g.
  - . a finite line (two linearly connected points)
  - . a triangle
  - . a circle

For point-like elements the location estimation results obtained in the described way are exactly valid with perspective projection, for other elements failures occur depending on the degree of violation of the condition of perspective normal projection.

Analytical result for location determination are obtained with respect to several aspects:

A. There is a complete analytical solution for location estimation with the physically adequate number of remaining free variables.

B. There is a complete analytical solution for location estimation without remaining free variables.

C. There is a complete analytical solution for location verification for a specified class of location constraints. Regarded location constraints are characterized by only one degree of freedom of object rotation and only two degrees of freedom of object translation perpendicular to the rotation axis.

D. There is an adequate analytical solution of location determination by reducing to location estimation and verification of subelements of ray type for a specified class of location constraints.

E. There is an analytical location determination solution at all.

Table 1 summariezes the results for a subset of the regarded geometric elements, the details can be found in /20/.

	ray	angle	planar 3-corner	spatial 3-corner	line	circle	triangle
A	+	+	+	-	+(1)	+(1)	+(1)
B	-	-	+	-	-	-	+(1)
C	+	-	+	-	+(1)	+(1)	+(1)
D	+	+	+	+	+		+
E	+	+	+	+	+	+(1)	+

(1) - solution assumes that perspective normal projection is valid.

Table 1

With the exeption of the element type ray all final solutions are overdeterminated, i.e. there is information to decide and to evaluate the reliability of a concrete location determination result. So one can decide if the accumulator should be updated and how.

For example, the specified location constraints hold in the case of an object lying in a stable position on a supporting plane. Because the verification algorithm works with arbitrary camera position and orientation the analytical results for the elements ray and line generalize the results reported in /21/ where perspective projection was also supposed but camera axis and planes normal had to be colliniar.

AKNOWLEDGEMENT

We express our thanks to Ch.Stiel, J.Suess and H.Hausfeld for fruitful discussions and for the support given by implementing and testing of algorithms on a CM-computer.

REFERENCES

/ 1/ Villers,P., Recent Proliferation of Industrial Vision Applications, Proc.13.ISIR(1983),pp. 3.1-3.20
/ 2/ Ishi,M., Nagata,T.,Feature Extraction for Three Dimensional Objects and Visual Processing in a Hand-eye System Using Laser Tracker, PR 8(1976),pp. 229-237
/ 3/ Vamos,T. and Bathor,M., 3-D Complex Object Recognition Using Programmed Illumination, Proc.ICPR (1980),1091-1093
/ 4/ Nimrod,N., Margolith,A. and Mergler,W.H., A Laser-based Scanning Range Finder for Robotic Applications, Proc. 2.RoViSeC.(1982), 241-252
/ 5/ Will,P.M. and Pennington,K.S., Grid Coding:A Novel Technique for Image Processing, Proc.IEEE 60,(1972),No.6,669-680
/ 6/ Shirai,Y. and Suwa,M., Recognition of Polyhedrons with a Range Finder, Proc.IJCAI 1973, 629-640
/ 7/ Rybak,W.I. et. al., Visual Perception of Robots Environment - Methods and Techniques of Constructing, ISAI 83, Leningrad
/ 8/ Florath,P., 3-D Object Recognition with Location Constraints Control in:Plander,I., Artificial Intelligence and Information Systems of Robots, North-Holland,1984
/ 9/ Stanke.G., Florath,P., Acquisition of Data for 3-D Vision Systems, in: Plander,I., Artificial Intelligence and Information Control Systems of Robots, North-Holland,1984
/10/ Rioux,M.,3-D Camera Based on Synchronized Scanning, Proc. 13.ISIR, pp.17.48-17.60
/11/ Altschuler,M.D., et.al., The numerical Stereo Camera, Proc. of SPIE 283, 15-24
/12/ Rosenfeld,A., Davis,L.S., A Note on Thinning, IEEE Trans.SMC-25 (1976),226-228
/13/ Roesler U.,Schwarze,G., Maskenverfahren zur Manipulation von binaeren Rasterbildern linienfoermiger Objekte, EIK-16(1980) Nr.4, 171-184
/14/ Zhang Shengxung,Fu,K.S., A Thinning Algorithm for Discrete Binary Images, in: 1.Int.Conference on Computers and Applications, June 1984, IEEE 84CH2039-6
/15/ Harris,J.F.,et.al., A Modular System for Interpreting Binary Pixel Representation of Line-Structured Data, in:J.Kittler, K.S.Fu, and L.F.Pau(eds.),Pattern Recognition and Applications, Pattern Recognition Theory and Application, 311-351
/16/ Florath,P., et.al., Modelle und Verfahren der 3-D Erkennung, unpublished research report, Central Institute of Cybernetics and Information Processes, Berlin, 1984
/17/ Shapiro,L.G., Haralick,R.M., Structural Descriptions and Inexact Matching, PAMI-3, Sept.1981, No.5, 504-519
/18/ Ballard,D.H., Brown,C.M., Computer Vision, Prentice Hall,1982
/19/ Ballard,D.H., Generalizing the Hough-transform to Detect Arbitrary Shapes, Pattern Recognition 13 (1981),No.2, 111-122
/20/ Florath,P., Location Estimation and Verification in a Generalized Hough-transform Approach to 3-D Interpretation, to be published
/21/ Fang,T.J., et.al., Three Dimensional Object Recognition Using a Transformation Clustering Technique, Proc.IJCPR 1982, 678-681

ARTIFICIAL INTELLIGENCE: Methodology, Systems, Applications
W. Bibel and B. Petkoff (Editors)
Elsevier Science Publishers B.V. (North-Holland)

SCULPTOR-2: REPRESENTING, GENERATING AND EDITING SMOOTH PLANAR SHAPES

Lina Massone, Pietro Morasso

Department of Communication, Computer and Systems Science
Via All'Opera Pia 11a - 16145 Genoa - Italy

In this paper a representation scheme based on MAT transform is presented, as a powerful tool to manage the main structure of shapes. An editing system is then introduced, SCULPTOR-2, allowing generation and editing of smooth planar shapes by means of a symbolic description of shapes topology.

INTRODUCTION

A considerable amount of attention has been devoted to the computational treatment of shape in the field of geometric modeling. Among others, Requicha and his coworkers (Requicha (1980), Tilove (1980)) were very careful in pointing out the importance of a well defined mathematical formulation of the concept of object for deriving meaningful computational schemes. They embedded the notion of rigid object in the topology of the Euclidean (2D or 3D) space by defining regularized-sets (shortly r-sets), i.e. point sets which are characterized by the fact that they coincide with the closure of their interior. They also developed a representation scheme called CSG (Constructive Solid Geometry) which is based on "regularized" set operations (union, intersection, subtraction). Even if CSG is very attractive for its mathematical clarity, it fails to capture the notion of "smoothness"; CSG shapes are bound indeed to display sharp edges or corners, i.e. discontinuities.

However, following the formulation by Requicha, we may define "smooth shapes" as connected r-sets (CSG may generate disjoint r-sets) whose boundary is continuous up to a certain level: if the boundary is expressed in terms of parametric equations, we assume at least continuity of the second derivative for planar shapes (it determines curvature) and of the third derivative in the 3D case (it determines torsion and the Gaussian curvature). Our goal is to deal with "smooth r-sets", looking for their structure.

An additional intuitive notion that we deem important to understand "shapeness" is the distinction, in the structure of an object, between a "main structure" and the overlying "details" or "textures". For example, different door keys might be characterized by a similar structure (an oblongated protuberance linked to a rounded body) but by different details (the teeth of the keys); the profile of a mountain ridge will show, in different times of the year, different "textures" superimposed on the same underlying structure or the other way around if we consider different mountain ridges with a similar "foliage". These two entities can be separated in terms of frequency analysis, the low frequency component being associated with the main structure, and the high frequency component with details/textures.

The proposed representation of shape consists of two complemetary components: (i) the "skeletal representation" of the main structure, which uses the concept of Medial Axis Transform (Blum (1978)), and (ii) the "zero-crossing representation" of the details/textures which extends to the contours of shapes the theorem by Logan (Logan (1977)) already applied to problems of vision (Marr (1979)).

This paper deals with the structural aspects, i.e. with the low frequency component of the objects boundary. The mathematical aspects of skeletal representation have been discussed in (Gaglio (1983)); here the focus is mainly on the transformation from the numerical representation based on skeletons and on associated thickness profiles, to a symbolic description in which the topology of shapes is encoded in a way suitable for further symbolic processing. An interactive editing system is then presented, SCULPTOR-2, which, exploiting the symbolic description allows the user to build a 2-D shape and then to incrementally refine it, adding new details until the desired shape is generated. After each editing operation, the corresponding symbolic description is updated to code correctly the new shape. The geometric constraints which guarantee validity and consistency of results are automatically taken into account by the editor.

SKELETAL REPRESENTATION

Numerical aspects

An appropriate representation of the low frequency component of the objects boundary, that we call skeletal representation, can be obtained by means of the MAT (Medial Axis Transform (Blum (1978))). The MAT has long been considered as a useful methodological tool to explicit the structure of a shape but its practical use has been shadowed by the apparent hypersensitivity to high frequency components, in which noise and/or texture are predominant. MAT, anyway, can be used correctly, i.e. with respect to a really smooth boundary, using a different representation for the high frequency component of the boundary and still keeping all the information about the shape. In qualitative terms, the choice of a cutoff frequency should be made in order to maximize the stability of the representation, i.e. in such a way that the structural and textural representations are as insensitive as possible to variations of the chosen frequency.

The medial axis, or skeleton, is defined as the set of points inside a shape which are centers of circles which are all contained in the shape, have maximum size (let us call them m-circles) and therefore are tangent to the boundary in one or more points. The boundary is the envelope of the one-parameter family of m-circles (see Rektoris (1969) for the definition of one-parameter families of planar curves; in our case, the parameter is the running variable along the skeleton). The size of the m-circles is a measure of the local "thickness" of the shape and we can define a thickness function as a scalar function of the running variable along the skeleton.

The skeleton of a smooth r-set (SRS) is composed of several open or closed segments which may intersect at "fork points" and may have "open endings". Such "singular points" of the skeleton are in biunivocal correspondance with the type of tangency between the boundary and the m-circles:
(i) points of minimum curvature of the boundary usually determine skeleton open endings, where m-circles have a radius equal to the radius of curvature of the boundary and are tangent to the boundary only in the point of minimum curvature (the exception occurs when the local thickness is smaller than the radius of curvature and in that case the points of minimum curvature of the boundary do not determine singular points of the skeleton); when points of minimum curvature of the boundary do determine open endings, the latter can be computed by tracing the normal to the boundary in the point of minimum curvature and by advancing inside by an amount equal to the radius of curvature.
(ii) m-circles centered on fork-points of the skeleton are tangent to the boundary in three or more points. The number of intersecting skeleton branches is equal to the number of tangent points and the unit-vectors tangent to each skeletal segment departing from a fork point bisect the angles formed between the radii of the m-circle which reach the tangent points on the boundary.

Apart from the "singular points" (open endings and fork points) which form a finite set, the skeleton consists of curved segments of "regular points", characterized by the fact that the associated m-circle is tangent to the boundary in two distinct points.

The skeleton of a shape without holes is topologically a tree where each terminal node corresponds to an open ending, each non-terminal node corresponds to a fork point, and the links correspond to the branches of the skeleton. If the shape has holes, it is possible to have loops (i.e. closed chains of one or more links) and the topological structure is that of an oriented graph.

For each branch of the shape, the differential geometry of SRS's determines a constraint among the boundary, the skeleton, and the thickness function which can be expressed as follows:

let $s=s(t)$ be the natural curvilinear coordinate along the skeleton as a function of the running variable t;

let d=d(t) be the thickness profile, function of the same running variable;

let alfa be the angle between the two radii of the m-circle which join its center on the skeleton to the boundary, where the angle is measured counterclockwise from the left to the right radius (we may call it "aperture angle");

then

cos alfa/2 = d-dot/s-dot

Among the various mathematical properties which have been discussed in (Gaglio (1983)), it is worth recalling the relation between skeletal representation and boundary:

C = s + R(+alfa/2)*d*tau

where C is a point of the contour (two points in the cartesian plane), R(alfa/2) is the rotation matrix and tau is the unit vector tangent to the skeletal curve. It is important to point out that this relation is by itself an explicit algorithm to recover the low frequency boundary.

Symbolic Representation

The skeletal representation of the main structure of a SRS can be symbolically described in terms of a graph composed of vertices and connection branches as follows.

<Skeletal-Representation> ::= (<shape-name><vertices><branches>)
<vertices> ::= ({<vertex-descriptor>})
<vertex-descriptor> ::= <open-ending>/<fork-point>
<open-ending> ::= (OPEN <ending-name><thickness> <branch-name>)
<fork-point> ::= (FORK <fork-name><thickness><order> ({<branch-name><aperture-angle>}))
<branches> ::= ({<branch-descriptor>})
<branch-descriptor> ::= (<branch-name><initial-vertex> <final-vertex> <skeleton-segment> <thickness-profile><length><average-thickness>)
<shape-name>,<ending-name>,<fork-name>,<branch-name> ::= ATOM
<initial-vertex>,<final-vertex> ::= ATOM
<thickness>,<average-thickness>,<length> ::= positive real number
<aperture-angle> ::= positive real number not greater than 2 pi
<order> ::= positive integer number greater than 2
<skeleton-segment> ::= (parameters of a Bezier curve expressed in a local reference)
<thickness-profile> ::= (parameters of a Bezier function)

The Bezier polynomials (Bezier (1983)) have been chosen for computational convenience, but any other parametric representation is equally acceptable. The thickness-profile gives a description which is obviously independent of translation/rotation. For the skeleton-segment it is possible to use a translation/rotation independent representation, which is the curvature profile, but this is not very convenient computationally; however, it is possible to normalize a Cartesian representation of the curve by expressing the parameters (in the Bezier representation they are the guiding points of the curve) in a naturally local reference frame which we chose with the x axis directed as the tangent unit-vector in the origin of the curve.

A certain redundance is present in the symbolic description, but this may be convenient for two types of reasons: (i) the redundance helps in defining and implementing consistency tests, (ii) it is convenient to represent explictly certain macro-parameters, even if they can be derived from parts of the representation, when they are "meaningful" at some coarse level of shape analysis and their computation is rather expensive. An example of the redundance of the first type is given by the fact that the specification of the <aperture-angles> in the <vertex-descriptor> must match the value of the derivative of the <thickness> profile in the corresponding <branch-descriptor> and an example of the redundance of the second type is given by the <length> of a <branch-descriptor> which otherwise would require, i every timef needed, to integrate every time the Bezier curve.

SCULPTOR-2

In this section an editing system is presented based on skeletal representation which allows generating interactively planar shapes; starting from a single-branch shape it is possible to add singular points (i.e. other branches) modifying both structure and thickness function until the desired shape is generated. After each editing operation the corresponding symbolic description is updated to code correctly the new shape. The effects of each operation are presented on-line on a 512x512x8 raster graphic system.

The user can access 3 groups of commands:
A) general commands
B) structural commands
C) local commands
General commands are the following:
A1) (STORESHAPE <filename>) ---> stores on a file the symbolic description of a shape;
A2) (LOADSHAPE <filename>) ---> reads from a file a symbolic description;
A3) (STRUCTURE) ---> prints on TTY the actual symbolic description;
A4) (RUBBER) ---> removes the effects of last editing operation and restores the old shape;
A5) (OK) ---> confirms last editing operation and updates symbolic description;
A6) (NOSKEL) ---> deletes skeleton of shape;

A7) (SKEL) ---> redraws skeleton of shape;
A8) (NAME <shapename>) ---> gives a name to the actual shape;
A9) (BYE) ---> exits from SCULPTOR-2.

Commands of B group allow adding branches introducing singular points.
B1) (FIRST-BRANCH <skeleton-params> <thickness-values>) ---> generates a branch named S1 with ending vertices V1 and V2; the skeleton is generated by means of <skeleton-params> which are Bezier parameters expressed in absolute coordinates; the thickness function is generated by means of <thickness -values>: each <thickness-value> is a pair (value.position) where position refers to the local abscissa along the skeleton branch. All parameters are later converted into local Bezier paprameters.
B2) (SINGULAR-POINT <vertex-name> (<branch-name> <aperture-angle> <skel-params> <thick-values>) .....(<branch-name> <aperture-angle> <skel-params> <thick-values>) ---> introduces a singular point in <vertex-name> adding n branches where n is the number of branch descriptors in the command. All data necessary to update symbolic description are also computed (ending points, average thickness ....).

With C group commands it is possible to modify locally a single branch and the associated thickness function. "Locally" means that they have no effect on the global structure of the shape but only on branch parameters.
C1) (CHANGE-BRANCH <branch-name>) ---> shows the actual Bezier parameters of the branch and allows changing some of them by means of a cursor;
C2) (CHANGE-THICK <branch-name>) ---> shows the actual thickness values of the branch and allows changing some of them by means of a cursor.

CONCLUDING REMARKS

The skeletal representation has been introduced as a powerful tool to represent the low frequency component of a planar shape boundary and to emphasize its topological properties. An editing system has then be introduced, SCULPTOR-2, whose main features are high interactivity and incrementality. A symbolic approach has been followed which is extremely useful to perform operations like name generation, condition verification and so on. This fact, together with the graphic interface, makes SCULPTOR-2 a powerful and easy-to-use tool.

The commands interpreter and the processing operations on symbolic descriptions have been implemented in Franz Lisp, while all mathematical computations have been done in Fortran 77. A software interface between the two levels has been designed hiding the numerical level and allowing the user to interact only with the interpreter level. A VAX 11-750 connected to a VDS-701 raster graphic system has been used.

As far as the future is concerned, the following topics are a matter of study:
(i) extension of SCULPTOR-2 to high frequency components to allow the user to add to the main structure some local details;
(ii) extension of the theory to three-dimensional shapes;
(iii) applications to problems like planning, obstacle avoidance, puzzle fitting and so on.

REFERENCES

[1] Requicha, A.G., Representation of rigid solids: theory, methods and systems, ACM Comp. Surveys, 12 (1980) 437-475.
[2] Tilove, R.B., Set membership classification: a unified approach to geometric intersection problem, IEEE Trans. on Comp., C-29 (1980) 874-883.
[3] Blum, H. and Nagel R., Shape description using symmetrix axis features, Pattern Rec., 10 (1978) 167-180.
[4] Logan, B.F., Information in the zero crossing and bandpass signal, Bell Syst. Tech. Jrnl., 56 (1977) 487-510.
[5] Marr, D. and Poggio, T. A computational theory of human stereo vision, Proc. R. Soc. London, 204 (1979) 301-328.
[6] Gaglio, S., Massone, L. and Morasso P., Representing shape for visuo-motor processes in robots, Proc. Int. Symp. on Art. Int. ,Leningrad, October 1983.
[7] Rektoris, K., Survey od applicable mathematics (MIT Press, Cambridge, 1969).
[8] Bezier, P.E. and Sioussiou, S., Semiautomatic system for defining free form curves and surfaces, CAD, 15 (1983) 65-72.

ACKNOWLEDGEMENTS

This work has been partially supported by the Italian Research Council under a Grant for Bioengineering and Anthropomorphic Robotics.

ARTIFICIAL INTELLIGENCE: Methodology, Systems, Applications
W. Bibel and B. Petkoff (Editors)
Elsevier Science Publishers B.V. (North-Holland)

LOGIC PROGRAMMING ON REDUCTION/DATAFLOW MACHINES

S.Gaglio, G.Marino, R.Zaccaria

Department of Computer, Communication and System Sciences
University of Genova, Italy

Next generation computer systems will be characterized by very high level functions; most of them will be based on Logic Programming. In this paper a non-Von Neumann abstract machine is presented, based on a "fine" functional language, suitable for parallel realization, well suited to support Logic Programming. The machine, called nSASL, features both Dataflow and Reduction mechanisms, and uses a novel principle of "potentially useful" computation. Simulation results are presented on an implementation of a rule-based deduction system.

1. Logic Programming and Architectures

Next generation computer systems will be characterized by very high level functions, as: (1) Problem Solving and Inference, (2) Knowledge Base management, and (3) Intelligent Interface.

Functions (1) and (2) will require a speed performance which has been estimated in 100M-1GLIPS[1], whereas actual systems at present range from approximately 10^4 to 10^5 LIPS[5]. Logic Programming has a key role in the realization of (1) and (2) functions.

The research activity in this field basically relates to two aspects:

1) Logic itself (knowledge representation, production systems, hypothesis formulation, languages for logic programming, etc.) to improve problem representation and

2) machines (architectures, systems, languages) to improve performance and properly exploit the technology.

The last aspect is the subject of this paper.

As relates to architectures, three general approaches are being carried out:

---

[1] Logical Inferences Per Second.

1) strictly architectural (Data Flow Machines[1], Connection Machine[3], etc.);

2) language-driven (LISP Machine[7], Reduction Machine[8], PROLOG Machines, etc.);

3) system-wide (as Hewitt's "Actor System"[2] for knowledge bases and problem solving).

The common feature is, obviously, the idea of a highly parallel architecture. This is an extremely interesting challenge for a future Logic Machine, in which a huge amount of parallel activities is foreseable. We will simply add the idea that the future machine will require, besides a 1 G LIPS performance, other characteristics such as: a "fine" machine language (i.e. a purely functional language), a highly reliable or, possibly, a fault-tolerant (or better gracefully degradable) system.

Our approach is language driven. In this paper we will briefly introduce a virtual machine based on a purely functional language, called nSASL. It is a new definition of Turner's SASL[9] with the same syntax, but suitable to execute programs on a (not necessarily limited) number of processors. The underlying hardware is, at present, an abstract set of interconnected elementary processors, with no costs or overheads in communications. The nSASL virtual machine uses both the Data Flow and Reduction mechanisms; it also implements a new idea of "potentially useful computations", which is meant to take into account all possible "hypotheses" on the program execution before selecting the right one. We have implemented an emulator of the virtual machine that monitors the parallelism of the execution. Some results of parallel executions will be presented in a graphic form.

In Sect. 2 the nSASL machine is briefly described, and in Sect. 3 some experimental results, related to logic programming systems, are illustrated.

2. The nSASL machine

In nSASL, the atomic mechanism is the **Event**. We define an **event** the (n+1)-ple **[PO, arg1, arg2,...,argn]** where PO is a Primitive Operator and [argi] a list of arguments, possibly still needing to be evaluated. An event is a "future result" inside a functional expression: it can be referenced by several nodes in the program graph[2]. Events are evaluated inside the whole static environment, hence concurrent evaluations can be carried out.

The evaluation of an event produces an **Object** (atom, list, function) that, in turn, can give raise to other events. A program terminates

---

[2] As it is well known, a purely functional program can be represented by a graph: SASL is based on such an internal form.

when there are no more events to be evaluated. A non-terminating program can give "partial answers", even though new events are generated along non-terminating branches of the program's graph: this is the desired behaviour of a "lazy" interpreter.

A rule for event evaluation with respect to PO has been defined as follows. Two classes of POs in SASL can be devised: "strict" and "lazy" POs. The former class includes basic functions (**+**, **-**, **and**, **or**, **hd** (CAR), **tl** (CDR) and so on); basically, they are related to data production and consumption. The latter includes combinators[10] which are symbolic operators that work on "names" of arguments without requiring their evaluation; they control function applications, hence they are related to the program graph reduction. Events are associated to the nodes of the program graph.

2.1. Event Evaluation for Strict Operators

The nSASL uses a proper data structure to hold the dependencies graph for strict events. We call it **Event Associative Storage** (**EAS**). It plays the role of the stack in a conventional machine, and keeps track of the recursive calls of nested PO applications. Unlike stacks, EAS is a structure suitable to be processed in parallel. Any cell of the EAS is addressed by the name of an object, and holds the name of an event suspended on (or waiting for) it; it also holds a counter of the number of arguments to wait for.

This is basically a Data Flow mechanism.

2.2. Event evaluation for Functions

In SASL's semantics another dependencies graph among events can be found: the (Partial) Functions' Activation Order. SASL, in fact, manages Curried Functions, as to say, partial functions of one argument only. For example,

plus x y = x+y

can be read as

(plus x) y

where "(plus x)" is a function of one argument, whose action is adding x to that argument.

The nSASL machine is able to suspend an event **f x** waiting for evaluation of **f**. This is carried out by keeping a graph of dependencies of reduction of functions, besides the described "data flow" graph.

2.3. Look-Ahead Events

The two mechanisms introduced above can be resumed as follows:

1) a data-flow mechanism, for computing strict operators, and

2) a reduction mechanism for computing functions.

Both are implemented by events. Moreover, the proposed machine also features a much more interesting evaluation mechanism.

Let us define **Look-Ahead Event** (**LAE**) an event which can be statically (i.e. following the program graph) triggered, but whose result may be useless. The nSASL allows two cases in which LAEs may occur:

1) conditional operators
Whenever an "if branch" is found during evaluation of a function, both alternatives are eligible for evaluation, together with the predicates of the conditional expression. Once the proper branch is chosen, the other alternative becomes "wasteful computations".

2) non deterministic operators
Unlike strict operators, non-det operators are those which may evaluate without needing complete evaluation of their arguments. In our interpreter, logical operations (**and**, **or**, etc) evaluate in non-det way. For example, the expression **(and e1 e2)** causes simultaneous evaluation of both e1 and e2; if, for instance, **e1** returns **FALSE, and** evaluates to **FALSE** without waiting for **e2** (whose associated computation becomes "wasteful").

In all cases LAEs produce wasteful computations. In some cases such computations terminate; however, in many cases LAEs may trigger non-terminating computations.

However, we must point out that wasteful computations are not a drawback "per se", though they involve time and space overhead. In a VLSI architecture, a large number of processors is easy and cheap to achieve; therefore, the fact that part of them may carry out of work that will be disposed is unimportant. The same applies for large (local) memory.

LAEs play the role of "elementary hypotheses" on the computational flow, suitable to be performed in parallel to save time, waiting for an event to verify which was the correct solution (if any).

In simulation runs, LAEs are allowed up to a tunable upper bound of events, expressed as a percentage of the number of "normal" events; usually, it ranges from 0 (no LAEs allowed) to 100-300%.

The problem of controlling LAEs has been solved as follows: a Primitive Operator **KILL** is triggered by an event that states the "disposability" of a graph branch **B**; **KILL** recursively (i.e., generating other **KILL** events) marks all events depending on **B** as disposable; disposed events are flagged in the associative memory, and garbage-collected on intervention of the unique general garbage collector, that unifies both functions. **KILL** events, obviously, operate in parallel.

2.3.1. A Classical Example: Factorial

The simplest definition of Factorial in SASL looks like:

```
fact 0 = 1
fact n = n * fact(n-1)
```

This algorithm is usually considered to be sequential (each recursive call cannot be activated but in sequence).

In fig. 1 performances of **fact 30** are compared for a number of processors ranging from 1 to 22 and for different percentages of LAEs ; it can be seen that, in spite of the apparent sequentiality of the algorithm, a quantity of parallel action is discovered by the machine.

This result is very important. It shows how the proposed machine is able to evaluate in parallel, with enhanced overall speed, "normal" programs, as to say, without requiring nor formulation in terms of processes, communication etc., nor special versions of the algorithm more suitable for parallel execution. Moreover, the non-det machine exhibits a "tolerant" behaviour with respect to the number of processors: the same program can successfully run on machines with different number of processors [3] (possibly only one); as the number increases, the execution speed increases, at least until enough parallelism is found in the program.

3. nSASL as Inference Machine

In order to investigate more deeply the possibility of using nSASL as a machine for Logic Programming, a rule-based deduction system,

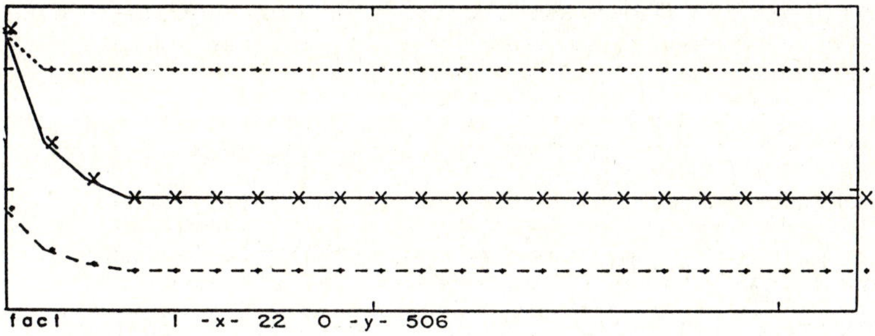

Fig.1 - Computational time (expressed in time slots) of **fact 30** versus the number of available processors, for three values of allowed LAEs: dotted: no LAEs; solid: 150% of LAEs; dashed: 200% of LAEs. X axis: no. processors, y axis: time slots.

---

[3] This implies the possibility of "graceful degradations" of the system.

called nSTP[4], has been implemented under nSASL. It is inspired by a work by Wallace[11] on a LISP implementation of PROLOG. The nSTP program manages facts and rules expressed as lists, where the first clause is the consequent (if any), and the following are the antecedent (variables are conventionally symbols starting with the '$' sign). For example, the rule

```
(grand_son, $x, $y), (son, $x, $z), (son, $z, $y)
```

stands for

```
SON (x, z)  SON (z, y) -> GRAND_SON (x, y)
```

The heart of nSTP is a backtracking mechanism (implemented by a function **prove** that derives from Wallace's PROVE) and a **unify**[6] algorithm. The function **prove** is called by passing it a formula **F** to be proved and a list of **axioms; prove** gives back the list of necessary substitutions to prove **F.** Successively, substitutions are performed by other functions and the answer is given as a list of facts.

An analysis of nTSP would lead us too far. We will restrict ourselves to some preliminary results on a non trivial subset of it. For this purpose, we used a simple data base consisting of the following clauses:

```
((DOG, FIDO), ), ((NOT_BARKS, FIDO), )
,((WAGS_TAIL, FIDO), ), ((MEOWS, MYRTLE), )
,((FRIENDLY, $x1), (WAGS_TAIL, $x1), (DOG, $x1))
,((DOG, BAU), ), ((NOT_AFRAID, $y2, $x2)
,(FRIENDLY, $x2), (NOT_BARKS, $x2))
,((ANIMAL, $x3), (DOG, $x3))
,((ANIMAL, $x4), (CAT, $x4))
,((CAT, $x5), (MEOWS, $x5))
,((WAGS_TAIL, BAU), ), ((DOG, WHISKY), )
,(MEOWS, PUSSY), ), ((MEOWS, KIM), )
,((NOT_BARKS, WHISKY), ), ((WAGS_TAIL, WHISKY), )
```

We asked **prove** to find the substitution list that proves the goal

```
(DOG, $x), (CAT, $y), (NOT_AFRAID, $y, $x)
```

As it could be shown, the solution consists of 18 terms, whereas the substitution list is obviously longer. Results are given in figs. 2 and 3, considering the time **T1** at which the first substitution

---

[4] nSTP stands for **nSASL** **T**heorem **P**rover.

[5] nSASL features "Lazy Evaluation", hence list elements are available as soon they are evaluated, without waiting for completion of the whole list.

becomes available [5] as a measure of the speed[6]. If we consider that on a sequential execution **Tl** is about 3500 time slots, we can see that

1) with no LAEs allowed (fig. 3) the computation can spread only over a little number of processors (approximately 6), owing to the small data base; nevertheless, **Tl** decreases to about 1500 time slots;

2) with high percentage of LAEs (in this case 150 %), a large amount of tentative evaluations is performed (fig. 2), giving the result of a low **Tl** (approx. 400 time slots).

This demonstrates how the proposed machine may significantly increase the speed performances of Logic Programming. It seems reasonable that more realistic (and complex) problems will take much greater advantages: in[4] it is shown how a NP-complete problem, for example, might be solved by nSASL in linear time.

4. Conclusions

A non-Von Neumann machine has been presented that: i) is based on a "fine" functional language, ii) fits well with parallel hardware (VLSI or distributed systems), iii) is transparent with respect to

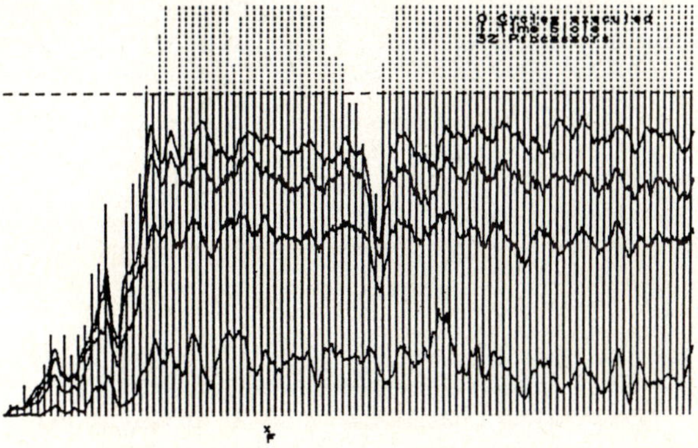

Fig.2 - A trace showing the number of processor involved on the execution of the first 1088 time slots of **prove**, with 150 % LAEs; x axis: time (in time slots); y axis: number of processors executing strict operators (1st band from bottom) or lazy operators (2nd band from bottom). The first result (**(F, $x)**) is marked on the x axis (at approx. 415 time slots). The upper bands (not discussed in this paper) show the number of suspended events for the two mechanisms "Dataflow" and "Reduction". The y axis range is 1 - 32.

---

6 the first substitution, which is **(FIDO, $x)**, is marked on the x-axis.

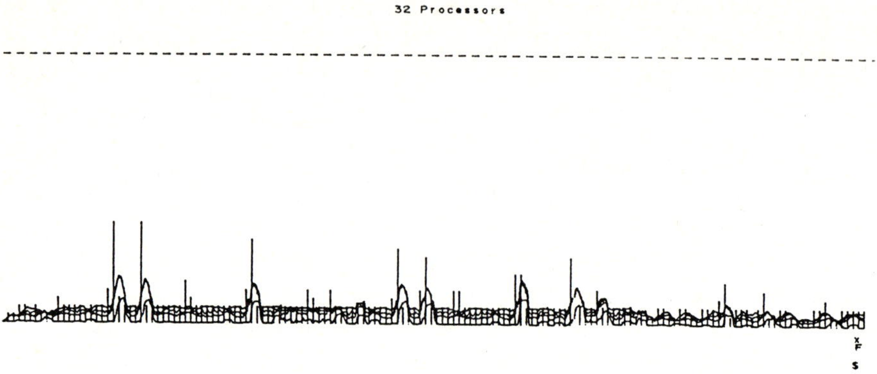

Fig.3 - Trace of the first 1525 time slots of **prove**, with no LAEs allowed. The first result is at approx. 1500 time slots, but only less than 7 processors are used by the machine. Scale factors are the same as in fig. 2.

the number of processors, iv) can widely use a look-ahead mechanism which gives a good increase in performance by massive, automatic use of parallel hardware, v) does not need particular formulations of algorithms, vi) is well suited to support Logic Programming.

Simulation results show a stable and monotonic behaviour. Such results support the present work that is in the line of moving nSASL to a real distributed environment, and, on the other hand, encourage to explore its applications to the field of A.I. and Robotics as well.

REFERENCES

1. J. B. Dennis, C. K. C. Leung, and D. P. Misunas, "A Highly Parallel Processor using a Data Flow Machine Language", CSG Memo 134-1, Lab. for Computer Science, M.I.T. (June 1979).
2. C. E. Hewitt, "Viewing Control Structures as Patterns of Passing Messages", Journal of Artificial Intelligence Vol. **8**(3) pp. 323-364 (June 1977).
3. Daniel W. Hillis, "The Connection Machine", A.I. Memo No. 646, M.I.T. (Sept. 1981).
4. G. Marino, "A Non Deterministic Interpreter for the Sasl Functional Language (in Italian)", Int. Rep. DIST-TR-5-84, Communication, Comp. and System Sciences Dept Univ. of Genova (May 1984).
5. Tohru Moto-oka and al., "Challenge for Knowledge Information Processing Systems (Preliminary Report on 5th Generation Computer Systems)", Proc. of Intern. Conf. on Fifth Generation Computer Systems, (Oct. 1981).

6. Nils J. Nilsson, "", in Principles of Artificial Intelligence, Tioga Pubbl. Co., Palo Alto, Ca. (1980).

7. G. L. Steele and G. J. Sussman, "The SCHEME 79 Chip", Computer, (July 1981).

8. P. C. Treleaven and G. F. Mole, "A Multi-Processor Reduction Machine for User-Defined Reduction Languages", Proc. 7th Int. Symp. Computer Architecture, pp. 121-129 , New YorkIEEE, (May 1980).

9. D. A. Turner, "A New Implementation Technique for Applicative Languages", Soft. Pract. Exper. Vol. **9** pp. 31-49 (sept 1979).

10. D. A. Turner, "Another Algorithm for Bracket Abstraction", J. Symbol. Logic Vol. **44**(2) pp. 267-270 (June 1979).

11. Richard S. Wallace, "An Easy Implementation of PiL (Prolog in Lisp)", SIGART Newsletter, (85)(July 1983).

ARTIFICIAL INTELLIGENCE: Methodology, Systems, Applications
W. Bibel and B. Petkoff (Editors)
Elsevier Science Publishers B.V. (North-Holland)

ARCHITECTURE AND APPLICATIONS OF PARALLEL COMPUTER FOR ARTIFICIAL INTELLIGENCE

D.R. Avresky, S. Marinov, N. Patchev, S. Ovcharov, G. Slavov

Computer department
Higher institute for mechanical and electrical engineering
Sofia 1156
Bulgaria

In this report we outline the hardware and software of a highly parallel hypertree structured machine. A small (15 microcomputers) prototype of the machine, constructed from Intel 8086 Family components, has to become operational in 1985. The parallel computer can support many artificial intelligence applications, including the rapid execution of programmes, written in RED, a high-level functional language for parallel computations.

INTRODUCTION

To support the application of AI and research in AI, more powerfull computers are needed. One possible approach is to improve gradually current computers, but probably this conservative extension would be greatly insufficient to apply even in a limited part of AI to the real world. The other approach is to build and use Lisp-like and Prolog-like language machines, for example the LMI Lambda machine. The current architecture of these machines is not fundamentally different from present computer architecture, but they are a good start toward the future architecture. In order to obtain the greater power of a parallel computer for AI (Stolfo (1983)), a distributed control system is needed.

ARCHITECTURE OF A PARALLEL COMPUTER FOR AI

A most exciting prospect in computer architecture today is the opportunity to organize a very large number of inexpensive microporcessors into a high reliable multimicroprocessor system. Hypertree combines the best features of the binary tree and the n-dimensional hypercube (Goodman & Séquin (1981)). The basic skelleton of hypertree is a binary tree structure. A fault-tolerant communication architecture for distributed systems is proposed by (Pradhan (1981)).

The Parallel Computer for Artificial Intelligence, proposed in this paper, has a fault-tolerant structure (Avresky (1983)), which can continue to operate correctly in the presence of multiple failures of links or nodes - Figure 1. The basic skelleton of the structure is also a binary tree structure. A triple modular redundancy (TMR) microcomputer is used at the root.

If the root node fails, the nodes 2 (or 3) can perform its function. Each node is a microcomputer with its own memory and peripherals. Links are communication lines between microcomputers.

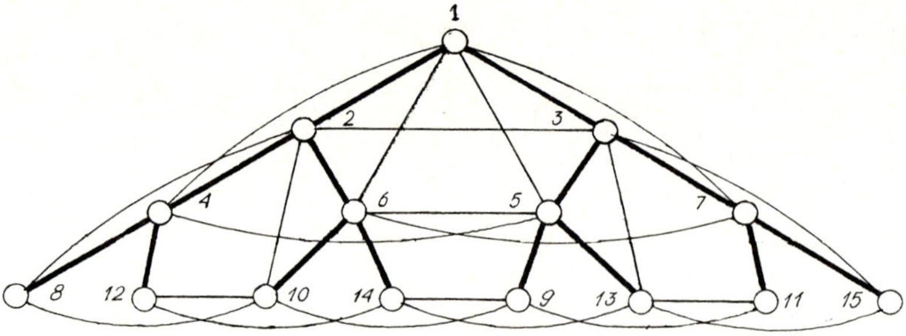

Figure 1

Each microcomputer in the prototype computer is 16 bit microcomputer, based on Intel 8086. It is located on four Double Europe Standard PC-boards.

CPU module - This module is a general purpose MULTIBUS compatible computer. It consisits of a Numeric Data Processor (8086+8087); 16K-bytes dual-port static RAM, realized on 6116; 8÷64-Kbytes EPROM, realized on 2716 (2732/27128); 3 individual timer/counters; 2x8 bit Parallel I/O with Handshake; 8 normal interrupt levels; 1 serial Sync./Async. I/O channel; on-board parity check.

RAM module - This memory module contains maximum 128K-bytes of dynamic read/write memory, realized on 2164 and 8203. It offers a very high degree of reliability due to the on-board Hamming code for single-bit-error-correction and double-bit-error-detection (with 8206) and data bus parity check.

EPROM - module - This memory module contains 64K-bytes read-only memory, realized on 2732. It offers a very high degree of reliability due to the on-board Hamming code for single-bit-error-correction and double-bit-error-detection (with 8206), address check by module three and data bus parity check.

Communication module (Avresky (1984)) - This is an 4(8) - channel communication module (CM) with DMA controller-I8237A. The CM posses the following properties: to provide exchange of message between nodes; to distinguish a message, destined for its private node and to transfer it to it, in the opposite case, to transmit it to its destination; to service on a priority basis concurrently entering requests; to check the information in exchange; to prevent dead-lock in the system; to provide a possibility for building of different structures; to inform its neighbours in case of a failure in the node or its communication lines; to go round a neighbour, from wich it has received a signal for failure, or to take its functions when it is a destination. The CM provides exchange of message of the following format:

TAG	SOURCE	DESTINATION	DATA	CHECK

where TAG forms the route of the message from the source to the destination. The information between nodes is transferred up to 1 M Bytes/second.

PROGRAMMING OF PARALLEL COMPUTER FOR AI

In the report is presented an interpreter for applicative language RED, which will be the basic unit in the Parallel Computer for Artificial Intelligence. The realized version of RED belongs to the class of the reduction languages, described by (Backus (1978)). The reduction languages are a subset of the expression-oriented languages.

Unlike the imperative languages, the Reduction language allows for continuous explicit presentation in literal form both the operators and the operands in the operational array (without reference to memory). As a result of this isomorphism the realization of entirely implicit program sequencing is possible - i.e. of imposed structured programming. Far more significant is the opportunity to use the names of the functions as arguments and vice versa. This allows for full or partial recursion and even modification of the program at the run-time.

The basic linguistic unit in the RED grammar is the expression. According to the language syntax, the expressions are constant (inactive): atoms, sequences, false condition - or active: applications. The constant expressions are names, arguments or values of functions. The active ones define a transition function as a single-operand operation in prefix notation:
<OPR ␣ OPD>,
where < , > are delimiters; ␣ is separator; OPR is an expression-operator specifying lexically and semantically the transition function; OPD is an expression-operand consisting of a list of arguments (dependent and/or independent), or a single independent argument. When OPR and OPD are constant expressions, the transition function is simply defined and computable (composible or reducible according to its semantic type). Thus the computing process is reduced to alternative finding out the defined single-valued transition functions and computing of the values.

There are several equivalent formal presentations. Linear-list parenthetical presentation is, for example, a RED-program consisting of well-formed RED-expressions. The most illustrative model of the computing process is the graphic one - through composition and reduction of an "execution tree". This is a tree in left-preorder form and for its graphic composing three elements (syntax units) are enough: '<' (left applicative delimiter), '(' (left sequential delimiter) and atomic expression. They are arranged in nodes observing the following restrictions: the root is '<', while the atomic expressions could only be leaves. Each active expression is presented by a binary subtree with three nodes: root '<', specifying the application, left daughter node - arbitrary expression - operator and right daughter node - arbitrary expression-operand. On their turn '('-nodes, specifying the sequential expressions could be roots of n-ary ($n \geqslant 0$) subtrees. Each branch of such subtree could represent arbitrary (including active) expression. Practically, this means that the subtrees presenting active expressions and having a common generation node '(' are independent in the operational array. The transition functions specified by them are of different explicitly given definition areas, which provide their unambiguity. This spatial parallelism allows, in the presence of suitable hardware, the realization of time parallelism. For this purpose language primitives for parallel processing of types SIMD and MIMD are provided in the RED syntax. The program sequencing with such a tree-type program is reduced to scan the tree of execution over the '<' nodes according to a certain algorithm.

The substratum basis of the semantic system are the rules of language syntax and the set of primitive transition functions. The structure of the semantic system is formed according to the following substratum-determined criteria: a/ the defining of the transition function in the applications is positionally dependent; b/ the transition function which is defined is always single-valued and its value is determined by the syntax type of the expression-operator (atom, sequence, empty sequence, false condition) and its semantic type (regular or meta, compositional or reductional), specified by the expression-operator.

The basic elements (rules) of the semantic system are:
a/ Rule for determination. The transition function in an active expression is defined if and only if the expression-operator and the expression-operand are constant.
Consequence 1: The user's program is set as application with constant operator and operand expressions;
Consequence 2: The evaluation of the transition functions continues up to obtaining a constant expression.

b/ Regular composition rule. The evaluation of the transition function by this rule is illustrated by transformation of the execution tree at which the node of the current expression-operand is substituted by a binary subtree of an active expression in agreement with the following formulae:

$$<(CE_1\ CE_2\ \dots\ CE_p)\ OPD> \begin{cases} p>1 \rightarrow\ <CE_1<(CE_2\ \dots\ CE_p)\ OPD> \\ p=1 \rightarrow\ <CE_1\ OPD>, \end{cases}$$

where CE_1, ..., CE_p are constant expressions and CE_1 is a regular expression, and OPD is a constant expression-operand.

c/ Meta composition rule. Its application redefines the transition function - the operator and the operand - in the current active expression:

$$<(CE_1\ CE_2\ \dots\ CE_p)\ OPD> \rightarrow\ <CE_1((CE_1\ \dots\ CE_p)\ OPD)>,$$

where $CE_1 = (CE_{11}\ \dots\ CE_{1r})$; CE_{11}, ..., CE_{1r}, ..., CE_p are constant expressions and C_{11} =¤(empty sequence), and OPD is a constant expression-operand. The meta composition step itself does not directly change the structure of the execution tree if the resultant expressions are treated as leaves. However, it provides opportunity for the program sequencing through full or partial recursion.

d/ Regular reduction rule. The application of this rule implies evaluation of transition function in a determined active expression. In this active expression an atom, belonging to the subset of langage-defined regular primitives, is in the position of an expression-operator. The result of the evaluation under the indicated terms is a reduction of the active expression to a constant one:

$$<OPR\ OPD_{current}> \rightarrow OPD_{next}$$

This is shown in the execution tree through substitution of a binary terminal subtree with a leaf or a subtree, both not containing '<'.

The language-defined regular primitives are classified in the following groups by a functional feature:
- arithmetic (+, -, *, /);
- logical, comparative and conditional (AND, OR, NOT, ATOM, NULL, EQAT,

EQ, NE, GT, LT, GE, LE, COND);
- restructural (COMBINE, DBL, DISTL, DISTR, ROTL, ROTR, LENGTH, SEP, UN, SPLIT, TRANSPOSE);
- selectorial ($i \in N^{+}$, FRONT, REAR, LHEAD, LTAIL, SHEAD, STAIL, MAX, MIN, MULTIPLES, SINGLES, COMPRESS, FIND, SUBSTR, INSERT, DELETE, REPLACE);
- others (input-output, control) (SNAP, STOP, ¤).

They also differ syntactically - by the admissible type of the expression-operand.

e/ Meta reduction rule. Its application is specified by the syntactical structure: sequential type of the expression-operator in the application, the first element of the sequence being an atom, belonging to the subset of language-defined meta primitives. (The only exception is the meta primitive APPLY which is formulated as an atomic expression-operator).

The evaluation of the transition function according to this rule consists in the generation of the n-ary ($n \geq 1$) subtree of the execution tree through substitution of the current '<'-root with '(' and the generation of daughter '<'-nodes, representing roots of binary subtrees. Each meta primitive has its own specific semantics. This reflects also on the syntax of the application containing it, that's why all different cases are stated as follows (here f_i and $expr_j$ are constant expressions):

$<(AA\ f)\ (expr_1\ \ldots\ expr_p)> \rightarrow (<f\ expr_1>\ \ldots\ <f\ expr_p>)$

($p \geq 1$, SIMD - computation for $p > 1$)

$<(AL\ f)\ (expr_1\ \ldots\ expr_p)> \rightarrow (<f\ expr_1>\ \ldots\ expr_p)$

$<(AR\ f)\ (expr_1\ \ldots\ expr_p)> \rightarrow (expr_1\ \ldots\ <f\ expr_p>)$

$<(AS\ f)\ (expr_1\ expr_2\ \ldots\ expr_p)> \rightarrow <(AS\ <f\ expr_1>)\ (expr_2\ \ldots\ expr_p)>$

$<(REDUCE\ f)\ (expr_1\ \ldots\ expr_{p-1}\ expr_p)> \rightarrow$
$\rightarrow <f\ (expr_1\ \ldots\ <f\ (expr_{p-1}\ expr_p)>\ \ldots)>$

$<(NF\ f_1\ \ldots\ f_p)\ expr> \rightarrow (<f_1\ expr>\ \ldots <f_p\ expr>)$

(MISD - computation for $p > 1$)

$<(COLLECT\ (f_1\ f_2\ \ldots\ f_p))\ (expr_1\ \ldots\ expr_q)> \rightarrow$
$\rightarrow (\ (<f_1\ expr_1>\ \ldots\ <f_1\ expr_q>)$
$\ldots$
$(<f_p\ expr_1>\ \ldots\ <f_p\ expr_q>)\ )$

(MIMD - computation for $p, q > 1$)

$<APPLY\ (expr_1\ expr_2)> \rightarrow <expr_1\ expr_2>$

$<(BU\ f\ expr_1)\ expr_2> \rightarrow <f\ (expr_1\ expr_2)>$

$<(UB\ f)\ (expr_1\ expr_2)> \rightarrow <(f\ expr_1)\ expr_2>$

According to this rule both place-holders BU and UB are reduced. They are used for direct exchange of operand segments or control structures between the operator and the operand expressions.

Besides the described rules the semantic system involves a mechanism for macrogeneration as well. Not increasing the computing power of the language theoretically, it provides the following advantages: simplifies the notation and the structurizing of the RED-program; contracts the currently necessary volume of the linear operational array thus helping the increase of computation speed; gives opportunity to achieve contextual dependence of the transition function of the macros. Macrogeneration is carried out by means of literal substitution in the operational array itself, owing to the fact that the macroidentificator is an atom and the macrodefinition - a constant sequential expression.

Essentially the algorithm for the interpretation of RED-programs must realize one recursive processing of transition functions with literal arguments, which process is illustrated by composing and reducing of the execution tree. The partial recursive interpretation function INT is set analytically in the following way:

```
INT(ACTEX) =       if     RRA(ACTEX) then CONSTEX
             else if     MRA(ACTEX) then INT(MRR(ACTEX))
             else if ROPREX(ACTEX) then INT(RCR(ACTEX))
             else if MOPREX(ACTEX) then INT(MCR(ACTEX))
```

Here ACTEX (active expression) is a literal argument of INT of the simple function type; RRA (regular reducible application), MRA (meta reducible application), ROPREX (sequential regular expression operator) and MOPREX (sequential meta expression operator) are comparative functions for lexical and syntactical analysis: predicates in the conditional definition of INT; MRR (meta reduction rule), RCR (regular composition rule) and MCR (meta composition rule) are transition functions, corresponding to the rules of the semantic system and having for value ACTEX; CONSTEX (constant expression) is a value of ACTEX as a result of the regular reduction rule application. In separate case (in the last reduction step), that is the value of INT.

Presenting the RED-program by linear parenthetical list naturally leads to the choice of one-dimensional character array as an operational array. The maximum possible size exceeds 32000 which is quite sufficient. On the other hand, the array is significantly more suitable for processing than the character string.

Each '<' node in the execution tree is characterized by three parameters - Absolute Level Number /ALN/, Relative Level Number /RLN/ and Generation Node Number /GNN/. ALN signifies the level of embedding in relation to the root of the whole tree of the current '<' root in subtrees with '('-roots. Formally, if for the root of the whole tree ALN is 0, the current ALN is equal to the number of the '(' nodes on the way of the root. Informally, it shows how many meta reductions are realized up to the generation of the current '<' node. RLN is a parameter dependent on ALN and therefore accepts specific values for each one and also for the basic subtree. RLN specifies the serial number of the '<' node in the binary way (composed only of '<' nodes) and starting from the root of a given subtree. Parallel subtrees having common generating '(' node could not be identified by ALN - it is one and the same for these subtrees. The parameter GNN is provided for them and is dependent on ALN, which defines the serial number of the parallel branch (from left to right) in the n-ary subtree. The value of this parameter is 0 for the nodes not belonging to the parallel branch.

APPLICATIONS

The interpreter for applicative language RED was tested in the course of more than a year with programs from different applied areas. The most complex program was designed for solving a non-degenerated transport problem (travel salesman), closed model. Its execution includes several thousand reductions. Another series of test programs serves for the verification of programs written in PASCAL (Avresky (1984)). Programs realizing some graphic images and transformations with application in the computer graphics as well as for analysis of frames of natural language were worked out (Avresky (1983)).

The RED-programs are miraculously quickly constructed owing to the imposed structured programming and the convenient mechanism of the macrogeneration. The simple syntax and the functional semantics determines easy visual check. The only problem for the programmer is the necessity for geting accustomed to the algorithmization with the help of the execution tree, because of the unfitness of the block-diagrams for describing the computing process, realized through the applicative language. Besides, the right running of segments or whole RED-programs by the first execution was marked as a regular phenomenon.

The programs (expressions) written in functional language RED - are loaded into the system through the root node. Each node contents an interpreter 24 KB for RED, written in Assembler for Intel 8086.

REFERENCES:

[1] Avresky, D., Design of a fault-tolerant multimicroprocessor systems. FTSD-6, Brno, 1983.

[2] Avresky, D., S. Ovcharov, Reduction machine, implemented in fully distributed system, Avtomatika and izchislitelna technika, Sofia, No 2, 1982.

[3] Avresky, D., S. Ovcharov, S. Marinov, A. Popov, Z. Karakehaiov, N. Kuzev, Highly reliable microprocessor module for parallel processing, National Conference on "Microprocessor systems", Plovdiv, 1983.

[4] Avresky, D., ..., Method and processor for natural language processing.

[5] Avresky, D., B. Sirlestova, N. Patchev, Application of the functional language RED for verification of programs in Pascal for data structres, FTSD-7, International Conference on Computing System's Reliability, Sofia, 1984.

[6] Avresky, D., S. Marinov, N. Kuzev, S. Ovcharov, A communication unit for a fault-tolerant multimicroprocessor systems. FTSD-7, Internatiol Conference on Computing System's Reliability, Sofia, 1984.

[7] Backus J., "Can Programming be Liberated from the von Neuman Style? A Functional Style and Its Algebra of Programs", CACM Vol. 21, No 8 (August 1978) pp. 613-641.

[8] Henderson P., "Functional Programming. Application and Implementation", Prentice-Hall International, London, 1980.

[9] Goodman J.R., C.H. Séquin, Hypertree: A Multiprocessor Interconnection Topology, IEEE Trans. Computers, Vol. C-30, No 12, December 1981.

[10] Pradhan, D.K., S.M. Reddy, A fault-tolerant Communication architecture for distributed systems, pp. 214-220, FTCS-11.

[11] Stolfo, S.J., Miranker, D., Shaw, D.E., Architecture and applictions of DADO: a large-scale parallel computer for artifical intelligence, IJCAI-83, Karlsruhe, West Germany, 1983.

[12] Treleaven P., Mole G., "A Multimprocessor Reduction Machine for User-defined Reduction Language", Computing Laboratory, University of Newcastle upon Tyne, Techn. Reports No 150, (January 1980).